# PREP SCHOOL

# PREP SCHOOL

*An Anthology*

COMPILED BY

## Michael Gilbert

JOHN MURRAY

First published in 1991
by John Murray (Publishers) Ltd
50 Albemarle Street, London W1X 4BD

The catalogue record for this book is
available from the British Library

Typeset by Rowland Phototypesetting Ltd
Bury St Edmunds, Suffolk
Printed in Great Britain at the
University Press, Cambridge

In ancient shadows and twilights
  Where childhood has stray'd.
The world's great sorrows were born
  And its heroes were made.
In the lost boyhood of Judas
  Christ was betray'd.
                    AE

# CONTENTS

# INTRODUCTION

'No one,' says Graham Turner, 'however long he lives, forgets his first day at boarding school;' and the late Arthur Marshall described it as 'an experience that will be with me to the grave and beyond – if beyond there be.'

It is not only what Kenneth Grahame describes as being 'kicked out of his nest into the draughty uncomfortable outer world.' It is a new world, a world with frightening inhabitants, strange customs and rigid taboos; even with a language of its own.

Things which were easy and automatic at home suddenly present problems. Ian Hamilton, sent all the way down from Scotland at the age of nine to Cheam, in Surrey, says, 'My childhood thoughts, informed only by women, had not yet tumbled to the fact that the great unknown inventor of braces had foreseen the possibility that a man might wish to take his trousers down *after* he had put on a coat.' Discovered by a boy in the lavatory in his shirt-sleeves the news flew round the school: 'There was an ass among the new boys who didn't know how to let down his trousers.' Nicholas Monsarrat, as will be discovered, was even unluckier.

The first chapter in this book, 'Arrival', is inevitably the most traumatic. After that things do settle down into a more tolerable routine of lessons and games (organized and impromptu) mixed with crazes, pets and myths, with, as an ever-present background, the question of food, sometimes edible and sufficient, sometimes deplorably inadequate.

'I can remember no time', says the twelve-year-old Kipling, 'when we would not eat dry bread if we could steal it from the trays in the basement before tea.' And Monsarrat, 'There was no appetite like that appetite, the ravenous craving which made one steal, lie, scheme, borrow money at ruinous rates of interest and swop one's dearest possessions for a slab of chocolate.'

Summing it up, as a master, not as a boy, Cecil Day Lewis calls it, 'A world, insulated, self-important, artificial, anxiety-ridden, yet endeared by familiarity, not less than by the deposit of golden moments.'

The extracts which follow are from biographies and autobiographies; a list of these appears in the Sources and Acknowledgements. In some cases the subject has needed no introduction. In other cases I have played safe. Names which were once well known – 'Jack' Seely, William Goodenough, 'Sligger' Urquhart, Maurice Baring, the Powys brothers, Giles and Esmond Romilly, Richard Meinertzhagen, and many others, are starting to fade from the public memory. Generally I have inserted a full-length description only when the extracted passage is itself lengthy. In some cases a lack of description only indicates my lack of knowledge of the boy concerned and the man he became.

These biographical notes will sometimes suggest how the experiences of the boy may have affected the character of the man. In a few cases – for example, Hugh Walpole, Francis Chichester, Frank Benson and Ben Travers – the after-effects are confessed by the subject himself. In other cases they can be deduced from our knowledge of what transpired. Who would have guessed how dramatically Oscar Wilde's boyhood wish would be granted?

A point on chronology: a man cannot expect to be the subject of a biographical study until he has become reasonably well known; and that does not usually happen before he reaches middle-age. It follows that the extracts given here are, necessarily, accounts of prep school life at least forty years ago and sometimes much longer ago than that. Incidentally, this accounts for the fact that the subjects are, with few exceptions, boys and not girls. If a similar book is compiled twenty-five years hence, no doubt the balance will be restored.

So what is the picture today?

The Incorporated Association of Preparatory Schools (IAPS), which represents the majority of schools of any standing, has on its books at this moment 540 schools – the greatest number it has represented during the 99 years which have passed since the Revd. A.S. Tabor of Cheam convened a meeting of headmasters to consider the size of the cricket ball. What has changed, and is changing every year, is not the number of schools but their nature.

Sixty years ago the stereotype would have been a boarding school for boys only, often at the seaside, the breezes blowing off the Channel and the North Sea being considered useful adjuncts to the boys' health. Today there are only 20,000 boarders as against nearly 80,000 day pupils and weekly boarders. The number of girls has increased greatly and the coast is no longer a favoured location. With the emphasis having shifted to day schools, parents will select one as near as possible to their own front door; a choice particularly pertinent for the parent who has to drive the child to school.

Prep schools now are much more agreeable places than they used to be. There are a number of reasons for this. They are no longer in a seller's market. There may be long queues for urban day schools, but boarding schools are looking for pupils. Parents can pick and choose; and a school which acquired a reputation for ill-treating children would soon have no pupils at all.

A second reason, I am sure, is the abolition of corporal punishment. Boys and girls can be as unpleasant to each other as ever they were, but at least the cane is no longer in the headmaster's cupboard.

A final reason is that the modern mother claims an equal say in her children's upbringing. And a mother is less likely to be bamboozled than a father who may nurse a residual fear of headmasters. She will be less interested in the scholarship board and athletic successes and more concerned with the drains and the catering. A description of the care such a mother can take will be found in the extract from Sue Arnold's article at the end of the first chapter.

A final qualification. Donald Leinster-Mackay in his book *The Rise of the English Prep School* says 'Men of letters are prone to exaggeration,' and 'all evidence from general biography about schools should be tempered by a recognition of its subjective quality.' Bernard Shaw, for example, clearly disliked his school days. His biographer, St John Ervine, is unsympathetic. He says:

> In reading G.B.S.'s diatribes against his school and his
> teachers, it is well to bear in mind that they were written in his
> middle manhood and old age and may have derived more from
> his theories about education than from his experiences of it.
> He refers habitually to schools as if they were concentration
> camps or penitentiaries and to masters as if they were brutal
> warders or sadistic commandants. This fantastic bosh reads
> like the remarks of a man so far removed from boyhood by age
> and by ideas that have long ceased to have any relevance to
> facts, that his reminiscences have become romantic
> figments.

So there it is. Read on, but do not let anything in this book discourage you from sending your son or daughter to prep school. They may be ideally suited to it and obtain lasting benefit from the experience.

This book could not have been written without help, and help has been unstintingly given. Many people, when told what I was doing, supplied me with the names of books; books which the London Library and the specialized Theatrical Library of the Garrick Club were almost always able to produce. Particularly I must thank, for help and encouragement, Michael Coates, Secretary of the IAPS, Charles Malden of Windlesham High School, Mike Gover of the Dragon School, who sent me *A Dragon Century* by C.H. Jaques, Anne Kiggell of *Prep School*, the IAPS journal, and the late Judge Edward Clark. I must conclude my thanks with two particular names: Dick Usborne who lent me two invaluable books, *A Century of Summer Fields (1864–1964)* which he compiled and edited, and *Time to Spare* by his friend Nicholas Aldridge; and last, but by no means least, the former chairman of IAPS 'Mark' Hankey, who has helped me with unsparing kindness at every turn.

# ARRIVAL

'To have been removed from home at the age of nine,' wrote the late Arthur Marshall, 'and placed in cheerless and unsybaritic surroundings was an experience that will be with me to the grave and beyond – if beyond there be.'

And David Niven, 'Apart from the Chinese, the only people in the world who pack their sons off to the tender care of unknown and often homosexual schoolmasters at the precise age when they are most in need of parental love and influence are the British so-called upper and middle class.'

Both went to bad schools; which, in Niven's case, perished unlamented, and in Marshall's case, if it still exists (he keeps the name from us), must by now have perished, or be a very different sort of place.

'Removed from home' and 'packed off' must ring alarm bells in many a middle-aged mind. 'No one,' says Graham Turner, 'however long he lives, forgets his first day at boarding school.' Comfortable years later he may be able to be as light hearted about it as Kenneth Grahame:

It was on or about Michaelmas Day 1868 when a bright and eager (sullen, reluctant, very ordinary looking) youth of nine summers sprang lightly (descended reluctantly – was hauled ignominiously) onto the arrival platform of the Great Western railway station at Oxford. A small schoolboy, new kicked out of his nest into the draughty, uncomfortable outer world, his unfledged skin still craving the feathers into which he was wont to nestle. The barrack-like school, the arid cheerless classrooms, drove him to nature for redress; and under an alien sky he would go forth and wander, along the iron road, by impassive fields, so like, yet so unlike, those hitherto a part of him.

It is beyond dispute that the moment at which a boy of eight or nine finds himself whisked away from the security of home and plunged into the insecurity of a boarding school will rank as the most memorable and dramatic in his whole life. There will have been the miserable last lunch at home, followed by a taxi drive to the station. Says Max Beerbohm:

> It was always the most bitter thing in my drive to the station
> . . . to see other people, quite happy, with no upheaval of
> *their* lives; people in cabs, who were going out to dinner!
> Grown-up people! Then the impotent despair of those drives
> — I had exactly fifteen of them. I hope I shall never experience
> a more awful emotion. They have something, surely, akin
> to drowning. In their course the whole of a boy's home life
> passes before his eyes, every phase of it, standing out against
> the black curtain of the future.

If the journey to school was by car, this merely postponed the evil moment. But, provided that both parties behaved with proper British phlegm, says Christopher Robin Milne — son, of course, of A.A. — it could be carried off.

> The journey to school was always with my father alone. We
> did the Times crossword and then sat silent. School was all
> right, when I got there, but home was so very much nicer.
> We said our goodbyes while still in the car, when there was
> a mile or two to go. We said them looking straight ahead. It
> was easier that way.

After one attempt George Lyttelton, himself an experienced school-master, chickened out. Humphrey, the son he mentions, was to become, in later life, the famous jazz trumpeter. The school was one of many at Sunningdale.

> On his first evening at his prep school Humphrey sobbed
> frantically throughout tea with the Headmaster, and half an
> hour after we left was in uproarious spirits; which his mother
> was not. After that we always sent him back with the odd-job
> man, and there were no more tears, until the day he left
> school.

# ARRIVAL

Robert Mortimer, late Bishop of Exeter, spoke for many:

Twice I have taken a little eight-year-old to his preparatory
school for his first term. I suppose I shall never know how
miserable they felt. I do know how miserable I felt. The
crunch begins at the tea party. There are the parents, trying to
keep up bright chatter. And the little boys are trying to
pretend to enjoy the eats provided. Everybody is keeping a
stiff upper lip, and how! And in the end one drives away with
one last look at a forlorn diminutive figure waving farewell.
Is it for the children that our English boarding school system
is so cruel, or for the parents?

The tension of the moment did not always deprive a small boy of
his powers of observation. Maurice Baring was not only an accomplished writer. He was to demonstrate, during the First World War,
an ability to get on with all sorts of people in the Air Force; from
disconsolate ACs to formidable Air Vice-Marshals. Those shrewd eyes
which, says a contemporary 'seemed half shut much of the time, but
missed nothing', were already on the alert.

We were shown into a drawing room where the Headmaster
and his wife received us with dreadful geniality. There was
a small aquarium in the room, with goldfish in it. The
furniture was covered with black and yellow cretonne and there
were some low ebony bookcases and a great many
knick-knacks. Another parent was there with a pale looking
little boy called Arbuthnot, who was the picture of misery
and well he might look miserable, as I saw, at a glance, he was
wearing a made-up sailor's tie. Two days later the machinery
inside this tie was a valuable asset in another boy's collection.

There were exceptional boys, later to become exceptional men, who
took the whole thing in their stride. But they must have been few
and far between. In his *Life of Earl Wavell* John Connell writes:

At ten, Wavell was a sturdy, quiet-mannered boy, a trifle
small for his age, handsome and with a quick, shrewd gleam of
humour in his eyes. He never gave the slightest sign of being
home-sick; indeed, there was a family legend that as soon

as he arrived at Summer Fields he was introduced to a group of boys, began to play with them and after a few minutes strolled over to his parents, observing, 'You can go now. I shall be quite all right'.

At Abinger Hall, his second preparatory school, Peregrine Worsthorne encountered an even more remarkable example of self-possession.

> I remember my lot of new boys included a rather fat eight-year-old whose sang-froid was unforgettable. Our first class was taken by the Head, who, to put us at our ease read out an extract from, I think, one of Macaulay's essays. It was totally above my head, but agreeable to listen to. After about twenty minutes he stopped and asked us whether we had any questions. We were all, naturally enough, tongue-tied, except for this fat eight-year-old who was sitting next to me. To my astonishment, up went his podgy little hand. 'Yes, Edward?' said the Headmaster (who was progressive to the point of using Christian names), 'What is your question?'
> 'Not really a question, sir,' said my neighbour. 'More an observation. I just wanted to tell you that with your voice you could fill the Albert Hall'. The boy's name was Edward Boyle.

A full-scale version of an arrival and a First Night remembered with advantages, comes from the other side of the world. Ian Tearlach Dall, who was born in 1893, was sent, aged nine, after a happy childhood at Las Olmeidas in the Argentine, to St Botolph's which had clearly been set up on the English model.

> Before going to bed we all went into a tin barn for Evensong – a service – in which Canon Peckover said how grateful we should be that we were all together again at the beginning of a new term and we would now sing the School Hymn in Latin and stop coughing. He said he was glad to see some new-comers in our midst, but there was one in our midst who wasn't a new-comer and that was Sin, which he hoped God would put down. A master went over to an organ that a man was pumping with a handle and we made an awful noise, singing, after which the Canon leant over the pulpit like a

hawk and said, 'Lord be merciful to us miserable sinners.'

In the bedroom, afterwards, the boys began to throw their boots at one another and said that whoever got hit with the boots would have to clean them and as my bed was in the middle I got hit with the boots and they said I would have to clean them in the morning. They wanted to know what my name was, but when I told them they all laughed and the leader, a fat boy called Beastley major, started to bounce up and down on the bed as though something was making him choke.

A prefect put his head through the door and shouted 'Prayers' and immediately the three smaller boys knelt beside their beds and folded their hands. I thought I had better say my prayers too, but when I looked between my fingers I could see Beastley major swaggering up and down and not saying his as though he had no need to ask God for anything. I wondered if God would do anything to Beastley major on account of this and could He possibly get me home again somehow, or ought I to ask Him to bless the school and make me a credit?

The prefect put his head through the door again and shouted 'Time'. The lights went out and all I had been able to say was 'Oh Lord . . . Oh Lord.'

In the darkness I could just make out a hump on Beastley major's bed, so I think he must have been saying his prayers under the sheet.

In other cases it was the day or two immediately after arrival which posed the worst problems. Simple things, to which no attention had been necessary at home, grew to the size of catastrophes. The difficulties encountered by Ian Hamilton, who had always worn a kilt, in dealing with his first trousers; or the problem which faced young Brown.

Poor little Tom was made dreadfully unhappy in his first week by a catastrophe which happened to his first letter home. With huge labour he had managed to fill two sides of a sheet of letter paper with assurances of his love for his mamma, his happiness at school and his resolve to do all she would wish. The missive, with the help of the boy who sat next to him, also a new arrival, he managed to fold successfully; but this done, they were sadly put to it for means of sealing. Envelopes were then unknown. They had no wax and dared not disturb the stillness of the evening schoolroom by getting up to ask for some. At length Tom's friend, being of an ingenious turn of mind, suggested sealing with ink and the letter was accordingly stuck down with a blob of ink and duly handed to the housekeeper to be posted. It was not till four days afterwards that the good dame sent for him and produced the precious letter and some wax, saying, 'Oh, I forgot to tell you before, but your letter isn't sealed'. Poor Tom took the wax in silence, with a huge lump rising in his throat and ran away to a quiet corner of the playground and burst into an agony of tears. The idea of his mother waiting, day after day for the letter he had promised her at once was as bitter a grief as any he had to undergo for many a long year.

And, many years later, the novelist, Nicholas Monsarrat:

I had been unable to find out where the lavatories were. I didn't know whom to ask. I didn't know *how* to ask. We had been brought up to be secretive and rather ashamed of everything to do with lavatories. I couldn't think of a polite form of words. After twenty-four hours it was really impossible to ask anybody.

Thus I wandered round the building, miserable, afraid and often desperate to bursting point. I once heard one boy ask another, 'Where are the bogs?' But the word was new and meant nothing to me. I continued searching and suffering.

At the end of three unnerving days the worst happened, as it was bound to. My disgusting plight was discovered in the changing room.

'Monsarrat's bogged his pants', came the public announcement. It drew instant attention. The evidence was displayed. Everyone began to clutch at their noses and keep an exaggeratedly safe distance from me.

As we come nearer to the present the scene lightens. It is not only that headmasters become more practical, less likely to lecture on the prevalence of sin and more likely to indicate to new boys where they can find the lavatories; but under their guidance the ethos of the school may have changed. Tears, in a new boy, no longer evoke the kind of reaction they did in the days of Tom Brown. They may be the subject, if not of pity, at least of tact.

Bernard Darwin, the noted golfer and writer about golf, recalls the day of his arrival at Summer Fields:

Home had been a background and a refuge. This was the first real plunge. And though I was soon very happy the going there was agonising. It is still agonising to think of; though it is not now my small self I feel sorry for, but for my father. I made the parting very hard for him.

My own family has treated me far better. They went back to school, if not positively as a bridal, at any rate with a stiff upper lip, for which I cannot be too grateful. The first parting at Summer Fields is so blurred with tears that I cannot recall it in any detail. I feel as if I must have lost consciousness from grief, so that my father left me in my bedroom and crept stealthily and miserably away. The first clear picture I have is of myself cast down upon my bed, sobbing and bedraggled, with the room having grown dark in the gathering dusk. Presently the other two occupants of the room arrived, to find this poor little abject spectacle on the bed. In school story books they would either have mocked me heartlessly in my grief, or told me with angelic kindness that everybody was very happy at Summer Fields and I should be happy too. They did neither, but they behaved, as I probably thought 'awfully decently', affecting not to notice my condition and talking in a friendly way.

I am still grateful to them.

Was there almost the thought that life might have been more positive and less empty if there had been some opposition to face, something to fight against?

Hubert van Zeller, who grew up to write spiritual, monastic and devotional works, was at Downside Junior School.

In later years I have been able, without any effort at all, to recapture the feel of my first night in a dormitory. It was not that anything particularly dreadful happened. It was rather that nothing happened and that life seemed to stretch in front of me in an endless length of not happening. Life at home had been full, but life at home was over. Life from now on, I told myself, as I lay between the stiff sheets and listened to the springs of the wire mattress, was empty.

I was nine years old and life was over. I had, for weeks, been preparing myself to miss familiar people and things, but it had been no preparation at all. The very stuff of homesickness is to feel that one has wasted one's chances whilst at home. There might be a return, I told myself, but it would be no more than a geographical affair. The real thing would not be the same.

I am not sure I was not right.

There is, fortunately, a modern example to close this section; or parents might be driven by it to refrain from sending away their sons, though suited to boarding school life and able to benefit from it.

The extract comes from Sue Arnold's column in *The Observer*.

At precisely 10.28 a.m. on 6 September 1988 I hugged my eight-year-old son for the last time and handed him over to the matron of a prep school.

I've lost count of how many reverse charge telephone calls Tom made home that first week, one day alone it was eight. 'It's no good, Mum', came the small distant piping voice between gulps, 'I'm not cut out to go boarding, honestly. Every break I walk to the gates by myself and think about you'.

I had to remind myself of the perfectly logical reasons for packing him off. Boys need space . . . the answer seemed to be a weekly boarding school for Tom with acres of space and hundreds of boys to play with.

At the first mention of the plan Tom had been enchanted. If he was anything like his father, whose school days were undoubtedly the happiest days of his life, he would love it. We bought 'The Good School Guide' and combed an area within fifty miles for the best school for our lad. Heaven knows how many headmasters we interrogated, how many dorms we inspected, how many geography lessons, school play rehearsals and music rooms we crept in and out of until we came up with what seemed the perfect prep school. We took Tom to see it; 'When can I start?' he asked, his eyes shining.

Even when we left Tom on that fateful September morning everything was so well organised, the hand-over so smooth and Tom so excited with his brand new tuck-box he scarcely seemed to notice we had gone.

And then the phone calls started. It was the postal strike, remember, and this was the only means of communication. 'Promise you'll take me away on Saturday', sobbed Tom.

On the third day I telephoned a friend, whose son had also just started. 'Andrew's so wretched he's in the san with a temperature', she said.

Next day I had a call from another mother, who cried because her son *hadn't* telephoned, *wasn't* homesick. 'He's obviously much happier at school than he is at home', she wailed.

The second week Tom didn't ring. I called him. 'How's it going?' I asked. 'Brill,' came the small distant piping voice. 'Rugby and pottery are best. I'm making a big pot. Must go, there's a dorm raid'.

So now I have a secondary problem when friends ask, sympathetically, how can I bear sending my son away, don't I feel guilty and miss him dreadfully? Certainly I miss him, but he likes his school so well now I feel guilty about not feeling guilty.

You can't win.

# 2

# FOOD

'Food, glorious food,' sang the orphans in Lionel Bart's *Oliver*. Even more heartfelt is Nicholas Monsarrat.

> Ah, food! There was no appetite like that appetite, the ravenous craving which made one steal, lie, scheme, borrow money at ruinous rates of interest and swop one's dearest possessions for a slab of chocolate which would be gone by sundown. One might be addicted to many things in later life; drink, cigars, women, other men, money, power or press-cuttings – one might, indeed, lie or steal or borrow for any of these prizes. But at eleven years old for me it was food – the most innocent, the most desperate, the most unappeasable of a whole life time of devious lusts.

Boys from upper and middle class families would have been accustomed at home to good, well-cooked food. The initial shock was likely to occur on the morning after arrival, at the breakfast table.

Thomas Anstey Guthrie, who wrote under the name of F. Anstey, was born in 1856. He was the son of a flourishing and well-liked military tailor whose customers 'unusually in the case of a tradesman, accepted his invitations to luncheon and dinner'. A long remove from Mr Bultitude. After six years at 'Crichton House' – so-called – he went on to King's College School and to Cambridge. Of the many books he wrote only *Vice Versa* lives today. Here he describes his own schooldays:

> As for the food, at breakfast and tea there was nothing but piles of bread and butter, but if the butter was rather thinly spread, it and the bread were excellent and we had as much as we could eat.
>
> Meat at breakfast was an extra and was nothing but sardines or a thin slice of 'polony'; most boys had pots of anchovy or bloater paste, however, which they shared with less fortunate

neighbours, and at tea any boy who had a cake or a pot of
jam from home saw it handed round the tables, sometimes
with only an off chance of getting the final slice of cake or
spoonful of jam.

The midday meal was dreaded by myself and most of the
boys who were in the least fastidious. The meat was probably
good in quality but, the cook being no artist, it often required
an effort, even for healthy and hungry boys, to get it down and
there were one or two soups and dishes which gave dismal
notice of their imminence a good hour before we faced them. It
never dawned on 'Grimstone' that they were at all
unappetising and, to do him justice, he ate precisely the
same fare as we did, and with an enjoyment we were very far
from sharing. Any attempt on our part to leave unattractive
morsels uneaten was a most serious offence in his eyes.

On Sundays we were given cold beef and rhubarb or quince
pies and though we did not find these exactly exhilarating
– indeed few dishes can be more depressing than a cold and
untender rhubarb pie – they inspired no actual aversion.

And somehow, though the food generally was open to
criticism, we managed to thrive on it.

From the same period, the 'sixties' and 'seventies' of the last century,
evidence is available from both the Navy and the Army. Sir William
Goodenough (the naval hero who appears again under 'Clothes')
writes:

We were in the house of the second master at Temple Grove,
Mr Edgar, and fared better in the way of food than those in
the Main House, from whom we heard lurid stories of cabinet
pudding and reputed hashed cat and rat being pushed
behind the water pipes.

Major-General Sir Archibald Anson had also attended Temple
Grove. Possibly he was in the Main House.

We had for breakfast oblong chunks of bread, about four
inches long and one and a half wide and one inch thick, the first
pieces having a smudge of butter on them, the rest being dry.
This was washed down by an allowance of milk and water

served in a small white basin. For dinner there was a pudding, either rice with little milk, very dry and served in round tins similar to those used by soldiers in barracks, or a doughy sort of pudding with a few raisins in it. My share of this one day was a lump of mortar, of which I got a mouthful. Then there was a joint of either roast beef or mutton, or sometimes a stewed aitchbone of veal. The pudding was served before the meat. The supper was the same as the breakfast. The wife of a schoolmaster whom I was telling how we were fed at school said, 'If we could feed boys like that now we *could* make some profit'.

An aristocratic family was no guarantee of preferential treatment. In his *Life of Earl Granville* Lord Edward Fitzmaurice describes a private school at Beaconsfield kept by a Mr Bradford. It had so many noblemen's sons in it that it was known as 'The Little House of Lords'.

Lord Russell recounted how, having a great dislike for the mutton fat which every boy was ordered to eat with the meat, he had succeeded, as he hoped unobserved, in dropping it under the table. Having been discovered he was compelled, by a clerical pedagogue, to sweep it up off the dusty floor and eat it, dirt and all.

The quality of the food normally depended on the headmaster, who might be generous or mean, imaginative or pedestrian, or it might depend on circumstances outside his control, such as wartime short-ages. Nicholas Monsarrat was miserable at Winchester, but had been, after a shaky start, surprisingly happy at both of the preparatory schools he attended. The second of these was 'The Leas' at Hoylake. Of the food there he says:

On Sunday mornings came the best treat of all, sausages; real sausages from Palethorpes of Liverpool with none of the soya-bean-breadcrumb trash of later years. But there was another treat that had us licking our lips every day of the week; this was tea-time, when tea was served from a giant urn and a bun – a long, thick bun covered with icing sugar – was doled out to each applicant who queued up for it.

The buns were counted to the nearest dozen. Sometimes

boys were late, or (astonishingly) were not hungry. If one waited long enough there was a chance of collecting a second one. I waited every day.

Other boys were not so lucky. Sir Gerald du Maurier, writing to his mother, told her, 'We had such a fearful pudding today that I hid it with my spoon. It was made of blancmange and plums, clotted cream and small black beetles'. In the case of the publisher and man of letters Sir Rupert Hart-Davis, and others of his generation, there was some excuse, since their prep school days unhappily occurred in wartime.

By this time there were serious shortages and the food was appalling. My letters are full of requests for cake and jam. Twice a week, for breakfast, we were faced by a tepid orange-covered mess of curried lentils. Mr Bultitude didn't know how lucky he was to get those two sardines.

So, also, Arthur Harrison:

My own generation must still remember the endless artichokes substituting for potatoes, the minute squares of strong-tasting margarine and the bitterness of those rhubarb and gooseberry puddings with no sugar to sweeten them.

Or Paul Spillane, in his account of St Andrew's, Eastbourne:

On Fridays there was a sort of bread and butter pudding known as Resurrection Pudding as it was felt that everything left over during the week had been put into it. It had another name; for forty years it was the misfortune of Mr Thwaites, a chiropodist, to make a monthly visit to inspect the boys' nails, which were cut each Thursday by the maids. The abundance of caraway seeds in Friday's pudding led to it being known as Toenail Pudding.

The best guarantee of adequate food was a school where the head-master took his meals with the boys and ate the same food. Claude Martin Blagden, later Archdeacon of Warwick and Bishop of Peter-borough, was a pupil, in 1882, at the St Mary Magdalene Choir School in Westbourne Terrace. His recollections, like Paul Spillane's, centre on the pudding.

The midday meal was, naturally, the meal of the day and the headmaster and his wife shared it with us. This was a guarantee that we should be adequately fed, but there still lingers with me the memory of a flat wicker basket into which all the bread not consumed at one meal was swept, sometimes with butter on it, to be ready for the next; and to this day the thought of bread and butter pudding fills me with nausea.

There may have been good reason for this, if the instructions in *The Preparatory School Review* of 1902 were conscientiously followed:

After ordering the dinner get the servant who has the management of the bread to show you what is left over from the previous day. Have all the parts of the loaves remaining from the school and family meals used for the boys' early dinner, so that they are not left to get stale. And also insist that those in the servants' hall use them for their dinner. You then give out to the parlourmaid a sufficient quantity for the boys' bread and butter; and tell her to make fresh loaves early next day for the masters.

Thomas Pellatt, who appears again under 'Discipline', here couples that topic with food in his own special way. Says Laurence Irving:

I have hinted that T.P. was a gourmand, though it was later that I came to appreciate this. Be that as it may, in term time he mortified the flesh by sharing our school meals. T.P. in a commanding position in the centre of the hall, carved the joints. Nell dispensed the pudding. While he carved, T.P. made any necessary announcements. Now and again he made it the occasion of the public chastening of a boy, who usually deserved it.

As he meaningly steeled the carving knife his accusing eye would seek out his victim. At his deceptively jovial invitation, 'Stand up D'Arcy Hyphen Smith' the abashed son of a noble house would rise from his chair. 'No. Come here, nearer to me so that we can *all* see you. Your darling mum tells me that in a letter to your old governess, Miss Croop, you told her that you hated the liver you had for breakfast. You did, didn't you? Well, you mustn't suppose that the rest of us, who happen to like liver, are going to go without it to please Miss Croop. You don't, do you? I thought not. Stand up all those who don't like liver.' (No candidates for martyrdom.) 'Well, there you are, you wretched chap. Go back to your seat and the next time you write to Miss Croop tell her that you are the *only* boy in the *whole* school who doesn't like liver.'

Self-help was the solution for boys with money of their own. Returning to the Bishop of Peterborough:

> We were naturally eager to supplement school food, but parcels from home were few and 3d a week pocket money did not carry you far. Mr Hayter, the genial grocer at the corner of Westbourne Terrace, kept a good brand of Fry's chocolate cream and Garibaldi biscuits. The baker, farther down the street sold half-penny currant buns hot at seven for threepence; Stewarts in the Porchester Road sold three-cornered tarts . . .

But the champion self-helpers, without question, were A. A. Milne and his brother, Ken. After leaving their father's little school, which closed down shortly afterwards, they both went, in 1893, as boarders to the Westminster Junior School. There was no wartime excuse in their case.

> Even now, after forty years, I cannot think of the meals without disgust and indignation. After an hour's work from seven to eight we had breakfast. It consisted of tea, bread and butter. The bread was, to me, the dullest form of bread, the butter the one uneatable form of butter; otherwise I should have liked it, for I like bread and butter. Tea was tea and I was never fussy about tea, but the milk had been boiled and great lumps of skin floated about on the top of it . . . Well, that was breakfast . . . At one o'clock we had the usual 'joint and two veg', followed by pudding. The plates of meat had been carved well in advance and brought to the right degree of tepidity in some sort of gas cooler. In the fruit season we had rhubarb. Not liking luke-warm slabs of beef (or rhubarb), I made no sort of contact with the midday meal. Tea was

breakfast over again with a few of the slabs of meat, now
officially cold, for anybody who wanted them. Very few
people did. In all my years at Westminster I never ceased to
be hungry.

As a schoolmaster, father was unable to take our complaints
about food seriously. All boys complained about their food. And
even if he believed us, there was little that he could do. We
lived in College at the expense of the authorities and our
scholarships entitled us to no more than they chose to give us.
We were left to keep ourselves alive. Which we did. There
were various expenses each term which demanded ready
money. College subscriptions, entrance fees for competitions,
haircuts, journey money if we went out at the weekend;
perhaps a wedding present for a master who was getting married
or a wreath for a canon who was being buried. To meet these
expenses father was accustomed to advance us three or four
pounds at the beginning of term, for which we had to account
to him afterwards, handing back the balance. We soon got into
the habit of regarding this as our own money. We put by a
small balance to take home to him and spent the rest on the
biscuits and sweets for which our neglected stomachs shrieked.

The 'accounting' was child's play. Father couldn't know if
a master had been married that term and wouldn't know if
a canon had died; nor could he be dogmatic about the
subscriptions likely to be demanded from each boy on these glad
and sad occasions – 'Wreaths 15/-, Wedding presents 17/6d'
looked reasonable. Ken called our system the double-entry
system, because we entered every expense twice and he said
that all accountants used it, because it was a very good and
well-tried system.

# 3

# Friends

Stephen Pasmore says, 'Friendships with other boys were a blessing, but naturally those who most needed friendship were too disturbed to be able to make friends.'

It will be noted that he speaks of friendships in the plural, recognizing the unlikelihood, at that age, of a friendship lasting for four or five years. But there could be no doubt about it being a blessing whilst it lasted; a 'technique of survival', says Maurice Bowra, 'a life raft in stormy seas'.

Maurice Bowra was born in 1898 in China. His father brought him and his brother to England in 1903 and left them both there 'to be educated' – which they were. First at Cheltenham Preparatory School, then at the main college from which Maurice won the top scholarship to New College, Oxford. After fighting in the 1914–18 war he was awarded a tutorial fellowship at Wadham and in the words of the *Dictionary of National Biography* 'became a legend in the Oxford of his hour.'

He writes in his autobiography:

For a boy of twelve, I had seen a lot of the world and moved too much among grown-ups. I was used to talking when I had something to say and that was often. Nor had I the faintest inkling of the English convention that it was bad form to talk too much.

After a shaky and uncomfortable start I worked out a congenial way of life. My real discovery was that boys will forgive anything for a joke. I set out to amuse the other boys and by such simple devices as imitating the masters or inventing fantasies about their private lives, I got myself accepted. I was asked to tell stories after dark in the dormitory and, by drawing on what I had picked up in China, I did not find this difficult, although I did not always adhere strictly to the truth.

I even made a friend. His name was H. N. Crooke and like

me he was thought an oddity and not much liked. He was
rich in witticisms and, being the son of an Indian civil servant,
had a background not unlike mine. I went everywhere with
him and a sarcastic master compared us to a pair of turtle
doves. We did not mind, but did not think it very funny.

When we moved up to the senior school we were in different
houses and so were not allowed to speak to each other; and
later he was killed in France in the war.

But between us we had evolved a technique of survival in
a society which would not otherwise have found us easy to
digest.

In its simplest form this relationship might be the sort of feeling
that David Copperfield had for the glamorous Steerforth. It might be
unilateral and unreciprocated. The older boy might even be unaware
of the devotion of the younger one. But though one-sided it had the
elements of friendship in it.

R.H. Dundas, lecturer in Greek history at Christ Church, Oxford,
and a former officer in the Black Watch, writes to Lord Wavell's son:

Your father was a year or two senior to me. I'm glad to think
that, when I was ten, he was my first and greatest schoolboy
hero; a very solid little boy, with resolution and a low centre
of gravity and very hard to knock over at soccer. I thought
him terrific and am pleased to think how right I was. He went
to Winchester (he would have had a wider, if worse, field at
Eton) and came down a term or two after he had left Summer
Fields. I stood at the door of the fifth form room and gazed at
him in mute adoration, until he observed, quite kindly,
'Young Dundas. I'm not a peepshow.' I retired, a trifle
dashed, but still mute and still adoring.

From what sources did this power of attraction spring? Never, or
very rarely, from the wealth or position of the boy's family. It might
be skill at games, but it could be more subtle than that. The best
evidence and the fullest analysis comes from the Poet Laureate, Cecil
Day Lewis, who was able to view the matter from opposite vantage
points; first, as a schoolboy (at the school he calls 'Wilkies') and, later,
as a master at Summer Fields.

The boy whom he presents as an example of this extraordinary

magnetism is Nicholas (Nico) Llewellyn-Davies, the youngest of five
boys, out of Barrie's friendship with whom came *Peter Pan*.

Says Day Lewis:

The most remarkable boy at Wilkies was Nico
Llewellyn-Davies. He was remarkable, not for exceptional
intelligence, or prowess at games, though later he kept wicket
for Eton, but because he possessed the magnetism which, very
occasionally, distinguishes one small boy from the crowd of
his fellows and so often vanishes during adolescence. To
analyse such magnetism is impossible. Nico had great charm,
certainly, and poise, and a not unpleasing touch of arrogance
and a lively face with two prominent front teeth, but other
boys possessed these qualifications. Nico's magnetism,
however undefinable its source, was visible in its effect, for
we used to follow him around like the tail following a comet.
Leadership is a word which has been devalued by generations
of public school masters; one can, no doubt, up to a point,
be trained for it, but natural leadership – the kind that is
exercised without official authority or physical pre-eminence,
without even any apparent will to power or consciousness of
it – is an emanation of personality, a rare and often transient
gift, like beauty, which cannot be imparted.

When I became a preparatory schoolmaster myself, I found
only two or three examples of it in eight years of
acquaintance with young boys. One of them turned up before
I had given my first lesson. Walking through the dining hall
for breakfast, on the first day of term, I noticed a very small
boy reading a book of poetry. I leant over his shoulder to see its
title. He was reading *The Land*.

'Is that a good book? Do you like it?'

'Of course it's a good book,' he politely replied. 'My mother
wrote it.'

In the self-assured, somewhat pre-occupied, but charming
style of Nigel Nicolson's answer and in a kind of sparkle
that danced off his personality, I perceived a strong affinity
with the Nico Llewellyn-Davies of fifteen years before. There
was, besides, a certain physical resemblance and Nigel proved
to have the same magnetism for his fellows as Nico had had
for us.

Our next two witnesses are cheerful extroverts, who later made names for themselves in sport and in written and spoken commentary on sport.

In his autobiography, *The World that Fred Made*, Bernard Darwin touches on the instability of schoolboy friendship:

> The side wall of our playground was only on one side, on the
> other there were fives courts, 'fives' being our name for
> squash racquets with no back wall. Naturally among eighty
> boys or so a court only came to one at long intervals and
> the possessor of a court could confer no greater mark of favour
> than an invitation to play; an invitation, by the way, to be
> discreetly and modestly given, since it might suggest the
> awful crime of 'sucking up'. The withholding of an
> invitation afforded a subtle opportunity of wounding the
> feelings of one's best friend and boys of private school age live,
> in my recollection, in a constant state of having ostentatiously
> best friends and as ostentatiously quarrelling with them.

Raymond Robertson-Glasgow, cricketer, broadcaster about cricket and sought-for after-dinner speaker, wrote a number of books (one with the intriguing title *I was Himmler's Aunt*). He went to St Edmund's School, near Hindhead. He discusses the progress of schoolboy friendship, from its chancy start to its full flowering, in the agreeably adult tone of voice which made his talks so ensnaring. It would have occurred to very few boys to describe their communal sleeping quarters as a club; though possibly Mr Bultitude, who must have been a member of one, might have done so if he could, for a moment, have detached his mind from his own misfortunes.

> A school dormitory is a man's first club, with a self-appointed
> committee and a few difficult members. There was one who,
> from time to time, felt I would derive benefit from a midnight
> dip in the cold hip bath that each of us kept under his bed.
> Perhaps he was right. I hated him for one year, then, for three
> more, highly esteemed his company. He taught me the art
> of making paper jabber-wocks and ink-bombs, how to bottle
> blaeberry wine and mix it with sherbert when fermented by
> burial and how to hide conscious guilt under the mask of

innocence. At belching he was second only to the eldest son of
the Bishop of Salisbury, from whom I received tuition, as a
favour, in the senior changing-room. But at expectoration
he stood unrivalled, for distance combined with accuracy and
from ten yards he could hit the picture of Pericles on the
classroom wall three times out of four. A genial lad was
William Bunnett. At sixteen he enlisted in Canada for the First
World War and was killed in Flanders before his seventeenth
birthday.

A crowning difficulty was that a boy could not always attach himself
to the friend he would have preferred. The law of the attraction
of opposites governed the choice. Timidity was drawn to audacity,
unpopularity to popularity. A boy might need a friend. He might
need one desperately. But the more he yearned for one, the less likely
was he to find one. Two authors, L. A. G. Strong and Lawrence
Hanson, have touched on this; the former briefly and brutally, the
latter, under the guise of fiction, with more feeling.

In *Green Memory* Strong writes:

I began to make friends. The first of these was an outcast, a
slow, amiable, ugly boy in his fourth term, at whom his
companions jeered for his ineptitude at work and games.
Reduced each term to seek company among the new boys,
whom he propitiated by helping them and showing them the
ropes. He would have someone to walk with and sit next to for
a week or a fortnight, but seldom longer. One after another
his protégés came to despise him. He took these defections
as a law of nature.

'You'll soon get sick of me,' he told me one day, without
rancour. 'Everybody does.'

In his book, *Boy and Man*, Lawrence Hanson describes the same
process, more analytically, in greater detail and with more feeling for
the victim. Lance, the central character, is accompanied to school,
much to his embarrassment, by his father, whose plebeian accent is
the subject of mockery by the other boys, chief among them a red-
headed boy called Roberts, at that moment leading his triumphant
forces in a battle of toy soldiers:

'Supper' announced one of the maids loudly and, Lance
thought, a little unnecessarily as the trays were set down in
the midst of the battlefield. There was a momentary pause in
the mutual recrimination, claim and counterclaim, as victor and
vanquished alike seized a steaming mug, thick slice of bread
and butter and hunk of cheese. When the mob had withdrawn
from the table a solitary mug still stood there. The fat boy
picked it up, together with bread and cheese and brought them
over to Lance. 'Come on,' he urged, 'you'll need it. Nothing
more till brekker.' He took a vast bite from his own slice,
crumbs clinging to each side of his mouth.

Lance accepted the offering with an appearance of gratitude
and, to some degree, with gratitude in his heart. He had in that
moment discovered the humiliating fact that the people who
were kind to him were not necessarily those to whom he was
most drawn. The fat boy was plainly, in his way too, an
outcast but this bond was not enough for friendship, it was
not sufficient even for liking. Nor did his kindness do more
than prick Lance's conscience the harder. The truth was, he
recognised, with shame but without a moment's hesitation,
that the chief torturer himself, the red-haired boy, was the
one whom he admired and would have liked to call friend.
There was about him something dare-devil, something frank,
open and almost heroic, that compelled admiration, whereas
the fat boy was not only physically repulsive but bore the
unmistakable stigma of failure and – the decisive stroke – he
was not a free choice. He could no more admire him than
he could hate Roberts – no, not even when, a few minutes
later, the red-haired boy, mug in hand, face ruddy with
excitement, mischief in his eye, looked round with triumph,
caught sight of Lance, leapt on a desk, flourishing his mug
and cried, in a voice that turned all heads in his direction,
''Ullo lads. Wot cheer mates. Pleased to meet yer.'

Finally from Sir Osbert Sitwell. In 1903, aged ten, he was dis-
patched to a school which he christened 'Bloodsworth', but which,
from its location and other pointers, must have been Ludgrove. By
reputation it was one of the best of its time and was certainly one of
the most expensive.

The headmaster had been an international soccer player ('a *tremendous* dribbler; no one in England could touch him at it'). In Osbert's view it was 'a miniature model prison, with all the middle-class snobbery, but lacking the middle-class comforts'. He loathed it, but is fair enough to record that 'a few years ago, it was moved to a new house in another neighbourhood and I am told that since then it has come to deserve the reputation it has so long enjoyed'.

On his first Sunday there, Osbert was taken out on a formal perambulation:

> I was at the very end of the school crocodile and beside me trudged another new boy, a very young child he seemed. The master, about seven vertebrae in front of us, occasionally glanced round and gave him a particular look, as if he would have liked to throw him to the wild beasts. Perhaps the weather damped even his energy. But I think my companion liked the weather for he was homesick, plainly, almost audaciously homesick for some haunted Irish fastness which he had left for the first time only three or four days previously; homesick with the unabashed frankness of a child who as yet has developed no guile and thinks no ill of his fellows and his face was wetter than even the rain could make it.
>
> Presently he stopped crying and, thrusting his hand into mine, said, 'Let us be friends; let us promise.' By the prevailing code I should, of course, have shouted, 'Yah! Cry-baby!' but in fact I was inexpressibly touched, though I scarcely knew how to show it. It was such a friendship as might have sprung up between two early Christians in the arena, but it was not destined to prosper or endure. We were not in the same form and we slept in different dormitories, though they were next door and that term I could often hear the sound of his being beaten at night for being a cry-baby.

# 4

# Bullying and Counter-

# Bullying

Bullying is not confined to preparatory schools. There is enough and to spare in all schools. In the universities it is called ragging; in the armed services, training. It spills over, in a less physical form, into business and the professions. But the seed-bed of this vice was the old-fashioned private boarding school. So much so that a yardstick by which such an institution could be measured was the extent to which the headmaster supervised the leisure hours of his charges. The organization of leisure could certainly not be left, unsupervised, to the boys themselves.

In *The Crystal Box*, a limited edition which was privately published in 1924, the novelist, Sir Hugh Walpole, describes his experiences in a prep school at Marlow (the passage is quoted in Sir Rupert Hart-Davis's admired biography of Walpole). At this school the headmaster was so little in touch with the day-to-day lives of his charges, that on one occasion when Hugh was kept back for a week at the end of the holidays, the headmaster had not noticed his absence. As a result:

When I say that it wasn't all that it should be, I mean that
the food was inadequate, the morality was 'twisted' and
Terror — sheer, stark, unblinking Terror — stared down every
one of its passages. I had two years of it, and a passionate desire
to be liked, a longing for approval, and a frantic reaction to
anybody's geniality have been, for me, some of the results of
that time. I have been frightened since then. I was frightened
several times in the war rather badly, but I have never, after
those days, thank God, known continuous increasing terror
by night and day. There was a period, from half-past eight
to half-past nine in the evening, when the small boys (myself
with them) were dismissed to bed, but instead, spread
themselves into an empty classroom that is still, when I think

of it, damp green in retrospective colour. The bigger boys held during that hour what they called the Circus. Some of the small boys (I was always one) were made to stand on their heads, hang onto the gas and swing slowly round, fight one another with hair brushes, and jump from the top of the school lockers to the ground. Every night (owing, I suppose, to my then unrecognised short sight) was a horror to me. I would be pushed up onto the lockers, then, 'one, two, three, — Jump'. I can feel now again as I write the sick dizziness at my heart as I looked down at the shining floor, bent myself to jump, pulled myself together, fell, to be caught generally by some bigger boy, who would push me into the arms of someone else, thence on again and so round the room. Swinging round the gas was worse than the lockers — being roasted in front of the fire (shades of Tom Brown) worse than the gas. Worst of all was being forced to strip naked and stand then on a bench before them all while some boy catalogued ones various physical deficiencies and the general company ended by sticking pins and pen-nibs into tender places to see whether they were real or not.

Worse than the hour itself was the anticipation of the hour. First thought on waking was that eight-thirty was far away! Then, slowly through the day, it grew ever closer and closer until, by tea time, tears of anticipatory fear would fall into one's cup and salten one's hunk of bread.

To those who would say, 'We've all been through those private schools; a little roughing it does no one any harm. You ought to have stood up for yourself', my reply is, 'Quite so. But I did not stand up for myself then, and I'm not trying to stand up for myself now'. The point is that I was a miserable child, and one month at Marlow was enough to make me sycophantic, dirty in body and mind, a prey to every conceivable terror, so that the banging of a door or the dropping of a book sent my heart into my cranium; sentimental, too, like a little dog, fawning on anyone who was for a moment kind and — worst of all these, I think — muddle-headed and confused beyond any grown human's conception.

Sometimes there were not even the trappings of rough fun about the performance. It was cold and simple sadism. The Hon. Henry Coke's first prep school was Temple Grove. He went when he was seven. 'We were half starved and exceedingly dirty; we were systematically bullied and we were flogged and caned as though the master's pleasure was in inverse ratio to ours'. Moving him on, his uncle, Admiral Keppel, took him to the naval academy at Gosport. It was no improvement.

> The very first afternoon of my admittance I had three fights
> with three different boys. After that the new boy was left
> to his own devices. I have spoken of the starvation at
> Temple Grove, here it was the bullying that left its impression
> on me – literally left its mark, for I still bear the scar upon
> my hand.
> Most boys, I presume, know the toy called a whirligig,
> made by stringing a button on a loop of thread, the twisting
> and untwisting of which causes the button to revolve. Upon
> this design, and by substituting a jagged disc of slate, the senior
> boys constructed a very simple instrument of torture. One big
> boy spun the whirligig, while another held the small boy's
> palm till the sharp edge gashed it. The wound was severe. For
> many years a long white cicatrice recorded the fact on my
> right hand.

More than once, rather than face such ordeals, a boy ended them by taking his own life. We have an account of one such occasion when the boy who faced the possibility, was to demonstrate, in later life, physical courage of a high order. After leaving school Ian Hamilton served in almost every war with which the British Army was concerned; on the North West Frontier of India, in Natal, Burma, the Sudan and South Africa, where, at the Battle of Elandslaagte, he showed such conspicuous courage that he was recommended for the Victoria Cross; a recommendation which the Duke of Cambridge rejected on the grounds that the decoration had never previously been awarded to a Brigadier-General. Personal gallantry should be confined to junior officers.

He had gone, in 1863, at the age of nine, to Cheam, reputed to be the most famous preparatory school in England.

> At 6 a.m. a big bell rang – damn that bell! said every boy –
> and everyone was supposed to leap out of bed. In our
> dormitory the boys did not leap out of bed – only me. I had

26

to do the leaping onto the cold floor and pull out the small baskets that were under the bed of each of the five other boys. The clothes had then to be laid out neatly, so that each one had his things quite handy; the shoes had to be collected from outside the door, and each pair put by the right bed. If I made mistakes, I would be shown during the day a spillikin of wood being shaved and carved with a pocket-knife. My punishment (like the present-day League of Nations sanctions) must cause no bloodshed, must leave no mark. An ingenious instrument for inflicting this invisible wound had been patented by a small and swarthy Hebrew (whom I could have licked, as I proved later on) who had the advantage over me of a term's seniority. My hair was thick and curly and the spillikin being put into this mop and twisted round, a small tuft could be plucked out by the roots without anyone, but me and my executioner, being the wiser. The tug hurt, and my imagination helped my tormentors, for I got to think it was the same as having a tooth pulled, which was nonsense. However, imagination or not, the sight of the preparation of that spillikin sufficed to embitter what anyway was likely to be a pretty harsh day.

[Later that term Sir Ian was given a leave-out to visit his uncle's house at Carshalton.] Uncle John had long, light brown hair and whiskers, a long light brown face, bright blue eyes and a long thinnish nose. He was really an awfully jolly uncle . . . Coming from hateful, spy-ridden pi-jaw Cheam, Carshalton, with its jokes and bright, friendly, open welcome struck me all of a heap; and when they told me to run out and amuse myself until supper, I didn't quite know whether to laugh or cry and was really as drunk as any lord with the boiling up of queer thoughts within me as I danced and skipped down the smooth slope of the lawn towards the river, which had a punt moored to the bank, as if waiting there for me like a magic boat in a fairy tale. So out I poled, into the middle of the stream; floated down round a bend and out of sight of the house; anchored myself with a little anchor and gazed into the crystalline current with my face about two inches above the surface as it slipped, slipped, slipped away to sea.

Photographed for ever on my mind's eye are the long waving

strips of dark green water-weeds and here and there slim speckly semi-transparent shapes only asking, it seemed, to be caught. Quite another peep into another sort of life from that I used to get, wading through the chain of pools linked together by miniature cataracts where the Eccy ran at the back of Benmore. Here, I just looked, with no wish to catch these paradise fish of Carshalton, which moved like dancers in tune with the gliding water and waving water-weeds. Life was wonderful, after all. And then, like the backwash of a wave, a terrible thought gripped me close as clasp and seemed to be trying to pull me down under. Very soon I must go back to Cheam. Why go back? Why not stay by the river – in the river? An intolerable feeling of utter friendlessness and of my enemies in the dormitory shot like an arrow through my heart. I began to sing to the old Scot's tune, 'We're a noddin, nid nid nodding' the words 'Je suis misérable – mi-sé-ra-a-ble' and set to sobbing and crying. The impulse to sleep, enfolded by this haunted stream, grew stronger.

> One brave leap:
> Sleep, sleep, sleep.
> Now or never –
> In the river.

'Ian! Ian I-a-a-an! Where are you? What a fright you've given us. Come in, you naughty boy and get your supper at once.'

So now I know how, and why, boys do it.

Patrick Campbell, Lord Glenavy, owner of a pen tipped with Irish inconsequence and humour, may be best remembered as Frank Muir's opposite number in the television programme *Call my Bluff*. He derived from his experiences at school a novel idea, that anger and violence were a waste of time.

My father pushed me into Crawley's Preparatory School, St Stephen's Green in Dublin. He'd gone there himself and was proud of his academic record, but the only memory I retain of Crawley's is a dark cellar and a terror so dreadful that the only way I could contain it was by trying to stand outside myself and telling myself that it must come to an end, that sooner or later I would be safe on the top deck of the No. 15

tram, going home. Crawley's was a day school, or I might not have survived it.

The trouble was two enormous brothers. To me they looked like fully grown men. One had flaming red hair and a temper that became more and more demoniac the longer he persecuted me. The other was dark and sinister and invented new tortures for his brother to carry out.

These ceremonies – they had the feeling of ceremonies in their set form and fixed dénouement – were conducted in the cloakroom, a cellar in this old Georgian house, and they terminated in my head being shoved into a revolting lavatory bowl by the red haired brother, while the dark one pulled the chain.

I imagine they picked on me because I was very tall and very thin. My stammer made me almost completely inarticulate.

But those possessed and dreadful brothers did one thing for me. They gave me a life-long conviction that anger and violence are an actual waste of time. I remember I had to walk half a mile every morning from our house to the tram terminus in Terenure and then sit in the tram for another half hour, with the brothers and the lavatory bowl getting nearer every minute and the only thing I really objected to, in an utterly numb and miserable way, was this waste of time.

I could have been doing anything else, but here I had to sit on top of the tram as it lurched and howled down the long drabness of the Rathmines Road, waiting for the moment to come when I walked into the cellar to hang up my coat and to provoke the brothers to their inexplicable furies – furies that no appeal to reason could disperse.

It was a comfort, on top of the tram, to look forward to my approaching misery as a waste of time – a period of hours in which no nice or funny or interesting thing would happen, a time of limbo, of non-life.

Years later, at a party in London, a jolly psychiatrist in an eccentric but exceedingly smart suit heard me telling someone that I regarded anger as a waste of time.

'But what would you prefer to do with this time which is wasted, you say, upon anger?' he wanted to know.

'Live it,' I said, to my own satisfaction, but not, as it turned out, to his. He thought it stemmed from a subconscious refusal to accept reality. But then, he hadn't known the demon brothers and, at his prices, I wasn't prepared to lay their record before him.

The bullying was not always physical. Francis Chichester was to become a man of courage, demonstrated in other fields than war. He made a remarkably hazardous round-Europe flight, often landing in ploughed fields and flying (and landing) blind; and made a London–Sydney flight in 1929, including the first solo crossing of the Tasman Sea. He then flew from Australia to Japan and from Japan to China, playing hide-and-seek with a typhoon and ending with a near fatal crash at Katsuura. After which he turned his attention to small boats and took part in, and won, the first single-handed Atlantic crossing. Later he was dubbed by the Queen with Drake's sword at Greenwich, following his return from sailing single-handed round the world. He went, as a boy, to a preparatory school called Ellerslie, in North Devon.

I do not know if I was born with a passion for spending all day alone in the wildest parts of the countryside. I suspect it was due to circumstances such as the start of my school life. When I was seven I was sent off to school at Ellerslie, about seven miles away. My parents drove me there in the family buggy. During my first term the senior boys of the school were having a game, which was to prevent some of them from entering the building. I was standing on the concrete floor of the wash place at the time, with a row of basins round two sides of the room and above the basins a row of oblong windows, which pushed outwards. Through one of these windows appeared the head and shoulders of my brother, trying to get into the building. I picked up a handful of sawdust from a box on the floor and threw it in his face. It was a silly, thoughtless thing to do, but certainly not done from malice, only excitement. A bit of this sawdust went into his eye and I can remember his bending over the basin and bathing it.

As a result of this I was 'put in Coventry' for three weeks and for the whole of that time not a single boy spoke to me. My brother, who was four and a half years older than me, was one of the senior boys. I do not know if he had any part in the 'Coventry' punishment, but he never spoke to me during the period of it. It seems hard to believe that senior boys would do such a thing to a seven year old new boy just because of a stupid joke that went wrong. I can assume only that I must have been very objectionable, perhaps precocious – I don't know. This episode turned me into a rebel against my fellows; every boy was an enemy unless he proved himself to be a friend.

Chichester may be right in thinking that this experience helped to turn him into a 'loner' – one of the most outstanding 'loners' of all time – compared by his biographer to Frobisher, Burton, Doughty and Shackleton. All he says himself is, 'One instance of the effect of such treatment is that, until recently, I would shake with fear if I had to get up and speak to more than half a dozen people, because the terror of doing or saying anything which would not be approved of by a mob code was so rooted in me'.

Guy Kendall, headmaster of University College School, Hampstead, for twenty years, puts his finger on the root trouble. Unsupervised discipline should never have been entrusted to boys of twelve or thirteen.

Bullying had been very bad in the school just before I came. My brother, who preceded me by a year, had encouraging stories to tell about boys who were made to climb trees and fall down, their nether portions being in a sort of jelly in consequence. One of the bullying gang remained and he succeeded in making our lives a terror to us. The Head had been at Rugby as a boy and, more than faithful to the Arnold tradition, he appointed monitors and left most of the discipline to them. But monitors unsupervised are a source of tyranny, not discipline, especially if they are of the age of twelve or thirteen at most.

The bullying came to a climax when a Scotch boy who had made himself objectionable to one Watkins (who, I think, was head monitor) was singled forth during a walk – for these walks were almost always unattended by a master – and told to go on some yards ahead. Each of us then, in turn, were ordered to go ahead and kick him. Many of us were friends of his, but this made no difference. Either through fear, or herd instinct, or bravado or the horrible sadism which seems to

lurk in most small boys, we all kicked as hard as we could.
Finally he was told to run on ahead. He did so (I can still
see his disappearing heels and his deerstalker cap), but he was
not heard of again that day. In due course the alarm
sounded. The excitement was intense, 'Maddison has run
away'.

Next day some of the senior boys were sent out on search
parties. The rest of us were gathered together in the 'Big
Room' and, one by one, were asked to give an account of what
had happened. Each of us did so faithfully, until it came to the
end when the tale finished off with, 'And then we kicked
him'. Finally the last search party, consisting of two very upright
boys, arrived and was called up. Their recital agreed with
ours, except that it finished with the words, 'And then Watkins
told us to kick him'.

'Thank you,' said the Head, turning to the rest of us. 'Now
then, none of you had the courage to say that that little
whipper-snapper told you to do it'. It was only too true. He
then proceeded to give us an account of the horrors of the past
night; how he had sat in the police station, listening to the
ticking of the clock and wondering under what hedge the poor
little victim was shivering. He spared no dramatic touch,
ending – 'That day when we have to stand before the
Almighty's throne and give an account' – etc., etc. Many of
us were weeping by this time, some because they could not
help it, others because they thought it was expected of them
and the rest because it is a catching thing.

The weeks that followed were like what I imagine the
populace feel when a tyrant has been deposed. Watkins was
kept in quod in the private side of the house for some days;
when he came back he realised that his reign was over.

The moral of it all is, do not make monitors on the plea of
'giving training in self-government', and then save yourself
trouble by leaving them to themselves, especially if none of
them exceeds fourteen years of age. It will bring more trouble
in the long run, besides much pain and possible torment to
the weaker boys.

It is a relief to find that, even in those early days, there were
exceptions. James Anthony Froude, historian and man of letters, now

chiefly remembered for his majestic twelve-volume *History of England*, went to Buckfastleigh School in Devon.

> Bullying was, by common consent, treated as a public crime. A lad who was guilty of persecuting any smaller boy was condemned by a Committee of Judge Lynch, made to kneel, with bare back, on the school-room floor and was flogged – buffeted we called it – every boy striking him one blow with a knotted handkerchief. The fear of the penalty was a sufficient deterrent. I never saw it inflicted but once. I can see the poor boy now, on his knees, with tears in his eyes, suffering more from the shame than the pain of the blows. He had not been very cruel after all and to me he had been uniformly kind.

If bullying loomed, there were boys who were not prepared to knuckle under. Tom Brown was an early exponent of the riposte direct. When he was found in tears over the failure of his first letter home, 'his wrath was proportionately violent when he was aware of two boys who stopped close by him and one of whom, a fat gaby of a fellow, pointed at him and called out, "Young mammy-sick". Whereupon Tom arose, smote his derider on the nose and made it bleed – which sent that young worthy howling to the usher'.

The results of this sort of individual rebellion were sometimes a great deal more dramatic. The boys who tried to bully George Millar chose the wrong victim. In his books *Horned Pigeon* and *Maquis* he has shown his ability, first to evade, then to fight back against the Gestapo in France. On an earlier occasion his private resistance movement was equally drastic and equally effective. He was at Notre Dame School in Fife, a school which took boys of all ages. The younger group were called Newts. Millar was twelve at the time of the incident described.

> During my second, third and fourth nights I watched my fellow 'newts' being 'hardened' by 'Mad' Carew and his assistant 'Screw' Gunn.
>
> The newt was held prone on the floor and 'thigh-cracked' (struck repeatedly with clenched fist on the muscles of arms and legs). A few more painful indignities followed. And finally his ankles were roped together and he was suspended, head down, outside one of the windows.
>
> This final stage in Carew's hardening process seemed

designed to expose my major physical weakness, an exaggerated, almost a phobic fear of heights.

Before going to our dormitory we were required to put on slippers. But I had a pair of house-shoes that my aunt had bought for me in Norway. They were made of hand-sewn reindeer skin, supple but solid.

On the fifth night I waited by my bed. My horror of heights had set me in a fury, a flexing and loosening of the muscles such as Conan Doyle's 'Brigadier Gerard' knew on the black night in the Spanish cell when, in order to save a woman from pain he let them cut off his ear.

At last the two bullies stood before me. The room, as usual, was hushed. Carew told me that it was my turn to be hardened, for my own good, and that of the school.

As his big hand snaked towards me, I stepped back, measured my distance, kept my eye on the target and kicked Carew with all my strength, every ounce I could summon, in the testicles. Mad Carew doubled up with a scream that faded as though a railway engine, blowing its whistle, had rushed into a tunnel. Clasping the damaged locality he fell to the floor. And before he was down I kicked him with equal savagery, this time on the side of the face. His face seemed to splinter and open under the reindeer foot.

There was no possibility of concealing the damage. Carew was removed to hospital. Millar was beaten by the headmaster. Oddly enough the victims who had not resisted united against him. However, when Carew came back he kept well clear of Millar. No one could predict the way that public opinion would swing. Sometimes it surprised the bullies.

Maurice Collis, historian, biographer, novelist, dramatist and art critic, was sent at the age of eight to Cordwalles, 'a select and expensive establishment at Maidenhead'. He rose to be head of the school, an elevation which was unpopular with three other boys, who considered they had prior claims to the post. They decided to make his life unbearable by emerging from their classroom every evening when Collis was superintending the smaller boys at prep and making rude gestures at him.

There was, no doubt, some counter-measure which I might

have devised, had I been resourceful enough to think of it, but as it was I pretended, at first, to take no notice. To the reader this prep school drama will sound highly ridiculous. But to me, aged 13, it was a real dilemma. If I showed that their antics hurt me, it was a triumph for my antagonists. If I did nothing to stop them, how long could I bear it?

Unable to resolve the problem, I continued mutely to endure, trusting they would get tired of their petty revenge. I did my work as head of the school and captained the eleven as if nothing whatever was wrong; and in my letters home made out that I was happy, enjoying my last term and my distinction. So much did I fear to abate my dignity that I would not even ask help from my friends.

The persecution came to an end as suddenly and unexpectedly as it had begun. Extraordinary to relate it was stopped by the audience before whom it was staged. The school came over to my side.

I do not know their reasons for deciding to squash my adversaries. One day, when we were all in the swimming bath, a number of boys turned on the little gang and ducked them; telling them, as they did so, that the school liked me. I was exceedingly relieved and pleased and pretended not to see the trio's discomfiture, just as I had refused to recognise their animosity. The ducking, accompanied by so universal a disapproval, alarmed them and they were never disagreeable to me again.

The really interesting cases, however, are where the younger boys used organization or ingenuity to defeat the older ones. The three boys concerned all became men of mark. First, Randolph Churchill.

There was a gang of bullies at Sandroyd, organised by two boys older than myself. They held the whole school in awe. They would send their minions to arrest any small boy like myself whom they did not like and frighten him by swinging and cracking whips round his head. I cannot recall whether any violence was ever used, but it was an alarming process.

Many small boys more inhibited than myself were terrorised

and enslaved by this process. Having been brought up with a due respect for law and order, I did not scruple (at the risk of being called a sneak) to denounce the aggressors to the authorities. This proved no more effective (as we were later to find) than did denunciations of a similar nature to the League of Nations and the United Nations. Throughout my life I have learned that it is better to rely on defensive alliances.

So, with childish prescience of the shape of things to come, I formed a counter-gang to resist these outrages. My gang consisted of a very tough boy called Benn, who was a nephew of a Member of Parliament called Sir Arthur Shirley Benn, and three Spanish princes, Alvaro, Alonzo and Atalfo of Orleans-Bourbon. Benn was my chief of staff and the Spanish princes were my body-guard. We got the better of the older bullies and we demoralised them. It was, I must admit, with some satisfaction that I heard, a few years later, that both our enemies had been sacked from their public schools.

For an even more remarkable example of organization we turn to a man, well known in his day, but little remembered now. 'Jack' Seely, later 1st Baron Mottistone, rose to be Secretary of State for War in the Liberal cabinet of 1912, lost his post over his mishandling of the so-called Curragh Mutiny, reverted to active soldiering and fought on the Western Front with scarcely a break from 1914 to 1918. His reference, in the passage now quoted, to his 'valiant Canadians' refers to the occasion on which, in the desperate days of March 1918, the Canadian Cavalry Brigade which he commanded recaptured the Forest of Moreuil, one of the turning points in that backs-to-the-wall campaign. His courage was undoubted. His mental ability less so. One of his critics said, 'If Jack had just a little more brains he'd be half-witted'; but this may have been reaction to the Curragh incident, in which he seems to have regarded Gough and his fellow cavalry officers in much the same light as he had viewed 'Sinister' and his accomplices so many years before.

There were about twenty new boys. After tea we were told there would be no lessons that evening and we could run away and play until bedtime. The headmaster and the assistant masters then left us alone. My enemy, whose name I remember, but we will call him Sinister came up to us with his attendant satellites and said to his friend, 'Well, we had better send these brats over the jumps. You stay where you are and we will come and fetch you when we are ready'. So there we sat, twenty little boys, frightened to death and wondering what was in store for us.

After about half an hour one of the four bullies came back and said, with a horrid grin, 'All ready. Come along'. We filed out down a long passage to the covered playground, a large room with a concrete floor. Set out at intervals were four improvised jumps, about two feet high, making the playground look like a miniature steeple-chase course. Sinister was standing in the middle armed with a strap. To my dismay, I observed that he held it by the end with the holes in it, with the buckle at the far end. The other three were similarly armed and there was one of them to each jump.

'We'll begin with the spawn of Satan', said Sinister; the others roared with laughter, one of them saying, 'Yes, let's have a go at the Liberal'.

I was told to go over the jumps. I said, 'I can't jump that. It's too high'.

'You'd better have a try', said Sinister, and caught me a whack with the strap.

I flew at him, but of course he was waiting for me, quickly tripped me up and sat on my head while the others came along and gave me a good basting with their straps. Then they pulled me into a corner and ordered me not to move. The command was hardly necessary, for I was so battered that I could scarcely stand up.

There I sat, with my back to the wall, while the four brutes flogged those unfortunate little boys round the course. As the boys approached each jump a bully would catch them a crack with his strap, of course putting them out of their stride, with the inevitable result that, nine times out of ten, they fell over the jump. It began to dawn upon me that, unless we could meet force with force, we little boys were going to have a pretty desperate time. There and then I thought out a plan.

Next morning I felt quite well. Of course I was stiff and sore from the beatings of the previous day, but I did not mind this, for I was full of my plan. I told each boy that I had thought out a way by which we could avoid being flogged

37

round the course. I told them to meet me at some place I would find where we could talk it over. I found the place and an appropriate time when the big boys were in school and we were out.

It has been my good fortune to plan and carry through many attacks in war; this was the first and not the least successful. First of all I asked each boy if he was prepared to take the risk. There were twenty of them and they all volunteered, so I chose fifteen who seemed the strongest and looked the most resolute. I swore them all to secrecy, then I expounded the plan.

We were to be divided into four groups of four each – one for each bully. On the next night that we were to be flogged over the jumps we would try to get each group near to its selected bully. On a signal which I would give the four would fly at their man. One, the leader, would catch him by the throat, another would throw his arms round his legs and hold on tight so that he would fall to the ground; the other two would take an arm each. The leader would beat the head of the bully on the concrete until he cried out for mercy.

These gallant little boys accepted the plan without demur. 'I expect they will kill us if we don't succeed', said one of them, 'but anything is better than going over those jumps for the rest of the term'. I showed them the way to make the attack and each group practised it several times on one of the boys not selected, only omitting the beating of the head upon the ground. Then I impressed upon them the need for ruthless violence and absolute loyalty; confided to them the signal, which was to be the word 'fight' shouted loudly by me; told off each group to their victim, taking Sinister for myself. It was a thrilling moment. Just as, thirty eight and a half years later, I knew that my valiant Canadians would not fail in our desperate onslaught on the victorious Germans in front of Amiens, so I knew that those little English boys would not fail in what seemed to them to be just as desperate a venture.

The next night there was no flogging round the course, but we managed to find out that we were for it on the following night. When the time arrived we filed, as before, into the covered playground. Sinister was there with his strap and the others too. Quickly we grouped ourselves about the four

38

bullies, I edging up to Sinister with my three comrades. He
turned to me and said, 'Hullo, spawn of Satan'. 'Fight'
I screamed and in a moment each group grabbed its man.

Oh, the joy of feeling Sinister falling backward to the
ground, his legs held tightly by my number two. I fell with
him and on top of him. His head hit the concrete, but not
hard, so I gave him an extra tap.

'Help', he shouted. I said, 'There's no help unless you give
in', and gave his head another crack.

Holding him still tightly by the throat I looked round.
There were the other bullies lying flat on the concrete floor,
equally helpless in the grip of their opponents. 'Now,' I
shouted, 'you four bullies, we have got you and unless you give
us your solemn promise, each one of you, that you will never
bully us again, we'll knock your brains out'. And to my
comrades, 'Give them another tap on the head'.

This was done. I looked down into the eyes of Sinister. I
have never seen such concentrated hate, even in war. Then the
light seemed to fade out of his eyes as he realised he was
powerless and he said, 'I promise'. I said, 'Do you swear?' and
he said, 'Yes, I swear'. 'On your honour'. 'Yes, on my honour'.

The same question was put to each of them. They all
promised, on their honour. 'Now boys', I said, 'let them go'.
We stood aside and the four bullies filed out. There was no
more 'flogging round the course' during my time at school.

So much for organization. For ingenuity we need look no further
than Compton Mackenzie, soldier, administrator, novelist, dramatist
and spy-master.

'C', a lout and a bully, had a habit of making smaller boys
run round outside the 'giant stride' in the playground pulling
on the ropes while he, in solitary splendour, rode on the one
particular rope he had marked as his private property.
Compton decided to retaliate. He and a boy called Scott (whose
odd jacket and breeches 'C' had jeered at while twisting his arm)
happened to be in different classes. By meticulous timing they
asked to be 'excused' at the same moment, and met in the
lavatory. Proceeding from this base to the playground they
had to run the gauntlet of possible observation from different

classes, but by crawling along the ground arrived undetected at the 'giant stride'.

We soon found 'C's' sacred rope, with his initials carved on the handle. 'Pull it out and keep it as tight as you can', I said. Then I pressed the catch of my Norwegian knife and drew out the blade. Slowly I cut through the strands of the rope on the inside. We looked at it critically when it was hanging motionless with the rest of the ropes round the giant stride and decided that 'C' would not notice anything.

The bell shrilled for break. 'C' was waiting by the door out onto the playground.

'Come on you kids. Come on young Scott. Hurry up if you don't want me to kick your arse'.

We were herded up to the giant stride. 'C' seized the handle of his sacred rope and took it round, outside the ropes of his galley slaves. My heart was beating. Suppose the rope broke too soon. Suppose 'C' noticed it had been cut. Suppose – but no. He had seen nothing and off we started. Almost immediately 'C' was in the air, out at right angles to the rest of us. He must have circled the giant stride half a dozen times when suddenly it happened. We saw 'C' flying through the air, over the fence and heard a crash as he landed in a cucumber frame on the other side.

'C's' arm was still in a sling when he returned to school about a fortnight later. His collar-bone had been broken and there were two or three patches on his face.

Neither Scott nor I ever breathed so much as a hint of what we had done to bring about the tyrant's fall. We prudently denied ourselves the renown of Damon and Pythias; we had no desire to be executed for the assassination of a tyrant.

# 5

# A Little Learning

In the years between the wars a number of educational theorists gave their names to what was, in effect, a system of free choice, involving a minimum of supervision. An assistant master, found smoking his pipe in the common room, being asked what he was doing would reply, with a glance at his watch, that he had adopted the Dalton System. He was, at that precise moment, he might say, taking the top form in English and History, diversified by a little Latin grammar.

Professor Dalton's idea was not original. It had been propagated more than a century before by Tolstoy. In his book *Boyhood*, written in 1845, he says:

> A little bell rang at eight o'clock every morning and half an hour later the children appeared. The teacher entered the classroom. On the floor is a pile of children, one upon the other, screaming and bawling. The teacher goes to the cupboard, takes out the books and distributes to those who have followed him. Those who are still on top of the pile ask for theirs. Gradually the pile grows smaller. The children sit where they please, on benches, on tables, on window sills, on the floor. The hours for lessons are most irregular. The children are not obliged to come to school nor to remain there nor are they required to pay attention when they are there.

He adds, 'The sole basis of education is freedom. The freedom of people to organize their own schools and of the pupil to make up his mind what he will learn and how he will learn it.'

One of the features of the English preparatory school system was that it rested on a largely untrained staff. This could produce effects which varied from a reign of terror for the boys to a life of misery for the master. But it had compensations. A boy, at his most receptive age, might find himself being taught science by H.G. Wells, dramatic construction by George Orwell, appreciation of poetry by C. Day Lewis or John Betjeman or of light verse by A. A. Milne. Or he might find himself having his block knocked off by a lout fresh from performing similar feats at his public school.

Golden opportunities were sometimes missed. If Evelyn Waugh had been better instructed in the art of instruction, or had taken his unwanted job more seriously, he might have inculcated into his charges the elements of his own fine prose style. However:

> I had no strong pure sympathy for little boys, nor they for me. 'In charge of a form' is not an accurate expression. 'Confronted by it' or 'exposed to it' would be better. I was appointed to take the eldest in history, the younger in Latin and Greek. The latter I kept under subjugation, finding positive relish in making their lessons as tedious as the subject (very easily) allowed; the former were disorderly. I never fully succeeded in keeping them quiet. One of my major defeats was when I cried wrathfully to a moon-faced vacuous creature, 'Are you deaf, boy?' To which all his fellows replied, 'Yes, sir, he is.' And he was.

The results of such a system are slated by H.G. Wells, who had taken a teaching appointment at Henley House, a private school in Hampstead which belonged to J.V., the father of A.A. Milne. (His broadside is not necessarily aimed at Henley House, which was by no means a bad school.)

> Schools with such untrained staffs were responsible for the education or want of education of a considerable fraction of the British middle class. They were under no public control at all. Anyone might own one, anyone might teach in one, no standard of attainment was required of them; the parents dipped their sons into them as they thought proper and took them out when they thought they were done . . . For the most part these private schools passed the middle-class youth of England on to business or professional life incapable of any foreign language, incapable indeed of writing or speaking their own except in the clumsiest manner, unable to use their eyes and hands to draw or handle apparatus, grossly ignorant of physical science, history or economics, contemptuous of the board-school boy and with just enough consciousness of their

own deficiencies to make them suspicious of and hostile to intellectual ability and equipment.

However, though himself untrained, he managed to repair the deficiencies of the teacher from whom he took over instruction in science and biology.

My predecessor had been a Frenchman and evidently a man of great persistence of character. His chemical teaching had apparently reached a climax in the production of oxygen by heating potassium permanganate in a glass flask. Young Roberts, the son of Arthur Roberts the comedian, said it had been a very great lesson indeed. These were primitive times in glass manufacture and the ordinary test-tube or Florentine flask was not of a special refractory glass as it is now and it cracked and flew at the slightest irregularity in its heating. My predecessor had put his permanganate in a flask, put the flask on a tripod, set a bunsen burner beneath it and made all the necessary arrangements for collecting his oxygen. But before there was any oxygen worth mentioning to collect the flask flew, with a loud crack, and its bottom descended upon the flame.

My predecessor rallied his forces and put a second Florentine flask into action, with exactly the same result. A certain joyousness invaded the class as, with the spirit of the French at Waterloo, a third flask was thrown into the struggle. And so on, *de capo*; joy increased and open demonstrations had to be repressed. At the end there were no more flasks and the applause broke out unhindered.

Later in the same book he explains the steps which he took to remedy matters:

I discussed matters with the headmaster. 'Mr Milne,' I said, 'I think experimental demonstrations before a class are a great mistake.'

'They certainly have a very bad effect on discipline,' he remarked.

'I propose,' I said, 'with your permission, to draw all my experiments upon the blackboard — in coloured chalks — to

43

explain clearly and fully exactly what happens and to make the class copy out these experiments in a notebook. I have never known an experiment *on a blackboard* go wrong. On the other hand, these attempts at an excessive realism –'

'I am quite of your mind,' he said.

'Later on, however, I may dissect a rabbit bit by bit and make them draw that. I may dissect it under water, because it is cleaner and prettier than a heap of viscera on a board. I shall have to buy a large baking dish and cork and lead and pins.'

'It will not be – indelicate?'

'It need not be. I will show them what to see on the blackboard.'

'One never knows what parents will find to object to. However – if you want to do it . . .'

The attention of the boys was not always secured by the instruction, though it might be attracted by the personal habits of the instructor. According to Giles Romilly:

The star period of our week was a scientific lecture given by a man called Mr Boil. Benches were placed in a square round the big classroom and Mr Boil dominated the scene from a high desk at the far end. With pencil and paper we waited to make notes of the words of knowledge which fell from his mouth, but the only person who really took notes was the headmaster, Mr Dobrell. We spent the hour in flipping pellets of paper, passing messages and making mass noises of astonishment and interest. Mr Dobrell would get to his feet with an oratorical gesture and an 'I say, you fellows, do try to take a little more interest.' Afterwards Mr Boil had lunch at the top table with Mr Dobrell. There was always currant pudding when Mr Boil came and always by the end of the meal a currant or two had got impaled on the sharp bristles of his moustache. With currants on his moustache Mr Boil was indeed a fascinating sight.

Mathematics was, for the most part, passed over in silence by the boys; either because it had bored them out of their minds, or because they felt there was nothing to say about it. The only commentator is a girl, Naomi Mitchison, who appears later in this chapter. She memorized the multiplication table by allotting colours to it. 'Twice two was too easy to need a colour. Three times a yellow, four orange, five blue. After that they were sombre dark forest tones in which one was lost, until ten became clear. But why did I never learn them properly?'

Instruction in Greek was normally confined to a few boys in the senior class, but the study of Latin began early – and systematically. This is Winston Churchill arriving, at the age of nine, at his preparatory school.

We quitted the headmaster's parlour and the comfortable private side of the house and entered the more bleak apartments reserved for the instruction and accommodation of the pupils. I was taken into a form room and told to sit at a desk. All the other boys were out of doors and I was alone with the form master. He produced a thin, greeny brown covered book filled with words in different types of print.

'You have never done any Latin before, have you?' he said.

'No, sir.'

'This is a Latin grammar.' He opened it at a well-thumbed page. 'You must learn this,' he said, pointing to a number of words in a frame of lines. 'I will come back in half an hour and see what you know.'

Behold me, then, on a gloomy evening, with an aching heart, seated in front of the First Declension.

| | |
|---|---|
| mensa | a table |
| mensa | O table |
| mensam | a table |
| mensae | of a table |
| mensae | to or for a table |
| mensa | by, with or from a table |

What on earth did it mean? Where was the sense in it? It seemed absolute rigmarole to me. However, there was one thing I could always do, I could learn by heart. And I thereupon proceeded, as far as my private sorrows would allow, to memorise the acrostic-looking task which had been set me.

In due course the master returned.

'Have you learnt it?' he asked.

45

'I think I can *say* it, sir,' I replied and I gabbled it off.

He seemed so satisfied with this that I was emboldened to ask a question.

'What does it mean, sir?'

'It means what it says. Mensa, a table. Mensa is a noun of the First Declension. There are five declensions. You have learned the singular of the First Declension.'

'But,' I repeated, 'what does it *mean?*'

'Mensa means a table.'

'Then why does mensa also mean O table?' I enquired. 'And what does O table mean?'

'Mensa, O table, is the vocative case.'

'But why O table?' I persisted, in genuine curiosity.

'O table – you would use that in addressing a table, in invoking a table.' And then, seeing he was not carrying me with him, 'You would use it in speaking to a table.'

'But I never do,' I blurted out, in honest amazement.

'If you are impertinent you will be punished and, let me tell you, very severely,' was his conclusive rejoinder.

Such was my first introduction to the classics from which, I have been told, many of our cleverest men have derived so much solace and profit.

Possibly because he was taught more imaginatively, at his little Welsh school, than Churchill at his fashionable English school, the actor Emlyn Williams received a very different impression of Latin grammar, its cases and meanings.

And there was Latin. 'Puellae pedes nautarum lavant'. The girls wash the feet of the sailors. I saw the Mediterranean sands, the purple sailed galley rocking in the bay, the bronzed boys in their togas, sandals in hand, the white-robed girls kneeling with bowls of sea-water. 'Ave Caesar' . . . And romantically intricated with the picture was the grammar; the nominative girls verb-ly washing the accusative feet of the possessive sailors.

But the supporters of classics did not have it all their own way. It was not so much, thought their opponents, that Latin should be abolished in favour of science, but that much that was taught was pointless.

46

Eustace North, himself a classical scholar, said to a committee of the Headmasters' Conference, 'We have discussed, at length, the pronunciation of Latin – a matter of extraordinary unimportance. We have convinced ourselves that Latin verse writing is a sheer waste of time. We have had the melancholy spectacle of clever men, in the hopes of galvanizing a corpse, teaching little boys to talk Latin – with about as much utility as training poodles to carry parasols.'

After mastering the elements of Latin grammar, boys might be led, through Caesar's commentaries and the odes of Horace to the delights of writing their own Latin verse. At Summer Fields Dr Williams had his own methods.

It is astonishing what can be done by providing boys with dozens of formulae for dealing with general ideas. The mere occurrence of such words as 'spring' 'girl' 'dawn' 'evening' 'shade' or 'meadow' would call to the mind of any Summer Fields fifth-former (in this era) a reassuring armoury of Ovidian tags which enabled him to build up synthetic Latin verse easily enough.

Some boys took to this exotic art like ducklings to water. At the age of ten Ronald Knox was able to address a farewell ode to a young lady who had been paying a visit to his sisters: 'Florens Jacobi cara sororibus, Fortuna qualis mobilis, hinc abis –' (O Florence James, to both my sisters dear, Like fickle fortune hence you go away).

By tradition the first period each morning was devoted to a subject referred to in the time-table as Scripture or Divinity; though, in fact, since even the headmaster may have been chary of explaining the structure of the Christian faith to small boys, it was more probably Bible-reading and was entrusted to members of the junior staff; sometimes with unfortunate results.

In his book *Life's Rich Pageant*, which he wrote four years before his death, the late and much-lamented Arthur Marshall describes the procedure.

At Stirling Court we 'did' Genesis in the sixth form (it was probably considered too sensational and disturbing for younger boys) and here my friend Williamson came into his own for he had a splendidly enquiring mind and was not at all averse to asking questions, especially when he suspected, and how right he usually was, that the full truth was being, for some adult reason, withheld from him. He had already caused considerable consternation among the teaching staff by insisting on having the word 'whore' explained to him ('an immoral woman who sells herself for gold and I don't want to hear another word from you this lesson, Williamson') and he had followed it up with 'eunuch', which he mistakenly pronounced ee-unch ('a handicapped male person sometimes in the service of an eastern prince and come and see me after prayers, Williamson').

As soon as we reached the Cities of the Plain, and Sodom in particular, Williamson's alert mind spotted that we were not being Told All. The story, as watered down for our youthful ears, was feeble in the extreme. Everything hung, as you'll recall, on a secondary meaning of the verb 'to know'. This, we were told by a blushing Mr Sinclair, just meant 'getting to know' and indicated a chummy exchange of names and visiting cards. But why, then, the fire and brimstone and why, most revealing of all, the blushes. As soon as the lesson was over Williamson flew to the school library and searching, in a high state of excitement, through Chambers' invaluable dictionary, found what he was looking for ('To have sexual commerce with') and next day a fresh persecution of poor Mr Sinclair began, by now in deep trouble over Lot's unconventional behaviour in the mountains behind Zoar. 'Please sir, what does "commerce" mean?'

The teaching of history could vary from an attempt to blind the boys with science (or, at least, to keep them quiet if the headmaster happened to be present) to a genuine attempt to enlist their interest.

Evelyn Waugh adopted the former course:

The best way, I found, was to talk myself, without giving my pupils the opportunity to 'participate', as the liturgical jargon terms it. Memories of the history sixth at Lancing and of the few lectures I had attended at Oxford lent me words. One morning, early in my career, the headmaster paid a surprise visit to my form and sat at the back, listening while I discoursed on the financial embarrassments of Charles I. I was quite eloquent about the principle 'that the King must live

48

of his own', about the alienation of crown lands by Elizabeth and James, the feudal dues, the decline in the value of silver. In the presence of Mr Vanhomrigh the boys were unusually silent. Afterwards he called me to his study and said, 'I was deeply impressed by your lecture, *deeply*. But, you know, it was far over their heads. Also I noticed you constantly referred to "Stafford". I have always called him "Strafford".'

At the other extreme was the novelist, L.A.G. Strong. With the help of a fellow enthusiast, the Reverend J.A.C. Lysaght, he made a real effort to turn a catalogue of facts into a sensible and entertaining story.

Faced with the problem of getting a skeleton of accurate historical fact into the children's minds without stultifying the more creative side of the work, we hit on a compromise. Our object was to make the scaffolding of fact painless, even amusing and so allow time for an intelligent view of what history was about. We therefore devised a series of pictures, which I drew and painted. Each cartoon represented a reign. After our first attempt we gave up all attempt to represent the reigning King in human terms, for fear that the boys should think he really resembled the figure drawn. Instead we symbolized him. Sometimes by an animal, sometimes by a human figure so grotesque that even the stupidest could not take it for a portrait. William the Conqueror was an elephant, trampling underfoot symbols of the various rebellions against him, bearing on his back a Norman castle instead of a howdah and on his ample side a target made of concentric circles to represent the feudal system. William Rufus was appropriately a fox, Henry the First a lion, 'The Lion of Justice'. Through each picture ran a story, or sequence of images, in which the important events were spaced at a proportionate distance, one from another. For instance, the reign of Henry the Fourth was a kind of bobsleigh run, the course being beset with obstacles which stood for rebellions, conspiracies and battles encountered by the King – whose sleigh, incidentally, ran on castors, lest anyone should forget that he belonged to the house of *Lancaster*.

Thus, by means of puns, caricatures and various kinds of

nonsense, we were innocent, if vulgar, pioneers in teaching
by means of visual aids.

Geography, the Cinderella of subjects, almost ignored or taught
perfunctorily at most schools, received short shrift at Summer Fields.
Dr Williams regarded the subject as one of the counters in the game
which he played against the Etonian examiners. Ronnie Knox recalls
how, after breakfast at the White Hart at Windsor, where he was
conducting his scholarship boys, he said, 'Let's see. What have you
got this morning? History and Geography. Of course, there's been all
this talk of federating Australia. I suppose you all know the provinces
of Australia and their capitals, but we'll just pass it round once. So',
Ronald continued, 'we passed it round once and it was the first question on the sheet that faced us in Upper School.'

In somewhat similar circumstances Winston Churchill, knowing
that he would have to draw the map of one or other of thirty-six
different countries and that he had time to perfect himself in one only,
was inspired to choose New Zealand – which turned out to be the one
the examiners required. He says, 'this was what is called at Monte
Carlo an 'en plein' and I ought to have been paid thirty-five times my
stake.'

French and German masters were traditionally the victims of, at the
worst, mindless buffoonery, more often of affectionate scorn. Alfred
Percival Graves was Robert Graves' father. His autobiography, *To
Return to All That*, appeared shortly after his son's more famous work
(which he criticizes for lack of accuracy in a number of places and for
lack of generosity in others). His school was at Windermere.

Our French and German master – 'Moshyou Stroovell' might
really have come out of Struwell Peter. He was a dark
fiercely-moustached, thick-set Alsatian with an imperfect
knowledge of English, a pet canary and no power of keeping
order except with the cane, or with a ferule which he threw
with great accuracy at the heads of offenders. In self
protection we would put up the lids of our desks and the ferule
would ricochet across the room, occasionally smashing a
window. This provided him with opportunities for the exercise
of acts of skill for which we greatly admired him. If he
noticed us employed upon anything that did not concern our
French or German studies – such as an apple, a Brazil nut, or

even a bunch of keys – he would not confiscate it, but with
beautiful certainty pitch it out of the window through one
of those broken diamond panes. Once he thus pitched a turnip
watch and chain into outer space and the good old watch, which
had stopped for some time past, was found ticking away gaily.

But if they had shown themselves to be courageous, they could be
regarded with a measure of respect, as at Henley House.

Mr Howard was of French extraction and had fought in the
Franco-German War. Indeed, he was said still to have a
German bullet in his head, but I may be confusing him with
a later acquaintance, a French master at Westminster, who was
said still to have a German bullet in his behind. They both
had bullets, but they may have had them the other way
round; and in one case (since both, I am sure, were brave men)
it must have been an accidental French bullet. No doubt all
foreign masters of those days were so credited.

There was another one at Henley House who had been
engaged for years on an invention to render the tops of
omnibuses waterproof. It took the form of a large umbrella in
the middle of the floor, but there were technical difficulties
about opening and shutting it which I never understood and
which Mr Steinhardt never properly surmounted. Perhaps he
was a little before his time.

Teachers of French and German could present a problem to the
headmaster. In his book, *Memories of Half a Century*, the Reverend
Hiley says:

I had resolved never to employ a Frenchman. If admirably
qualified he may do well as a visiting master, but even then
his patience is sorely tried by perverse and rebellious English
youth. Having a penchant for the Germans I tried one or
two of Prussian nationality. Here I encountered different
problems.

One Prussian was remarkably vain of his person and I
observed that he had commenced to wear gold spectacles.
One Saturday he asked leave of absence to visit a friend in
Manchester. On his return, after two or three days, there

51

was a lot of giggling, though the reason I knew not until some time after.

It had been suggested that so handsome a man ought to marry a rich English woman, that Manchester would be his most likely market and that the best plan was to advertise in a Manchester paper. This was done. Answers arrived, correspondence ensued. He was to appear in person and to be recognised by his gold spectacles.

On the day fixed he sallied forth to Manchester and on arrival a smartly dressed young lady accosted him, amiably, but modestly and suggested an adjournment from the crowded platform to meet her friends. The guileless youth accordingly called a cab and the pair were driven to a pavilion on the cricket ground where there were two other young ladies eager to enter into competition. It need scarcely be explained that all three were young men in disguise and the pavilion was crowded with the youth of Manchester enjoying the fun. The rest of his adventure I knew not, but the poor fellow eventually appealed to the police for protection and under their care was 'returned empty' to the school.

And what of their own language?
Dr Williams had his solution with English as with Latin verse.

Whatever the subject he would dictate to them an opening, consisting each year of a different trite aphorism and give them another to wind up with. What they wrote in between was, in his view, immaterial provided that certain elementary laws of grammar and punctuation were kept.

But most children seem to have progressed either by encouragement in the home or by their own efforts. Rupert Hart-Davis had massive support from his home circle, not only from his mother, but from his uncle, Duff Cooper.

My love of learning, reading and speaking poetry was steadily growing, encouraged by Duff's gift of a pound as a reward for reciting all of Macaulay's Horatius to him. In June my mother copied out all three hundred lines of 'Charles Edward at Versailles' from Aytoun's 'Lays of the Scottish Cavaliers', so

that I could learn them under the dormitory bed-clothes with a
torch. I did so and they are still in my head, as so often
happens with things absorbed of one's own free will at an
impressionable age. Altogether during the next six years I
learnt more than a hundred poems by heart, most of them short,
but some longish. After a time I could not remember exactly
which I knew, so I entered them all alphabetically, under
poets, in a tiny leather bound address book and whenever my
mother asked me to recite something I gave her the book
to see what she would like. She was a perfect audience.

But the most striking evidence comes from Naomi Mary Margaret
Haldane who, under the name of Naomi Mitchison, wrote many
acclaimed historical and other novels. She had an unusually cultivated
background. Her father was an eminent physiologist and philosopher.
Her aunt Elizabeth is given a place in the *Dictionary of National Biography*
where she is described as 'having been educated in a highly cultivated atmosphere'. Her uncle, Richard Viscount Haldane, was
accounted by many to have been the greatest Minister of War ever
produced by this country.

Naomi went to the Dragon School. For most of the time, she says,
she was the only girl there, but found this no disadvantage.

At school we early got onto Macaulay, *The Revenge* and *Lays
of Ancient Rome*. How idiotic that one remembers masses of
this when things that would be valuable to remember are
totally not there. And it is not as if Lordly Volaterra or even
the Forty Prophets were in any way relevant to my life.

First I was taught writing in a copy book with 'pot-hooks
and hangers', the clerkly curves which used thin or thick ink
lines which one had to follow. This progressed to copying
whole sentences right down a page. But it was dreadfully
boring and curiously ink-spreading.

After a term or two, or maybe a year, we were told that we
were going to learn English grammar. I can't imagine what
the mental process was, but it came to me very clearly that
this would be in some way damaging and I was not going
to touch it. I was quite right, in a way; formal English
grammar would certainly have harmed me as a writer, but I had
not consciously known that I was a writer at that time, nor

would the amount of grammar we were likely to learn have
been either here or there. A glance at the early diaries shows
that I was in little need of it and had a very wide vocabulary.
But I refused to learn any of it, which must have been
annoying for dear Miss Williams, my form mistress.

Lord Dunsany was better known as a writer in the first half of this
century than he is now. He specialized in short stories and one act
plays and was a well-loved figure in the Irish literary renaissance. Lord
Longford says of him, 'He followed no fashion, founded no school and
had no use for self-consciously modern writing.' In a letter to Frank
Harris he says:

When I went to Cheam School I was given a lot of the Bible
to read. This turned my thoughts Eastward. For years no
style seemed to me natural but that of the Bible, and I feared
I would never become a writer when I saw that other people did
not use it.

His biographer, Mark Amory, says:

All boys of his generation and class knew the Bible well. He
knew and loved it better than most. When told to read the
lament of David for Jonathan and then to write out a précis
from memory, he instantly saw that no précis could be adequate
and so learnt it by heart and wrote it out. This display of
precocious good taste earned him no credit and he supposed
the master had merely thought he had been cheating and
cheating in a most unimaginative way.

There were other teachers of English who were more perceptive.
One in particular, Sir Jasper Hollom's brother, Vincent, writing of
life at Heddon Court School, Cockfosters, says:

Memories of John Betjeman tend to remain clear while others
become hazy, which is an indication of the intense impresssion
he made, mainly in his teaching of English Literature. The
hitherto familiar and laborious hours of 'parsing' and grammar
were transformed into the sounds and usage and rhythms of
words conveyed with such inspiration that sparks of

understanding seemed to be struck from every single and different boy in the classroom. Few, if any, were insulated from J.B's. electrifying and entirely communicable vision of literature.

For a summing up here is Arthur Symons, poet, translator and editor. He was educated, says the *Dictionary of National Biography* cautiously, 'in various Devonshire schools'. In his *Life*, by Roger Llombreaud, his own words are quoted:

I never understood a single proposition in Euclid; I never could learn geography or draw a map. Arithmetic or algebra I could do, moderately, so long as I merely had to follow the rules. The moment common sense was required I was helpless. History I found entertaining and I could even remember the dates, because they had to do with facts, which were like stories. French and Latin I picked up easily – Greek with more difficulty. German I was never able to master. I had an instinctive aversion to the mere sound of it, and I could not remember the words. There were no pegs in my memory for them to hang upon, as there were for the words in the Romance languages. When a thing did not interest me, nothing could make me learn it.

# 6

# Games

In the third quarter of the nineteenth century Crichton House School and its headmaster, Dr Grimstone, almost displaced Wackford Squeers and Dotheboys Hall as prototypes of the horrors of juvenile education. The popularity of *Vice Versa* had one unforeseen result. Whilst several originals were tentatively suggested for Squeers, Anstey's friends all knew which prep school *he* had attended. Anstey denied the attribution, but readers of his autobiography *A Long Retrospect* could be forgiven for spotting more than one resemblance. In food and in games, the ghost of Mr Bultitude lingers across the years.

I was not good at games and I doubt whether I should have found football or cricket much more attractive even if they had been better organised than they were. A few of the older fellows played with energy, but not much skill, the rest of us occasionally backing them up more or less half-heartedly. Now and then at football, generally when 'Grimstone' was present, I would rouse myself to charge some bigger boy who was dribbling the ball in my direction, with the usual result of finding myself on my back and the ball well on its original course. At cricket I was usually placed at some point which the ball was unlikely to reach and as there were no overs I could pursue my own thoughts undisturbed till the other side was out. When I went in to bat the field closed in all round in what I considered an uncomplimentary manner, and if I was not bowled out first I obliged with an easy catch and retired, quite unabashed and rather relieved to have got it over.

There was no spirit of emulation; nobody cared which side won, we never played other schools, and no one was a hero among us on account of his prowess at football or cricket. 'Grimstone' would appear and captain a side at cricket or football and he would bowl at cricket – unless I am mistaken – for both sides.

Ernest Raymond was one of the most prolific popular novelists of the early years of this century. He was the author of more than fifty novels, biographies and plays; the first and best known of his books was a school story *Tell England*. Colet Court, the junior establishment of St Paul's School, was the scene of his first experience of football – unhappier even than Mr Bultitude's.

In the first days of my first term I suffered a withering
humiliation. It was on a small asphalt football ground and
we were playing six-a-side. Since I was the newest footballer,
I was inevitably told to keep goal. There I stood, on the asphalt,
framed by the white goal posts. A nimble and fleet boy got
the ball somewhere near the centre line and out-running all he
came, with the ball at his foot, towards me, unimpeded for
about twenty yards. I did not know what one did in these
alarming circumstances, so I stayed where I was, waiting to
receive anything he might offer. Of course, he just footed
the ball into the goal yards away from where I was standing.
Howls of execration from the members of my side, roars of
delight from the other side, uncontrollable laughter from the
spectators.
     Though I was less of an incompetent in later years, I still
think this early scene on the asphalt is a fair picture of my failure
to be anything but a solitary at school.

Such scenes – pickups in which the headmaster took a dignified part, and games played on asphalt – must have seemed primitive, almost indecorous, to the strenuous and competitive young athletes of this century. Sport soon ceased to be something you did to fill up morning breaks and blank afternoons. It had become an all-absorbing passion. Stratton-Ferrier, who captained the Summer Fields soccer team in 1936, writes with a depth of feeling that would not have been out of place if he had been describing a climactic religious experience.

On Saturday, 5th December 1936, we played Horris Hill at
home, the last match of the season. So far we were unbeaten.
     None of us had been able to concentrate during that last
week and I was afraid lest one of the side should earn himself
a whacking or be put in the Black Book for inattention, with

disastrous effects on his morale. In the event nobody got so much as a double-sided 'copy'. I think none of the staff dared risk Geoffrey Bolton's wrath by demoralizing any of his precious First Eleven.

In Fifth Form the tension was unbearable. Saturday's match was in the forefront of all minds and the whole of ancient literature seemed crammed with subtle references to the impending decisive battle. On the Friday evening we sang the Psalm usually reserved for the day before Common Entrance. 'The ploughers ploughed along my back and made long furrows'. It 'wished us good luck in the name of the Lord'.

And finally Saturday came.

A few hurried last-minute conferences and the plan of campaign was complete. 'We must have a goal *quickly*,' G.B. said for the umpteenth time, 'so get in there with everything you've got and score ὡς τάχιστα . . . !'

So there we were, trotting on to the field at last, neat adrenalin pumping through our veins. There was G.B., his matchstick legs in long blue shorts and those crazy boots of his, his face trying desperately to register a referee's impartiality and refusing to talk to us now that we were under starter's orders. He looked grim and tired.

He blew his whistle and we kicked off. What immediately happened is a blur, but about thirty seconds later an image like a photograph impinged indelibly on my mind. In this picture we are attacking Horris Hill's goal and Gerald Seager is poised high in the air like Nijinski among a crowd of defenders, his clever head having found a good centre from the left wing. He deflected it in a high, slow, lob towards the goalkeeper. The goalie fumbled. The ball dropped on the line. He, two Horris Hill full backs, Gerald, Tommy Carlyon and I reached it about the same time. There was a great impact and a moment later there were the two full backs, the goalkeeper, ball and all in a heap at the back of the net.

I shall never forget Geoffrey Bolton's face as he came running up after blowing his whistle to register a goal. He was laughing, laughing in great uncontrollable giggles of glee, all pretence of judicial calm abandoned in this one moment of overwhelming victory.

For it was all over and we knew it and they knew it. We won quite easily after that.

One hopes that the boys, at least, behaved with decorum. If they did not, they would have earned the displeasure of A.P. Herbert, novelist, playwright and rhymester, formerly a promising soccer player at the Grange School at Folkestone.

It may sound smug, but I remember vividly how one behaved in those far-off days, when one scored a goal. You did not fling your arms in the air in arrogant exultation, even if it was the goal that won the match. None of your fellows approached you, patted, slapped or embraced you. Not even your captain. You trotted quietly back to your place with your modest eyes directed to the ground, as if you were almost ashamed to have attracted special attention. Applause was, rightly, left to the spectators.

I am sorry to see that the disgusting ecstasies of the professional footballer are beginning to invade the cricket field. A famous international batsman comes in. All expect and many hope that he will make a hundred. A good ball, or a poor stroke and he is out for two. By the fielding side at least the Fall of the hero might be observed in respectful silence, but no. Four or five players leap in the air. There is back slapping and happy huddling. However, the cricketers have some way to go. I have not seen Cowdrey kiss the wicket-keeper. Not yet.

There were boys, even then, who did not take football over seriously. Bernard Newman, author of more than a hundred books, first and most realistic of all spy-story writers, was one of them.

You are a junior, but by some accident you are called upon to play in the first eleven. With the scores level, and only a minute to go, you kick the winning goal.

Hundreds of books have been founded on this fantasy. But in my case, it really happened. I was a very undistinguished member of the school second eleven. One afternoon, having no match, I went with the first eleven as linesman. One of the team, kicking about before the game, sprained his ankle and I was co-opted. I was placed on the wing, where I could do least harm.

Five minutes before time we were three goals all and then, by some fluke, I found myself in front of goal with only the goalkeeper to beat. I kicked with great force – that was one thing I could do. Unfortunately I kicked the ground, not the ball which merely trickled forward. The goalkeeper, a hefty fellow, did not even trouble to pick it up. He came running out to kick the ball hard up field. I turned my back – and the ball hit me on the behind and rebounded into the net.

There seems to be something typical in the incident. More than once in my life I have achieved spectacular results, but not in spectacular fashion. I am more susceptible, it seems, to anti-climax than to climax.


As might have been expected, it was rugby football that attracted young Douglas Bader, flying ace and hero of the book and film *Reach for the Sky*.


Temple Grove was a pleasant old school with plenty of playing fields. The regime quickly drew the new boy into organised games and overnight he seemed to flare up, like a Roman candle, with eagerness. It was the perfect outlet for his mercurial nature and he literally threw himself into rugger, a gritty and indestructible small boy, bouncing up as fast as he was knocked down, which was often.

Fast on his feet and fast-thinking, he shone as a fly-half and after the first few games was promoted to more senior teams finding himself, as in all his fights, matched against bigger boys.

In the gym he limbered up on the parallel bars, on the horizontal bar, the vaulting horse, or in the boxing ring. He would try anything, not just once, but till he had mastered it, hating to let anything beat him; or anyone. People lost count of the times he fell off the parallel bars, but he learnt to fall without hurting himself. In fact, he lost all fear of falling, which was one of the most important things that ever happened to him.

Even rugby football had its lighter side, which can be found by turning to another Oxford prep school, as famous as Summer Fields, but less conventional. This is Lynam's, known as the Dragon School. A contributor to an educational journal commented on the difference between these schools when he wrote of Lynam's: 'Despite the compulsion to play games, there is no Cult of Games, no enforced watching, no frenzy over winning.' And in his book, *A Dragon Century*, C.H. Jaques remembers how, 'during the 1962 rugger season an unbeaten prep school side arrived with an army of excited parental supporters on an afternoon of fog so thick that from the touch line the play could only be followed by ear. The visiting supporters were soon encroaching on the field of play in search of the action, to such an extent that the Noter of the Term credited the only try to a visiting mum.'

A form of exercise which was almost universal in schools (and almost universally disliked) was 'gym' or physical training; now, in an effort to make it more acceptable, re-named physical education. Boys had several reasons for disliking it. First because what one did seemed pointless and non-competitive, and, worst of all, it was meant to be good for them. Let Graham Greene speak for all:

> The only class I actively hated was held in the gym. I was
> very bad at gymnastics and all life long my instinct has
> been to abandon anything for which I have no talent; tennis,
> golf, dancing, sailing, have all been abandoned and perhaps it
> is only desperation which keeps me writing, like someone who
> clings to an unhappy marriage for fear of solitude. I particularly
> disliked trying to vault or climb a rope. I suffered, in those
> days, like a character of mine, Jones, in *The Comedians*, from flat
> feet and I had to wear supports in my shoes and have massage
> from a gym mistress. The massage tickled and my soles
> sometimes ached, but on the whole I found the treatment
> agreeable, perhaps because it was given by a woman.

Equally unpopular, until their skills had been mastered, were swimming and diving. Splendid once the rudiments had been acquired. Off-putting until then. Paul Spillane writes about St Andrew's School, Eastbourne, under the great Edwin Leece Browne.

> No account of swimming would be complete without a
> mention of the plunge bath, which was built at the turn of

the century. It was about fourteen feet long, six feet wide and
nearly six feet deep. Steps and bricks set into one wall served
as diving platforms. First thing every morning the boys were
obliged to leap into its invigorating, icy waters. E.L.B. put coins
at the bottom of the bath to encourage the divers, and it was in
the 'plunge' that he taught generations of St Andrew's boys to
swim. After he had mastered the basic strokes, lying over a
piano stool, the boy would be put in a rubber ring at the end
of a broomstick fishing rod and trawled up and down the bath.
Then E.L.B. crying, 'Now swim for it', would command the boy
to jump into the bath and fend for himself. He held the ring
just out of the boy's reach. Nobody drowned.

Boxing seems to have faded out altogether. Possibly it was never
taken very seriously. One of the early magazines of St Peter's, Seaford,
records that an ex-sailor called Bob Willis used to come up, on Thursday evenings, dressed in a blue suit, high-necked sweater and a cloth
cap which blended with a broken nose and cauliflower ear to confirm
his pugilistic status. One of his pupils says:

> I will not say that he taught us boxing. He made no attempt
> to do so, but made two of us, of roughly the same size, have it
> out with eight-ounce gloves. No. 3 classroom was the ring,
> desks having been pushed aside and a chair, basins and towels
> provided for the young pugilists. Rounds might go on for five
> minutes or more, depending on how Willis was getting on with
> some highly improbable account of his life in sail.

In one or two of the leading schools there was one sport which had
the valuable effect of teaching a boy something he could continue to
enjoy when violent exercise was beyond him. Lieutenant-General Lord
Norrie, later Governor-General of South Australia and Governor-
General and Commander-in-Chief of New Zealand, reports:

> I found myself in the final of the Junior Schools Golf
> Championship, against Eric Ednam, now Earl of Dudley.
> Eric's father was a keen golfer. As we went round the course
> Eric said to me, 'Look, Willoughby, I'm going to have the devil
> of a bad report this term.' He paused and glanced at me. 'I
> suppose you wouldn't –?'

'You mean, let you win?'

He nodded, rather embarrassed. 'Well, you see, it's more important for me than you, isn't it? It would make all the difference with my father if I win this championship.' He has since reminded me that he offered me a bag of bulls eyes and all his golf balls into the bargain.

Anyhow, I did miss a twelve-inch putt at the last hole and Eric was victor by one stroke. Lord Dudley was more than delighted and went round his London clubs saying, 'My son at Summer Fields has won the Golf Championship. I'm going to present a silver medal each year to perpetuate the competition.'

When he died in 1930 Lord Dudley forgot to leave, in his Will, a sum of money to pay for this annual trophy, which is still known as the Dudley Medal. And for the last thirty years the present Lord Dudley has had to fork out a substantial sum for it. He much regrets that I did not win the competition.

But of all sports and games cricket was King.

Much of the attention of the first meeting of the Association of Headmasters of Preparatory Schools was devoted to a discussion of the size of cricket balls and the length of the pitch. For cricket demanded very different abilities and talents from football of either code. Quickness of foot, quickness of thought, strength of wrist and arm were important. But they were not of vital importance. What really counted was a sense of timing and a certain inherent talent. To the prep school master this represented a fascinating challenge. Well coached, a boy of thirteen or fourteen could be as finished a cricketer, lacking only adult muscle, as he would ever become. The flair had only to be spotted, the talent nursed.

Lord Home of the Hirsel, later Prime Minister of England, went to Ludgrove in 1912, at the age of nine.

Coming from Scotland where, because of the climate, cricketers were thin on the ground, I had never seriously considered the possibility that I could compete with my English contemporaries at that game. It was a master, W.S. Bird, later killed in the War, who had kept wicket for Middlesex, who banished that particular inferiority

63

complex. I was playing 'stump cricket' (one stump to bowl at, with a softish ball) when I overheard him saying, 'That boy is worth watching. He can bowl.' That modest encouragement was enough.

There were, of course, nigglers. In his contribution to *The Early Years of St Peter*'s, Christopher Pirie-Gordon says:

Rugger, with soccer and holy Cricket, formed the trinity of the school's established religion. I remember the awful tones of the headmaster's rebuke one day at lunch when some of us were talking about a murder trial at our end of the table when he suddenly banged his hand down, barking out, 'Whether a criminal be innocent or guilty has no importance compared with the matter I am discussing – namely whether English cricket is in a decline.' We started hastily to discuss the Test Match.

Equally disenchanted was George Melly, blues singer, journalist and screen writer, at school in the mid-1930s.

During the summer term, if a Test Match was being played we were expected to eat our bright pink mince and leaden jam roll in attentive silence and listen, with real or simulated interest to the BBC commentary. Any whispering, if detected, led to a slippering. In me the headmaster sensed a contrary spirit, and almost every day would fire questions as to who bowled the last over or was fielding at silly mid off. As I never knew ('Give me your slipper, Melly') I was very relieved when rain stopped play and even now the announcement, 'and we return to the studio', holds a certain irrational beauty.

For a final comment, Maurice Baring. A contemporary described him as 'urbane and artful' and it is possible to read this extract from *The Puppet Show of Memory* without being quite sure whether his tongue is in his cheek or not.

One day we were looking on at a cricket match which was being played against another school. Our school was getting beaten, the day was hot, the match was long and tedious and

Broadwood and another boy called Bell and myself wandered away from the match; two of us climbed up the wooden platform which was used for letting off fireworks on the 5th of November. Bell remained below and we threw horse chestnuts at him, which he caught in his mouth. Presently one of the masters advanced towards us, biting his knuckles, which he did when he was in a great rage. He ordered us indoors and gave us two hours' work to do. We went in as happy as larks and glad to be in the cool.

At tea we saw there was something seriously amiss. The rival eleven, who had beaten us, were present, but not a word was spoken. There was an atmosphere of impending doom over the school, charged with the thunder of a coming row. After tea, when the guests had gone, the school was summoned into the hall and the Head, gowned and frowning, addressed us and accused the school in general and Broadwood, Bell and myself in particular, of want of patriotism, bad manners, inattention and vulgarity. He was disgusted, he said, with the behaviour of the school before strangers. We were especially guilty, but the whole school had shown want of attention and gross callousness and indifference to the cricket match (which was all too true).

There was to have been an expedition to the New Forest next week. That expedition would not come off. The speech ended and the school trooped out in gloomy silence and broke up into furtive whispering groups. That night in my cubicle I said to Worthington that I thought Campbell minor, who had been scoring during the match, had behaved well all day. Didn't he deserve to go to the New Forest? 'No,' said Worthington. 'He whistled twice.' 'Oh,' I said, 'then of course he can't go.'

# 7

# STEPS TO THE STAGE

Laurence Olivier, whose choral start at All Saints, Margaret Street, is recorded in the next chapter, comments in his autobiography, 'My first acting opportunity was accidental – whose isn't?' But it is clear that when Chance whisked past, the Lady's hand was pretty firmly grabbed.

I had been cast for the second citizen in *Julius Caesar*, our Christmas play. At the early rehearsals I found myself undoubtedly and delightedly, scoring, eliciting enthusiastic laughter from boys and clergy alike. Our Cassius was not happily cast and Brutus, an older boy named Ralph Taylor, whose mother was the actress Mary Forbes, and who was showing himself a born actor, was switched to Cassius and I was raised from second citizen to Brutus. The original Cassius was made to feel happier as the second citizen.

Our performance was graced by highly august persons, one staggering example of which was none other than the magical Ellen Terry. Also there was Sir Johnston Forbes-Robertson, to whom my father wangled an introduction. Sir Johnston was, of course, courtesy itself, seeing my father's dog-collar and priestly silk tunic under the frock-coat. My father reported that Sir Johnston said to him, 'My dear man, your boy does not play Brutus. He *is* Brutus'. I cannot vouch for the truth of this anecdote. I never myself believed it.

The production was successful enough to be revived. I was nine the first year we presented a show; I felt an old hand the following year when I was ten.

The chance might slip away altogether – or it might simply be postponed, as it was for Roland Culver.

One master, Mr Featherstone, found in me something other than the pleasant idiot that I had previously been accepted as. I had committed some crime, the nature of which I cannot recall and Mr Featherstone decreed that I should be kept in from swimming for the following two days. During the two mornings of restraint I was to learn two speeches from Shakespeare; Hamlet's well-known advice to the players and Henry V's rejection of Falstaff – 'I know thee not, old man. Fall to thy prayers –'

I was anxious to avoid losing two swims and easily crammed in those two speeches the first morning. After prep I knocked on Mr Featherstone's study door.

'Please, sir. I know them.'

'Know what? Those speeches. I don't believe it. Let's hear them.'

I reeled them off without a hitch.

'Very good, Culver. Very good indeed. But it's a pity you seem only to concentrate under duress.'

'Oh, but I enjoyed it. It was easy.'

'Was it, Culver? Well, well. Your punishment seems to have discovered something you do easily. Have you ever thought of the theatre?'

'You mean, play in it, sir?'

'Yes, boy. Be an actor. You do? Then I'll have a word with the headmaster and, perhaps, your parents.'

Unfortunately, says Roland Culver, this was the year 1914. Mr Featherstone, who was on the Reserve of Officers, was called up before he could make good his promise and was killed in action in 1915. This, Culver reckons, postponed his own entry into the theatrical profession for a number of years.

Like Lord Olivier, John Gielgud made an early transfer from music to drama. At the age of nine he went to a preparatory school called 'Hillside', near Godalming.

I thought I sang rather well. At Sunday services my shrill treble would soar above the other voices during the hymns, as I stood with my head thrown back, hoping to be seen as well as heard. My histrionic cravings found another, more legitimate outlet. We were encouraged to act in the winter and spring terms and it was then that I appeared for the first time before an audience. My performance of the Mock Turtle

in *Alice* was duly tearful and I sang 'Soup of the Evening.
Beautiful Soup' with increased volume and shrillness in every
verse. I was a bland Humpty-Dumpty and an impassioned
Shylock. (My Portia was John Cheatle who afterwards
understudied me in 'Musical Chairs'). Another term I played
Mark Antony. I remember waiting for my entrance, standing
on the icy cold conservatory floor, shivering in my toga. I
warmed up, however, as soon as I began to act and as my
courage grew I must have played with all my might, for I
succeeded in reducing the only titled parents to tears.

Rex Harrison does not explain how he got his first dramatic role,
but it seems appropriate that the man who, as Professor Henry Higgins,
was to show such an informed interest in language, should early have
spotted the comic possibilities inherent in words. In his autobiography, *Rex*, he says:

> I played first in 'A Midsummer Night's Dream', as Flute the
> bellows-mender who doubles with Thisbe, a fair maiden. My
> mother made me a corn-coloured wig that went on like a
> basin, and a long dress; and I decided to go for an ample bosom
> and a lisp.
>
> > 'Oh wall, full often hast thou heard
> > my moanth
> > For parting my fair Pyramuth and me
> > My cherry lipth have often kithed thy
> > stoneth —'
>
> and so on. Getting, I may say, my fair share of laughs.
> Success obviously went straight to my head and I proceeded
> to fall in love with the small boy playing Titania, only
> because he looked so beautifully like a girl. His name, I
> remember, was Hay junior and I followed him everywhere
> back stage. I should add that my affection did not go beyond
> his costume and when he took it off I had no use for him at all.
> Nor can I remember anyone following me around as Thisbe.

Though modesty may be a pleasing characteristic in a boy, it is
clear that a measure of aggressive self-confidence is necessary if he is
to stand out from the crowd. The great actor-manager Sir Frank
Benson was at a preparatory school (unnamed) near Brighton.

One occasion I remember with priggish satisfaction. The boys were all asked to walk from their position in the numbered ranks, once round the gymnasium and back to their place. My number was 35 on a muster roll of 35.

All my seniors had failed to satisfy the instructor. They giggled, blushed, stumbled, ran nervously, fidgetted or were self conscious. The instructor was an old sergeant major who had served with the Guards in the Crimea. When it came to my turn, to the intense amusement of the class, I gravely paraded round the building, silently, solemnly, steadily, without shyness. On my return to my humble position I was promoted to the top of the class, as being the only boy who had carried out his orders correctly.

For long afterwards I remembered my embarrassment when the big guardsman led me out and prophesied to my classmates that one day that little boy would march ahead of them all towards some definite and important goal, and that many would follow him.


James Mason showed similar initiative. He was at a small preparatory school called 'The Old College', near Windermere. His headmaster was a Mr Raikes.


On a Sunday at the beginning of the Summer Term of 1919, in the Library, after Evening Prayers Mr Raikes turned the meeting into what theatre people refer to as a casting session. He picked on one or two of the smaller boys and briefed them as follows:

> 'I want you to imagine that some of those boys at the other end of the room are fooling about. You have to shout at them and tell them to be quiet.'

Three or four boys made pitiful attempts to comply. They were dismissed. Then he came to me. There was no need for him to repeat his instructions. I went straight into my act.

> 'You fellows down there,' I screamed. 'Stop fooling. If you don't keep quiet, you'll be kept in.'

Mr Raikes laughed, in a manner which suggested that I had passed some sort of test and it transpired that I was to tell a funny story at the forthcoming school concert about a passenger on an ocean liner who stuttered badly, especially in times of stress.

As he happened to be the sole witness of a dreadful accident, he rushed up to the bridge and tried to report the accident to the Captain.

Waving frantically towards the ocean, he worked his stutter into total unintelligibility.

'If you can't say it, sing it,' roared the Captain. So, to the tune of Auld Lang Syne, the passenger sang:

> 'Should auld acquaintance be forgot,
> And never brought to mind,
> The blooming cook fell overboard,
> He's twenty miles behind.'

Gratifying applause.

But the first truly professional touch is produced by the young Alec Guinness. He was at a school called Roborough, near Eastbourne.

As a change from Gilbert and Sullivan the Dramatic Society was doing Macbeth and he was given the brief and unremarkable role of a messenger, on the principle that, though he was bound to mess it up, he could not mess it up too much.

This was, to him, his big chance and he went about the preparation of the role with what, with hindsight, we can see as characteristic care and methodical attention to detail.

He first of all firmly memorised the brief speech and then set himself to consider how he could best create the illusion of having rushed home from the battle field to deliver his message. No unconscious exponent of Method acting, even at that early stage, he decided, more prosaically that something like the actuality was preferable to any artful illusion. So, after precisely timing the scene preceding his entrance, he sneaked out and stationed himself, in the dark, at the other end of the playing fields. When the time was ripe he set off, in a pell-mell sprint, back into the school hall and onto the stage, right on cue; giving an amazing impersonation of breathlessness and near physical collapse, because it was no impersonation, but the real thing.

Flabbergasted, the audience gave the messenger a spontaneous round of applause. And quite possibly at that moment the die of Alec's future was cast.

Six of the seven boys mentioned above were to become stars of the large and the small screen; but such a step belongs to a later stage in their life. Two exceptions, one named and one unnamed.

In her biography of Peter Finch, Elaine Dundy quotes John Carter and Keith Gill in their vivid recollections of a precociously talented boy.

A restless, energetic boy, he always 'connected', always made contact. And the only way he could do so . . . was to do what he could do best. He became an entertainer. 'I was regarded,' says Peter, 'as the comic of the class'. But he was more than that. Ingenious, enthusiastic, enterprising with a theoretical know-how that came straight from heaven, he organised other boys into putting on skits for the school's amusement; with himself, quite naturally, in the leading role.

'Most vividly,' says his friend John Carter, 'I remember his skit on Hamlet when he was in his last year (twelve years old). Written, produced, dressed and taking the title role etc., etc., etc. So good that the headmaster had him perform it to each of the three senior classes. Most of us then had never heard of Hamlet. It was a riot.'

'I think I must have been his first leading lady,' says Keith Gill, who had played Lady Macbeth to Peter's Macbeth. He wore one of his mother's night-gowns, tied with a green sash and the ghost chased them both round the class room.

In his earlier days, Peter had revealed an extraordinary talent. 'This shy, well-mannered, courteous, amiable boy,' says John Carter, 'was able to vomit at will. For a small fee he would vomit on the floor of the lunch room for those of his class-mates who wanted a day off school. They'd plead sickness and after clearing up the mess be permitted to go home.'

It was a fitting metaphor for such a rending actor as Peter was to become; spilling his guts out for a small fee so that the audience could take a half day off.

71

Then there was the equally remarkable Archibald Alec Leach. The son of lower middle-class parents, he was born in Bristol in 1904 and was sent, at the age of eight, to Fairfield, 'a respectable middle-class school', a mile from the centre of the town.

> For most of the time he was simply a mischievous, wilful boy with a rebellious and insolent streak that brought him into regular contact with the headmaster's cane. When he was caught at some misdeed he had the ability to open his dark brown eyes and raise a single eyebrow quizzically, as if in proof of his innocence. As he stood waiting for his punishment, in his scruffy sweater, twisting his ink stained hands behind his back, with his socks pushed down to his ankles, he seemed desperate to be noticed. A frail boy, with sad eyes and an almost girlish face, he looked like a belligerent fawn.
>
> The journey into adolescence brought with it a vanity that was to remain throughout his life. When another boy knocked him over accidentally that winter, he fell flat on his face on the icy ground. His front tooth snapped in half, straight across. Anxious to preserve the features that he was aware, were beginning to attract some attention among the girls at the school he decided to have the remaining piece of the tooth pulled out at the local hospital. For weeks after the extraction he kept his mouth shut as much as possible while the gap between his front teeth gradually closed. As a result he perfected the tight lipped smile that became famous.

Which, indeed, it was destined to do when he attained stardom in films under the name of Cary Grant.

The final extract poses a question one would like to answer; or perhaps not, since it might cause embarrassment. Hermione Williams, the wife of the then headmaster of Summer Fields, was a woman who kept a maternal eye on timid new boys. She is quoted in Richard Usborne's *A Century of Summer Fields*:

> One boy was nervous and highly strung and his mother very anxious about him. We had fireworks on the lawn on 5th November and the boys watched from the class-room windows. This mother asked 'If Christopher could watch

from the drawing room window and hold Mrs Williams's hand'. He out-grew his nerves, I am glad to say and has become a film star and usually takes the chief part in horror films. I always go eagerly to see them. I am sorry to say that I have not met him since he left. I always hope I shall do so.

Christopher who?

# 8

# Music

Cathedral and choir schools, which differ only from normal preparatory schools by reason of their attachment to a cathedral or a church foundation, are the institutions most likely to nourish all forms of musical ability in a boy. 'Music was taken seriously at the Chapel Royal', says Arthur Sullivan. 'Young M. was caned yesterday because he did not know the meaning of fortissimo'.

Geoffrey Bush, the well-known composer of church and other music, attended the Cathedral School at Salisbury from 1928 when he was aged eight, until 1933. Speaking on Radio 3 he said:

My own strong inclination to music may not have been apparent before I went to Salisbury, but it had emerged unmistakably soon after I was ten. From then on I filled dozens of manuscript books with juvenile compositions. By counting each of a series of Anglican chants as a separate unit I got to Opus 100 by the time I was thirteen.

All that I produced at first was a series of meaningless jottings, rather like the pot hooks toddlers draw in imitation of their parents' handwriting. But gradually what I wrote began to make a bit of sense. One day I was discovered scribbling away by Bernard Rose, now Organist and Informator of the choristers at Magdalen College, Oxford, but then our Bishop's Boy, or senior chorister. He grabbed the manuscript from me – it was, I think, a setting of the story of Jonah – and played it through to a group of boys standing round the piano. This was, I suppose, the greatest artistic triumph of my life. One of my contemporaries came up to me and said, 'It sounded like a real oratorio'.

Nothing much was done about actually teaching us music. Piano lessons were extra. They were given, I'm sorry to say, not by an expert, but by whoever happened to be sub-organist at the time. If he was a good teacher we prospered; if not, not.

There was no provision for any other instrumental teaching and this, I think, was a major deficiency. Nor were there any facilities for an apprentice composer to learn his craft. In my last year I saved 3/6d (a pretty good sum in those days) out of my pocket money to buy Sir John Stainer's *Harmony*, and I worked through that on my own.

Once I summoned up the courage to show the Cathedral Organist Dr (later Sir Walter) Alcock what he called 'a little composement'. It was a waltz in C minor. I can remember the first eight bars but, luckily, nothing else. Sir Walter was kindness itself; but that didn't constitute a lesson. On the other hand, in spite of the absence of formal teaching, we learned a prodigious amount by simply doing. Music was around us all the time. We absorbed it as children absorb a foreign language when they live abroad – effortlessly.

Laurence Olivier, whose early aspirations were musical, not dramatic, is of the same mind.

Why I was sent to quite so many prep schools I had not discovered. I only knew that the number of them was grist to the mill of fault-finding schoolmasters who would add my personal history to my other faults. '*How* many schools do you say you've already been to before you came here?' The extra admonition inevitably followed, 'All those schools and you don't even know . . .'

The fact is that my mother nursed a private ambition that I should follow my brother's successful entry into the choir of All Saints Margaret Street. This extremely High Anglican church possessed a rarely fine group of choristers reputed, and I believe with justice, to be the finest of all choirs in London . . . It was my repeated failure to win a place in this wonderful singing machine that pushed me, time and again, to some new prep school.

At last I was offered a place in the choir. As a chorister I received a musical education of great worth which has given me for ever a passion and appreciation for this most God-given of all arts. All Saints musical repertoire was especially rich. Our training was nursed in the great hierarchy of classical composers, way skyward above the usual Church of England

aspirations: Mozart, Handel, Bach, Beethoven (masses in C
*and* D), Schubert, Mendelssohn, Gounod, Dvorak,
Palestrina, supported by the more usual Attwood, Tallis,
Tinel, Gibbs, Wesley, Stainer and Stanford; masses, evensongs,
choral services of every kind, anthems and requiems. All these
and more were presented for the rapture of the congregations
which attended this highly fashionable, unimaginably
beautiful, though small, place of worship.

Even at a non-choral school a shrewd headmaster could appreciate
the value of a boy with musical talent. Malcolm Sargent obtained, by
competition, at the age of twelve one of the free places as a boarder
at Stamford School. The headmaster was Edwin Lovegrove, described
as a 'brisk innovator'. One of his innovations was rugby football, at
which Malcolm suffered a shoulder dislocation. For years afterwards
he was able, by rotating his injured shoulder, to put it out and in
again. Malcolm's biographer, Charles Reid, writes:

Any master could see, with half an eye, that Malcolm had
more of the dreamer in him than the average boy. It was
conveyed to Lovegrove that Malcolm's dreams were about
music and that he had rare musical talent. Although without
any ear for music himself Lovegrove, after a while, let the boy
off games altogether. During the Games' periods 'Mal'
practised on the school piano. On speech days he officially
accompanied the school choir and was always at the piano
when the school song 'Dulce Domum' was called for. In a
community that observed uncommonly rigid discipline he
had a niche to himself; he was acknowledged to be rather
apart, the sort of personality for whom special rules are made as
a matter of course.

The life of a schoolboy musician was not always an easy one. Arthur
Sullivan found that popularity had its drawbacks.

Every time I have made up my mind to sit down and write,
some fellow or other is sure to turn me away from it by
asking me to come and lead our band; which, by the way,
consists of two French 'speakers', so called, which, by
singing through them, produce a twangy sound like the oboe,

two combs and the cover of a book for drum. I am organist.
Or else they ask me to go on composing something for the
band.

Humphrey Lyttelton became one of the most celebrated jazz stars
of the postwar years. He says that he only really grasped the full extent
of his own fame when, in 1948, a period of tight food rationing, his
cousin Charles, the Tenth Viscount Cobham, received an under-the-
counter portion of steak in a Birmingham restaurant on the strength
of being Humphrey Lyttelton's first cousin.

In the last concert at Sunningdale, we had a jazz band. That
is what we called it, anyway, and it was certainly nearer to
a jazz band than anything that had appeared on the stage there
before. It was composed of three or four boys playing kazoos, a
master on the Swannee Whistle and myself on the drums. I
had no idea my career would lie in the direction of jazz, but I
must have been impressed, because I remember our jazz band
more clearly than anything else. The tune we played was
'Whispering', well known in those days as the signature tune
of Roy Fox and his Band. It is a tune with a simple melody and
even simpler words. The rendering of it by the Sunningdale
Jazz Band was a great success with the audience, although one
or two parents must have wondered if their son's musical
education was in the right hands.

# 9

# ENTERTAINMENTS

It is difficult to decide whether dancing ranked as entertainment or not. A boy at St Peter's, Seaford, who wrote to his mother about 'a dance we had last Saturday against one of the local girls' schools' clearly equated it to sport. Giles Romilly maintains a level view.

> Once a week we had dancing lessons . . . The door would open and in would come a genteel lady in a black frock escorted by a no less genteel though substantial accomplice with a music case. 'Good afternoon, Miss Sutton,' would rise the well-bred chorus and 'Good afternoon boys' the genteel reply. Then, after the headmaster, Mr Dobrell, with much old world ceremony and flourish, had helped Miss Sutton off with her coat and established her accomplice at the piano, we would pair off for the foxtrot or the waltz; and perhaps, after a hard hour of orthodox foxtrotting and waltzing, we would be allowed to attempt a country dance or perhaps even a Charleston. Finally we formed up in a line and after shaking hands with Miss Sutton, filed out through the corridor to tea, which on these days was fish pie.

Dancing had, at least, the merit of movement. Lectures involved sitting still and, very often, being bored. In a letter to his mother the young Gerald du Maurier is brief, but brutal.

> We went to a lecture on Monday evening and the money was given to the Sailors' Daughters Home Girls. The girls sang at the beginning. I think they must have done it to get rid of some of the people. If so, it was a jolly good dodge.

Ian Carmichael is equally scathing.

> We had innumerable lantern lectures ('click-click, next slide please') on such arresting subjects as The Great Wall of China;

The Battlefields of Flanders; and Across Tanganyika on a
Mule. These were deathly dull. They were illuminated by
black-and-white slides made from photographs of
monumentally amateur standard, taken by the lecturer
himself and thrown onto a tatty white screen in the dining
room by a lantern powered by something contained in a metal
cylinder. There was no electricity in the old building. The
main attraction of these lectures was that we got off prep
on the night they were held.

There was, very occasionally, some alleviation of this boredom.
Nothing approaching the modern type of show, with up-to-date pro-
jectors and all the latest films. In Carmichael's case they were primitive
productions, but enlivened by an interesting sound track.

Once a term Mr Kettle, a local photographer, brought along
a 35mm cine projector which was powered via an electric
cable, festooned across from the new building and entertained
us with an actual movie, albeit a silent one. *Joan of Arc* I
remember, starring Fay Compton and an all action drama
called *The Battle of the Falkland Islands*.
   A senior boy was despatched to the kitchen by the
headmaster to acquire a large tin tray which, on his return, he
struck loudly with a gong-stick every time a man-of-war's
guns went off, thus adding verisimilitude to the
entertainment.

One cannot withhold some sympathy for the lecturer, with a bored
audience and, sometimes, an over-intrusive compère. Eden Phillpott's
*Human Boy* sums it up in his succinct way.

A man lectured us last night and instead of prep we listened
to him. It was a lecture on Egypt and the Doctor introduced
him with a long speech about the Pharaohs and the Shepherd
Kings and the extraordinary religion of the Ancient Egyptians
and so on. The Doctor knew such a fearful lot about Egypt
himself that it seemed a waste of money to hire this man,
and as he went on and on, telling us really everything that
matters about Egypt, the lecturer began to fidget and get
anxious and secretly look at his watch . . . So, after half an

hour of the Doctor, Mr Wilson stepped to his side and old Dunston didn't half like it, but had to break off . . . but I think he had thoroughly unnerved the lecturer. He was not so interesting as the Doctor and only talked about a lot of digging that he had done himself; and he hadn't had much luck in his diggings either. However, there were some good slides, though not moving ones; and after you've seen moving slides the still variety is rather tame.

Compared with lectures, a puppet show must have seemed a delightful novelty. In the following letter a nine-year-old boy demonstrates a balance of interest between such diversions and domestic tragedy – with a brief footnote for learning. The school is St Andrew's, Eastbourne, and the headmaster is the great Edwin Leece Browne, the school's true founder and presiding deity for forty years. The news of his death must have been broken to the boys when this letter was half written. ('Enter' is school slang for the regular Saturday night entertainment which seems to have been up-to-date and lavish.)

My dearest Mummy,

'Enter' tonight is a puppy show. Sorry, puppets. There was a very good film on Sunday called 'The curfew shall not ring tonight', followed by an Aesop's Fable, followed by a comedy film featuring Harold Lloyd called 'I couldn't tell you'. At least, that's what Mr Giddins said it was. Please try not to send my papers so late as they will soon run into next week's.

Mr Charlie says the headmaster won't get better in this world, but he'll get better in the next. Dr Sherwood has almost given him up and he has a Red Cross nurse and two other nurses. Some people say it's a matter of hours, others say days and some say weeks, but I think that there is no hope at all and I expect you agree. It is, of course, old age and I think we've seen him for the last time. Yes, we certainly have, for he is dead. No, I am not joking or anything like that. He is dead. Isn't it sad? He died last night, while we were having an extremely good 'enter'. You know, the puppet show. It was awfully well done. But now I want to change the subject about the headmaster, for it is not very pleasant. I can't find another pen anywhere. I know I've got one, but

we're not allowed to wander about, but as I'm going to
stop, Latin 2, Maths. 3 and French, as usual, 1.
        Lots of Love from
        David.


But of all entertainments, the most notable were those provided by
the boys themselves. Cyril Connolly recalls one such occasion.

Orwell proved to me that there existed an alternative to
character, Intelligence. Cecil Beaton showed me another.
Sensibility. He had a charming, dreamy face, enormous blue
eyes with long lashes and wore his hair in a fringe. His voice
was slow, affected and creamy. He was not good at games or
work, but he escaped persecution through good manners and a
baffling independence. From Orwell I learnt about literature,
from Cecil I learned about art.

On Saturday nights the school was entertained in the big
schoolroom by such talent as the place could offer. When
Mr Potter had shown lantern slides of *Scrooge* or Mr Smedley,
dressed up like a pirate at a P & O gala, had mouthed out
what he called 'Poethry' — there would be a hush; and Cecil
would step forward and sing, 'If you were the only girl in
the world and I was the only boy'. His voice was small, but
true and when he sang these sentimental songs, imitating
Violet Loraine or Beatrice Lillie, the eighty odd boys felt there
could be no other boy in the world for them; the beetling
chaplain forgot hell-fire and masturbation and the Irish
drill-sergeant his bayonet practice; the staff refrained from
disapproving and for a moment the whole structure of
character and duty tottered and even the principles of hanging
on, muddling through and building empires were called into
question.

The second was a more private occasion. The recounter and protagon-
ist is Michael Powell, producer of the films *A Matter of Life and Death*
and *Black Narcissus* among others. He was at Kings Canterbury Prep
School during the First World War and then at Dulwich College.

I was in a large dormitory divided into individual cubicles of
pitch-pine, one bed, chest of drawers, hooks, tuck box to

each cubicle, a green baize curtain to draw across the entrance, a red blanket on the bed. A prefect slept in the cubicle nearest the dormitory door to keep order. As a war-time economy lights were put out early. Nobody felt sleepy and the boy next to me would call out, 'Powell will tell a story'. Other voices would take it up, 'Story! Story!' and in the pause, during which I remained modestly silent, the prefect's voice would be heard magisterially, 'All right, Powell. Let's have it', and I would lie back in my bed, my hands behind my head and in a clear voice like my mother's I would tell another man's story in my own way.

It is interesting to me now to realise that I was, even then, an interpreter rather than an originator. I was a good narrator. My mother's reading aloud had taught me the value of pauses; of change of voice; of change of speed. I was never one of the school that holds a book should be read as a book, without emotion, without participation. I had a photographic memory and knew a lot of poetry by heart. Sometimes I would refuse to tell a story and would announce, amid groans of horror, that I proposed to recite. But when I persisted, the magic of rhyme soon quietened them. 'The Ballad of East and West' became a favourite, with Newbolt's 'Drakes Drum' and 'He Fell Among Thieves', with Alfred Noyes' 'The Highwayman' as a runner-up. I would drum on the wooden panel of the cubicle – Rub-a-dub-dub, rub-a-dub-dub – before the lines, 'We'll drum them up the Channel as we drummed them long ago'. And the boys, remembering the war, which was by no means over, and the part which the Navy had played in the U-boat campaign and thinking, no doubt, of the fathers, brothers and uncles who had disappeared in Flanders' mud and the sisters and mothers who were away from home in the hospitals and first-aid stations, would take up the drumming on their partitions – Rub-a-dub, rub-a-dub – and would shout, in the dimness of the night-light, 'He'll drum them up the Channel as he did so long ago'; and would shout, 'Recite it again, Powell. Say it again', and the noise would die down, and I would clear my throat and in a hushed voice start:

> 'Drake he's in his hammock till the
> great Armada's come

(Capten art tha sleepin' there below?)
Slung atween the round shot, listening'
for the drum
An' dreamin' arl the time of Plymouth
Hoe'

and then the door would open and the housemaster would put his head in and say, 'What's going on, Tyrwhitt-Drake? I could hear you in the Common-room'; and the prefect, who had been rub-dub-dubbing with the best of us would answer, 'Nothing, sir. Only Powell's been doing a bit of reciting'. To which:

'You seem to have dramatic talent, Powell'.

'No, sir'.

'I hope you're not going to display it in my English class'.

'No, sir'.

'What was the subject of your performance?'

'Drake's Drum, sir'.

A silence. Then, 'Hmm. Drake's Drum. He'll drum them up the Channel, eh?'

'Yes, sir'.

Footsteps back to the door. 'No more drumming. D'you hear me, Tyrwhitt-Drake? Goodnight all'.

A chorus of 'Goodnights' and I would lie there, staring up into the darkness, getting drunk on rhymes while the dormitory slept.

# LIFE

Life in the army, in wartime, was described as 'long periods of boredom interrupted briefly by terror'. So also at preparatory school. Between dramatic episodes of bullying, counter-bullying, fighting, unsatisfactory meals and painful interviews with the headmaster, there was a good deal of life to be lived.

'It was a world,' says C. Day Lewis, 'insulated, self-important, artificial, anxiety-ridden, yet endeared by familiarity, not less than by the deposit of golden moments.'

Sir John Masterman, Provost of Worcester College, Oxford, scholar, athlete and author of the double-cross system in the war of 1939 to 1945, writes:

A preparatory school at the turn of the century was a strange mixture of the hard and the easy life. Of course we were well housed and reasonably well fed (though we thought not), but we always started the day with a plunge into a rather cold swimming bath at 6.30 in the summer and 7.00 in the winter; and the classrooms were grim and cheerless, lacking the bright fittings and pictures of today. The gas lights and their smells and the carpetless passages are a vivid memory. No sweets were allowed and hampers, except gifts of fruit, were banned.

Outside events touched us little. The war, for us, was chiefly a matter of collecting boxes and emblems which bore the portraits of the generals – Buller, White, Methuen, Baden-Powell and the rest. The death of Queen Victoria seemed like the end of an age, but our interest in it was quickly swallowed up in excited anticipation of the Coronation. We were promised leave for three or four days and great was our disappointment when news of the King's illness began to trickle through. Godfrey Worsley assembled the School and told us, in grave and measured tones, of the monarch's dangerous illness – for appendicitis was then regarded with fear and awe. 'But,' he said, 'I have decided that as your parents expect you, you shall be allowed to have your holiday.' Boylike, we began to cheer, and were sternly reproved for our insensitivity and lack of proper feeling for our beloved monarch.

General Sir Archibald Anson was born in 1826 and went to Temple Grove in 1835. He lived to the age of ninety-nine and his biography, which appeared five years before his death, must have surprised the boys then at that school.

When the boys came down in the morning there was, from time to time, a head-washing carried out by the lady teachers. This took place in the writing-room, a room intermediate between the big and little school-rooms. Each boy had his head washed, over a basin of warm soap and water and then had a spongeful of rosemary and water squeezed over it. I can recall the smell of this, as it trickled down my nose, to this day. There was, in those days, no such thing as washing any other part of the body except the hands, face and feet and perhaps the neck and chest. The feet washing was a great ceremony, once a fortnight. A large oval tub was placed in the dining hall, with a long form on one side of it, on which about half a dozen boys would sit at a time, with their feet in the water in the tub. One or two maids would kneel on the opposite side of the tub and wash the boys' feet with soap.

   In the meantime, one of the lady teachers would sit at the end of one of the dinner tables and one boy at a time, after his feet were washed, would sit on the table, with his feet almost touching her chest, when she would proceed to cut his toe nails.

Equally surprising, on the other hand, was the measure of toughness and courage thought normal in a young boy of that period. The Reverend R.C. Fowles says:

I remember young Charles Kingsley climbing a tall tree to take a hawk's nest. Previously he had done this with impunity, but there came an afternoon when the hawk was on her nest and on the intruder putting his hand in, the results were disastrous. To most boys the surprise of the hawk's attack would have been fatal. They would have loosed their hold on the tree and fallen. Charles did not flinch. He came down as steadily as if nothing had happened, though his hand was streaming with blood. On one occasion, having a sore finger, he determined to cure it by cautery. He heated the poker red hot in the schoolroom fire and calmly applied it two or three times.

Tough boys, in a tough world. When they went to school, would they come back to the family unchanged? Kenneth Grahame, seeing off his older brother, Edward, to his first term at prep school writes:

Fortunately I was not old enough to realise that here, on this little platform, the old order lay at its last gasp and that Edward might come back to us, but it would not be the Edward of yore, but an alien being, ragged of attire and lawless of tongue, a scorner of tradition and an adept in strange new tortures, one who would, in the same half hour dismember a doll and shatter a hallowed belief.

At a later date, when life was not quite so primitive, the switch back might be achieved. Christopher Robin Milne thought it could be done — at a cost.

Life at boarding school is so very different from home life that the only way some boys can cope with it is to become two boys. They split themselves down the middle and become a schoolboy at school, a homeboy during the holidays. This is, I suspect, particularly true of introspective boys such as I was. In my case the split went deep. For it was now that I began the love–hate relationship with my fictional namesake that has continued to this day. At home I still liked him, indeed felt quite proud that I shared his name and could bask in some of his glory. At school I began to dislike him and found myself disliking him more the older I got. Was my father aware of this? I don't know.

An exceptional boy might succeed in adapting. Wilfred Thesiger, soldier, traveller and writer, holder of the Burton Memorial Medal of

the Royal Asiatic Society awarded for his two crossings of the Empty
Quarter, spent his early years in Abyssinia, where his father held a
diplomatic post. In 1920, shortly after his return with his brother,
Brian, to England, their father died. The boys were at St Aubyn's, a
school near Rottingdean.

Before Brian and I went to school we had hardly met any
other English boys. Suddenly at St Aubyn's we found
ourselves in a crowd of seventy, nearly all older. There was
no privacy anywhere; we were always among others, whether
in classroom, dining room or gymnasium, on the playing
fields or in the dormitory at night. School boys are very
conventional and quick to gang up on any boy who, in
behaviour or dress, does not conform. With our extraordinary
background Brian and I lacked the ability to cope with our
contemporaries; as English boys who had barely heard of
cricket we were natural targets.

Soon after we arrived I was interrogated about my parents
and our home life. At first I was a friendly, forthcoming
little boy, very ready to talk, perhaps to boast about journeys
I had made and things I had seen. My stories, however,
were greeted with disbelief and derision and I felt increasingly
rejected. As a result I withdrew into myself, treated overtures
of friendship with mistrust and was easily provoked. I made
few friends, but once I adapted to this life I do not think I
was particularly unhappy. I could comfort myself, especially
at night, by recalling the sights and scenery of Abyssinia, far
more real to me than the cold bleak English downs behind
the school.

Four writers cast their minds back. First, Cyril Connolly:

St Wulfric's was a well run and vigorous place which did me
a world of good. Though Spartan, the death rate was low, for
it was based on that stoicism which characterised the English
governing class and has since been under-estimated.
Character, character, character was the message which
emerged when we rattled the radiators or the fence round
the playing field. It reverberated from the rifles in the
armoury, the saws in the carpenter's shop and the hoofs of the
ponies on their trot to the downs.

Next, Maurice Baring:

We lived in an atmosphere of complete uncertainty. We never
knew if some quite harmless action would not be construed into
a mortal offence. Any criticism, explicit or implicit, of the
food was considered the gravest of crimes. The food was
good and the boys had nothing to complain of; nor did they,
but they were sometimes punished for looking as if they
didn't like the cottage pie.

One difficulty was the duality of the Law. 'We were always conscious of two codes,' says E.V. Knox. 'The authority imposed from
above and our own unwritten laws.'

Finally, viewing life through the eyes of a master, the poet C. Day
Lewis:

It was a world of bells and tattered books and football boots
and crazes and blackboards and piercing screams; of ink smells,
chalk duster smells, smells of mud and mown grass and the
mousey smell of little boys; of draughts, radiators,
chilblains, stringy meat and steamed puddings; of dismal
walks in the rain; of boring jokes and catchwords endlessly
repeated; of days when everything went right, hours when to
see the boys at cricket in the sunshine gave one illusions of
being blessed with eternal youth; a world of rewards and
punishments, reach-me-down justice and covert partiality, of
sadly unoriginal sin; a world where, under controlled
conditions, the workings of the herd instinct may be
observed in all their pristine innocence and mindless brutality,
but where also, as in an accelerated film of plant growth, one
can delightedly watch rapid unfoldings of intelligence,
courage, inventiveness and sensitivity.

What, apart from routine instruction, was taught and what was
not taught at these institutions so vividly remembered by boys and
masters? Christopher Hollis MP, a writer of the widest interests,
on the board of *The Tablet* and the Table at *Punch*, who was at Summer
Fields between 1911 and 1914, maintains that an additional matter
inculcated into them was 'reverence'.

In general we had little piety, but a general feeling that it was wrong to be 'irreverent'. No boy would have expressed any disbelief, or indifference to belief. I think he would honestly have felt that some thunderbolt on high would have fallen on him had he been guilty of such an impropriety.

But Christian faith was not a privilege. It was, rather, a faith imposed on us and from which, if imposed, there was no escape. We should have thought it very wicked to speak in disrespect of the Bible, or of any verse in it, or to have questioned the doctrines of the Church of England. On the other hand, one of the boys got hold of H.G. Wells' highly satirical account of the Last Judgement and the little mortals running up the sleeve of the Almighty. It was handed about from one to the other of us and read with huge amusement. As for any qualms of conscience about its irreverence, they were wholly, and to our minds satisfactorily, set at rest by one boy who explained, 'of course, he's an atheist, so he can say these things.'

Atheism was a privilege which some people enjoyed and which, possessed, carried with it perfect freedom.


Robert Speaight, actor and producer, who played Becket in *Murder in the Cathedral* both in the original performance at Canterbury and later in the West End, and was, as a boy, at The Wick School under Laurence Tring, thinks that 'kindness' should have been on the curriculum.


It is surely extraordinary that kindness, the quality most wanted in a world that does not get less brutal day by day, should not be instilled by an establishment that prides itself on the training of character. By character is meant courage, truthfulness and purity – a three line whip for purity – a modicum of industry and the responsible exercise of power. But, by some mysterious omission, character does not include kindness. Yet the English have a reputation for kindness, which may be well deserved. I doubt, however, if it is altogether deserved by the classes which used to govern and think they should be governing still.

A change of school could make a difference in outlook. David Niven went, first, to a very bad school (unnamed and now extinct) and then to a very good one, Heatherdown at Ascot:

> Gone were the sadistic masters and the school bullies tying small boys to radiators. Receding, like a bad dream, were the flinty playground, the evil smelling doorless lavatories, open both to the elements and the helpful advice of schoolmates. Instead I found a world of cleanliness and kindly masters; motherly matrons; green playing fields; a lake; delicious food and a swimming pool. In short, schoolboy heaven.

Robert Graves, in *Goodbye to all that*, also moved from a bad preparatory school at Rugby to a good one, which still flourishes, at Copthorne. He comments on the curious insensitivity of the schoolboy, particularly when clad in his school 'persona'.

> What surprised me most was when a boy of about twelve, whose father and mother were in India, heard by cable that they had both suddenly died of cholera. We all watched him sympathetically for weeks after, expecting him to die of grief, or turn black in the face, or do something to match the occasion. Yet he seemed entirely unmoved and because nobody dared discuss the tragedy with him he seemed oblivious of it – playing about and ragging just as he had done before. We found that rather monstrous. But he had not seen his parents for two years; and preparatory schoolboys live in a world completely dissociated from home life. They have a different vocabulary, a different moral system, even different voices. On their return to school from the holidays, the change over from home life to school life is almost instantaneous while the reverse process takes a fortnight at least. A preparatory schoolboy, caught off his guard will call his mother 'Please matron', and always addresses any male relative or friend of the family as 'sir', like a master. School life becomes the reality and home life the illusion. In England, parents of the governing classes virtually lose all intimate touch with their children from about the age of eight and any attempts on their part to insinuate home feeling into school life are resented.

Unhappiness was not always the fault of the school. Graham Greene, for instance, should clearly have been sent to any other school in England rather than the one (Berkhamsted) of which his father was headmaster. This unfortunate fact produced in him a complex of feelings of which the paramount one was betrayal; a theme he was to treat obsessively in his novels.

Some of the mental agony brought about by his lack of popularity and consequent difficulty in finding companions for his Sunday walks was relieved when his parents gave him permission to spend his Sunday afternoons at home. But it was a temporary relief. In the evening he had to rejoin his companions, tramping into the chapel and up the stairs to the dormitory.

It must have separated him still further from the other boys, for was he not receiving a special dispensation because he was Charles's son? And if he tried to gain popularity, would that not be betraying his father? At the same time his sense of failure in coping with the institution and its standards – which were those of his father – must also have been strong; and, in a way, a further betrayal.

And there were some boys, artistic, sensitive and self-centred who, as Sir Peregrine Worsthorne points out, should not have been sent to boarding school at all. Oliver Messel, the outstanding stage, film and architectural designer of the four decades between 1928 and 1965 was emphatically such a boy. Unfortunately his father, Colonel Messel, had decided that a dose of regimentation would be good for him. Oliver admits that his home life had been soft and comfortable. He says:

Schooldays were unadulterated hell to me, to be banished as far as possible for ever out of my mind. The abject misery of being plunged from the pampered life at home into a school of Dickensian horror, was a total ordeal. I realise now that such unhappiness, at an impressionable age, however painful, may have some advantages. For instance, life afterwards has seemed to me one glorious holiday by comparison. Also, loathing every minute of the day as I did, I could shut myself up alone, and create in my mind, an imaginary life, seeing vividly in dreams or pictures as I closed my eyes scenes and

people, or costumes that obliterated and compensated for all
I had dreaded during the day.

A different type of boy would almost certainly benefit from and
flourish in the same institution that young Messel found hateful.
Geoffrey Rawson was likely to be robust. His father, Commander
Wyatt Rawson RN, had led the British Army by night march across
the desert to the dawn attack on Tel-el-Kebir, at which he was mor-
tally wounded. In recognition of this service Queen Victoria stood
sponsor for his daughter, and young Geoffrey was given one of the
coveted places at 'The Royal Religious and Ancient Foundation of
Christ's Hospital'.

Young, innocent, immature, [he sees himself and his friends]
clad in our cloistral dress, young cenobites, grave beyond
our years, demure, unctuous, the heirs and beneficiaries of the
sad young Edward VI who had called us into existence. But of
course we were not, at heart, the holy young smugs we might
have seemed to a casual observer. Life, wild and barbarous,
coursed in our young veins.

Saints? Certainly not says Bernard Darwin.

We may legitimately thank heaven that we are not as we were
at eleven or twelve. It was an age of innocence, but an odious
one. By the time a boy reached thirteen, one might even be
reasonably happy. Provided one bore in mind what a Preparatory
School was preparation for.

The historian Sir Charles Oman found out. He says:

I rather enjoyed my last year at Malvern Wells (Preparatory
School) and was supposed to be getting on in a pretty satisfactory
way with my Latin and Greek, though composition was
considered my weak point. Also I found the boarders' round
by no means as rough as I had expected when I gave up the
comparatively easy life of a day boy. The food was good, if
simple, and very copious; the dormitories warm and
comfortable and the masters good disciplinarians, but perfectly
just.

I vainly imagined that I was inured to the trials that I should have to face when I went on [to Winchester] and thought that I could fend for myself, having no idea of what fagging would be, nor the expectation that I should find myself next year in a society where the prefect class were entrusted with the ground ash and thought it was their right, as well as their pleasure, to be using it all day long, for offences generally imaginary, on their unfortunate juniors. Nor did I suspect that I should find the task of getting enough to eat a serious problem. It had not occurred to me that a boy of twelve was a big boy in a prep school, but a very small one in a public school where the ages of the seniors ran up to nineteen. Nor did I know that the masters counted for very little in the life of such a place.

# CLOTHES

Boys, unlike their sisters, have one, simple ambition where clothes are concerned. They like to be indistinguishable from all other boys in the school. To be distinguishable is not to be distinguished. It will make them an object of comment and very possibly of scorn.

Fathers, with memories of their own prep school days, usually understand this. A wise mother will read the clothing list carefully, go to the recommended outfitter and buy precisely what is laid down, no more and no less. Osbert Sitwell's mother was not always very sensible, but on this occasion she stuck to the book. 'One pair of Black Oxford House Shoes (elastic sided) . . . well, that's plain enough . . . One pair best Bowling Trousers. Now what can they be? Perhaps it's these grey ones. One pair Association Football Boots (no steel caps) . . . That's so the boys shan't hurt one another'.

Nigel Nicolson's mother, Vita Sackville-West, having misread the clothing list, packed him off for his first term with three pairs of shorts – 'My bare knees became targets for derision until the trousers arrived, three long days later'.

Such carelessness could have unpredictable results. Siegfried Sassoon says:

I had on my mind, a single problem from which there was no
escaping. Its cause was neither complicated nor uncertain,
and merely amounted to this. My mother had sent my brother
Hamo and me to school without any shirts. Misled by her loyalty
to 'thick warm woollen underclothing' she had provided us
with starched 'dickeys' to our Eton collars and nothing else.
It seemed odd that Michael, my older brother, whose garments
were normal, hadn't drawn attention to the deficiency. But he
had overlooked it; and I suppose it was characteristic of me
that never having worn a shirt before, except in cricket matches,
I took it for granted that I could do quite well without one
at school. I probably wondered vaguely whether it was all right

and then hoped for the best. (Hamo didn't bother much about how he was dressed.) It was only when I was up in the big dormitory that my sense of humiliation became complete. This, I felt, was something I should never be able to live down. It was bad enough to be, for my age, only half educated. To be only half dressed as well was the finishing touch. Unconsoled by observing that, at any rate, I wasn't the only boy who didn't wear pyjamas, I hastened into my nightgown and said my prayers. (Hamo, in another dormitory, was probably quite unperturbed.) Next day I managed to get dressed without anyone noticing anything wrong. The crisis came in the middle of the morning when there was a half hour's break for cricket practice. I was eager to show Mr Jackson that I could play quite decently, but it wasn't possible for me to bat in my shirt-sleeves. When it came to bowling, he asked me why I didn't take my coat off. My embarrassment enabled him to discover what was amiss and he led me and Hamo off to the matron, who supplied shirts from somewhere. After that I became a different person and felt that I really was 'Sherston minor' instead of being a secretly shirtless absurdity.

And it could be the result of maternal wilfulness rather than carelessness. L.S. Lowry, the painter, was sent to Grafton House School. If he had a rough time there, his mother had much to answer for. His biographer Shelley Rohde writes:

Lowry's school life can hardly have been made any easier by the quaintly effeminate style in which his mother insisted on dressing him, and which can only have accentuated his awkwardness. She always took particular care with her son's appearance; as a baby she had dressed him in long frilly frocks and as a boy she put him into pretty sailor suits with smart leather gloves and highly polished shoes.

A type of boy who suffered more than most in this respect was one who had been brought up in a rough or a Bohemian fashion. Sir William Goodenough, now little remembered, was a remarkable figure of the First World War. He sank the light cruiser *Mainz* in ship-to-ship duel, distinguished himself at Scarborough and at Jutland where, according to Correlli Barnett, he handled his section of ships with great technical skill and more common sense than Beatty. His comments on food, fighting and his headmaster are found elsewhere in these chapters.

In 1875 my brother and I went to Temple Grove, then, with Eagle House – what shall I call them – two of the better known private schools of the day. Here I had to give up the ease and comfort of a seaman's dress and be restricted in the abomination of an Eton collar, almost as restricted as the ideas and conventions of that day.

Caspar John, though brought up by his painter father in a state of gypsy simplicity, seems to have taken kindly to formal dress. Not so the unhappy James Lees-Milne, author and adviser on historic buildings to the National Trust.

My natural lack of self-confidence was not mitigated by the strange garments I was obliged to wear for the first time in my life. To begin with I had, like the proverbial slum child of those days, never worn socks or shoes. It had been one of my mother's tenets that such impedimenta were bad for growing feet. The result was that mine were hard as iron, impervious to wounds and cuts and perfectly all right so long as they were not encumbered. But, the moment they found themselves imprisoned in wool and stiff leather, they practically ceased to function. I can scarcely believe the particular boots I was forced into on this occasion were too small when I recall how grotesquely over-size was everything else I was made to wear. Whether too small or too large, they were absolute agony and I could move only with the greatest difficulty. To add to the trouble, my adolescent cousin's trousers were far too big. The legs trailed over my feet like bedraggled hosepipes. I must have looked like some ghastly caricature of a dwarf hobbling on amputated stumps. Besides, no amount of pulling at the belt with its snake buckle would keep the beastly things up. This could only be achieved by my never letting go of the waist. The moment I did so, down they would fall literally to the ground. Furthermore, for the first time in my life – I was, let me remind you, eight – I was obliged to wear a shirt

with starched cuffs and collar, tie and waistcoat. Now in
the summer months I had been accustomed to wear nothing
beyond the briefest pair of shorts. In winter an additional
flimsy jersey was the utmost concession granted. My mother's
admiration of Captain Scott of the Antarctic was unbounded and
she had read and approved his dying instructions to his widow
to bring up their son, Peter, in the hard way. In Peter
Scott's case these directions were, I am the first to admit,
amply justified. In my own, either because I was not born in
the heroic mould, or because of the unnaturally abrupt manner
in which I was changed overnight from a potential Tarzan
of the Apes into a pantomime clown, they were not. The
shame of the transformation effected on 4 June 1917 has never
left me. I have been horribly clothes-conscious ever since.

In one or two accounts a theory is promulgated that to dress a boy
(or a girl) oddly might somehow act as a strengthener of character.
This has the feeling of an ex post facto judgement, but its two proposers
are worthy of a respectful hearing. The first is John Christie, of
Glyndebourne fame.

At the age of ten John went to St David's at Reigate, a
conventional prep school run by a Mr Churchill. John's mother,
'innocent', he said, 'of the ways of boys at a proper preparatory
school, despatched me there in a little Lord Fauntleroy
outfit. I fought a lot of the older boys and anyone who
commented on my clothes. My darling mother did not
understand these things and my father didn't help. I don't
suppose it was a bad thing. Perhaps it developed my character.
On the other hand I wonder whether I ought to have learnt
to fight on more important things. At any rate, boys who
laughed had to defend themselves and it did not disturb me'.

The second is Joyce Flecker, sister of the poet James Elroy Flecker.
The passage comes from the account of the poet's life, *No Golden
Journey* by John Sherwood.

A group photograph of Dean Close, taken in 1894 or 95,
shows row upon row of schoolboys in sober suits of Victorian
cut and, interrupting one of the rows, a small James Elroy in

a white sailor blouse. His sister, Joyce, who was also made
to go to the Cheltenham Ladies' College in sailor blouses
believed they had a character training significance.

'I think the idea was to make you strong against what
people said about you. You were not to be affected by what they
said. You were to be strong and do what was right; and there
were these perfectly good sailor blouses and they had to be worn
out'.

It is clear, too, that if criticism of a boy's uncommon clothes
led to a fight this might go far to restoring the reputation of the
boy concerned – particularly if he fought well. Douglas Ainslie and
his brother were sent down from their home in the North of
England to the fashionable Eton-oriented prep school, Aldin House
at Slough. Their ill-fitting pepper-and-salt suits were criticized
audibly by Douglas's form master.

However, criticism was not confined to him, but several of
the boys were not slow to condemn the sartorial efforts of
the far North. Among them was a bright boy named Reeve,
with smooth auburn hair and very brown staring eyes, whose
seat was exactly behind mine.

I was suddenly made aware of his critical disapproval by
receiving a series of sharp kicks. Turning round to
expostulate, I was blamed for talking and given a bad mark.
Immediately after school, in my turn, I handed a 'bad mark'
to Master Reeve, somewhere in the region of his right eye.

We were at once surrounded and separated by some bigger
boys who were passing. They told us not to worry. We should
have the honour of fighting it out next afternoon behind the
pavilion. My experience of the ring was limited to boxing with
my father's forefinger, which he would occasionally prod in
my chest. Reeve was an unknown quantity, but fortunately
turned out to be equally ignorant of the vile craft.

We set about our battle with a very good will and I can
still see before me Reeve's blazing brown eyes and ruffled hair
as we pummelled each other's countenances. After two pairs
of (eventually) polychrome eyes and a good deal of bleeding at
the nose on both sides, a draw was the verdict of the bigger
boys who had arranged the exhibition.

Reeve and I made friends afterwards and I found that my peculiar garments no longer met with open criticism. I never fought again – but I changed my tailor.

# 12

# HEADMASTERS

*L'Etat c'est moi.* In no institution was this truer than in the proprietary boarding school, before so many of them saw the tax advantage of operating under the umbrella of a trust. Even then, although theoretically subject to a body of trustees, in all the day-to-day running of the school the headmaster was King. (A fact which demonstrates the mistake made by fathers who, remembering their old schools with affection, sent their sons to them. If a different headmaster had taken over, it would be a different school.)

They might be good, and remembered with affection, bad, and remembered with horror, or eccentric and remembered with amusement. A prince of kindly eccentrics was Charles Cotterill Lynam, known to all as 'The Skipper'. He was headmaster of the Dragon School at Oxford from 1886 to 1920 and in those thirty-four years printed his personality on this, one of the half dozen most celebrated preparatory schools in England. As well as being a schoolmaster he was a small-boat enthusiast, sailing *Blue Dragon* round Scotland and across the North Sea in all weathers. His eccentricities, which were wide ranging, can be considered under separate headings.

Car Driving: His vagaries included the curious habit of accelerating sharply at each corner. Particularly the turn out to the Bardwell Road. For this, one of his staff offered an interesting explanation. 'He thinks he is still at the wheel of the Blue Dragon and has got to keep steerage way on her'.

Teaching: The unexpected was always happening and vitality was more important than sequence . . . The Skipper's use of coloured chalks established the artist as a scenic decorator of the first rank. There was a famous diagram of the Gulf Stream, as thick with arrows as the Battle of Hastings, for which he mistook it in his history class next day. Fresh from this triumph he embarked on the farewell between

Hecuba and Polyxena with a vigour that brings tears to my
eyes even now. On his English Literature lessons, let the world
which knows his pupils pronounce judgment. 'The Passing
of Arthur' still adorns the curriculum and the dusky barge
may yet be found on the walls of the Art Room.

Money: The Skipper was no financier. He dealt with money
matters by methods all his own, which gave rise at the time
to many surprising rumours, destined to pass into the realm
of Legend. Did he in fact make out the boys' accounts on
his way North to join the Blue Dragon with no other data
than his own guess at the wealth or otherwise of the parents?
And when Bills and Reports all went to the bottom of Oban
Harbour did he really substitute a short note to each parent
saying: 'Your boy is doing splendidly. Please pay what you
think you owe'? And was any difficulty over staff salaries dealt
with by the simple expedient of borrowing from one master
in order to pay another?

Eccentricity might be a matter of appearance more than conduct.
Colonel Sir Mike Ansell, who went to St Michael's, Westgate, in
1914 remembers his headmaster with mixed feelings.

Mr Hawtrey, known as Beetle, looked exactly like one as he
hobbled along on two sticks; this dear old gentleman always
wore a morning-coat and mortarboard, except while coaching
in cricket, when the mortarboard was exchanged for a top-hat.
He had other old fashioned ideas as well. I recollect the head
porter arriving in Mr Hawtrey's study (where I was awaiting
execution for some misdemeanour) carrying what looked like
a birch-broom. The noise it made was worse than the pain.
Blood drawn in a few places, but worst of all my mother found
among extras on the bill – 'one birch, ten shillings'. A very
expensive besom.

Provided that the eccentric conduct was largely directed to the
discomfiture of his family and the staff, the boys were prepared to
tolerate it. Professor C.S. Lewis, theologian, scholar and novelist,
author of *The Screwtape Letters*, was at Wynyard House, Watford. The
headmaster he calls 'Oldie' and his son 'Wee-Wee', the names by
which the boys knew them.

The ushers succeeded each other with great rapidity; one lasted for less than a week. Another was dismissed in the presence of the boys, with a rider from 'Oldie' to the effect that if he were not in Holy Orders he would kick him downstairs. This curious scene took place in dormitory, though I cannot remember why. All the ushers (except the one who stayed less than a week) were obviously as much in awe of 'Oldie' as we were. But there came a time when there were no more ushers and 'Oldie's' youngest daughter taught the junior pupils. By that time there were only five boarders and 'Oldie' finally gave up his school and sought a cure of souls.

He lived in a solitude of power, like a sea captain in the days of sail. No man or woman in that house spoke to him as an equal. No one except 'Wee-Wee' initiated conversation with him at all. At meal times we boys had a glimpse of his family life. His son sat on his right hand; they two had separate food. His wife and three grown-up daughters (silent), the usher (silent) and the boys (silent) munched their inferior messes. His wife, though I think she never addressed 'Oldie', was allowed to make something of a reply to him; the girls, three tragic figures dressed, summer and winter, in the same tragic black, never went beyond an almost whispered 'Yes, Papa', or 'No, Papa' on the rare occasions when they were addressed. Few visitors entered the house. Beer, which 'Oldie' and 'Wee-Wee' drank regularly at dinner was offered to the usher, but he was expected to refuse; the one who accepted got his pint, but was taught his place by being asked, a few moments later, in a voice of thunderous irony, 'Perhaps you would like a little *more* beer, Mr N'. Mr N, a man of spirit, replied casually, 'Well, thank you, Mr C. I think I would'. He was the one who did not stay till the end of his first week.

Headmasters could be harmless snobs. Rosslyn (or 'Rosy') Wester-Wemyss, Admiral of the Fleet and member of the War Cabinet in 1918, was at an extremely select prep school at Farnborough, kept by the Reverend A.H.A. Morton. Esme Howard, now Lord Howard of Penrith, says of 'Rosy':

I don't think I ever knew any man who changed so little from his school days. What I remember best was his keen enjoyment of anything humorous and his great love of fun. He had a critical side to his nature even in those days.

I well remember one Sunday when we were all out in our Eton jackets and top hats. He and I were walking together when suddenly our revered headmaster clasped his hands ecstatically and exclaimed, 'In what other school in England would you see the sons of three cabinet ministers walking together.'

Another small boy might have been impressed. Not so 'Rosy', who whispered to me, 'Did you ever hear such an old snob?'

They could impress parents as well as their sons. Paul Spillane's *History of St Andrew's School, Eastbourne* says:

Parents sometimes found Edwin Leece Browne alarming. The fussy ones got no encouragement from him and he often spoke to them with a certain bluntness, from which the cheerful smile and level voice removed any cause of offence. 'Now you know as well as I do, that you have no business to ask for that'. At Victoria, when the anxious mother of a new boy proposed to come and visit her son in the first fortnight of term 'to soften the sudden change from home', he replied, 'If you had a puppy, would you cut off its tail an inch at a time, or do it all at once?' He had a disconcerting method of dealing with pertinacious parents whose enquiries were ill-timed or obtuse, as is shown by the following conversation which took place on the long asphalt when he was surrounded by boys and parents.

'Well, Mr Brown, how is my boy getting on?'
'He stands up to fast bowling very well.'
'Yes, but in other ways how is he doing?'
'I think he is developing a natural off-break.'

They might be weak men, under the thumb of a wife who dominated the school. The historian, A.J.P. Taylor, went to a school called The Downs. It was not, in the strict classification, a Quaker school, but it happened that the Headmaster, H.W. Jones, was a Quaker.

He had started well, says Taylor. Twenty years before he had become Headmaster of Leighton Park, the high class Quaker school at Reading. He only lasted a single year. We were told that he had had a breakdown. We suspected worse things. Most of us thought he had made off with the money. A few, more knowing, spoke of 'a nameless offence'. He was rescued by his cousin, Ethel, who married him. Presumably she prescribed ownership of a preparatory school as a form of therapy.

Ostensibly Mr Jones was Headmaster. He was soft-hearted and occasionally bad-tempered. Although we had given up starched collars he always wore a stiff, tubular affair which, with his prominent nose, gave him the air of an apoplectic ostrich. He taught classics reasonably well and gave me private lessons in Greek. He even had some idea that, as a clever boy, I ought to be encouraged. But what he thought did not matter. For all practical purposes Mrs Jones ran the school, and dominated both it and him.

She was a formidable figure. She had a high corsetted bust, swathed in red velvet and hair piled up with the aid, as I now appreciate, of a chignon. Her bright lace collar was supported by bones. Character building was her obsession and for her this meant punctuality and cleanliness. The price of these, she believed, was eternal vigilance, a quality in which she was by no means lacking. Her sharp eyes were never dimmed.

After breakfast we made our beds. These were inspected three times – bottom sheet on, top blanket tucked in and finally coverlet on. It was particularly important that the foot of the bed should be made like a parcel. If anything went wrong, the bed was stripped and we had to begin again. If all went well, Mrs Jones uttered a strange cry which I thought was 'Turnip & Co.' It was, in fact, 'turn up and go'. It was much the same routine with shoe cleaning; one inspection when the dirt had been brushed off, one when the polish was put on and one when the shoe had been polished.

Meal times were a special trial, apart from the uneatable food, Mrs Jones was resolute in instilling good manners. If you spilled anything you went on plain fare – bread and water – for a meal. Even worse was to neglect your neighbour when his plate was empty. Mrs Jones's voice would ring out, 'So

and so, go on plain fare for a meal'. Or, if it happened more
than once, 'for a day'. The laxest offender was doomed to sit
between Mr and Mrs Jones, his eyes so rivetted to their
respective plates that he got little to eat himself. One of these
victims, greatly daring, made a score. Finding his own plate
empty, he said to Mr Jones, 'Herbert, dear. Plain food for a
day'.

For once Mrs Jones was amused.

He might be 'a beast, but a just beast'. H.W. Stubbs, later Lecturer
in Classics at Exeter University, recalls Geoffrey Bolton, headmaster
of Summer Fields in his time.

Will that titanic personality baffle all description? There are
plenty of fictional parallels for his sudden rages, real or assumed
(I still remember the outburst of mixed English and Greek
invective when I funked a rugger tackle on third game), and
his stern integrity is not uncommon. ('He's the ONLY master
who punishes you if you own up, and the ONLY master
who won't let you off if you blub'). But never in fact or fiction
have I come across so magnificent a teacher, one who touched
nothing that he did not illumine, one whose forceful
exuberance could leap in a moment over the gap between Cicero
and Burke, Troy and Vimy Ridge, Euripides and P.G.
Wodehouse. In class or out of it he talked to us as a man
of the world talking to men of the world.

He could be a skilful imparter of the sort of knowledge examiners
like. In his *Life of Ronald Knox*, Evelyn Waugh says of Dr Williams
of Summer Fields, Geoffrey Bolton's predecessor:

Dr Williams was then in early middle age. His rivals spoke
of him jealously as a 'crammer'. When he died, forty-three
years later, Ronald Knox wrote to The Times to refute this
charge. 'He was an amazingly successful educationalist', Ronald
said, 'with a genius for spotting ability. But I never persuaded
myself that we got only shop-window education. I believe we
had an admirable grounding, that steeping of the mind in the
first elements without which education never seems to "take".'

Nor were they necessarily consistent. Headmasters, like other men, could have insomnia or toothache or tax demands, and come into class and work their feelings off on the nearest boy, as Kenneth Grahame quickly discovered.

> The junior form, or class, was in session, so to speak and I
> was modestly occupying a position, at the very bottom,
> which seemed to me natural enough, when the Headmaster
> entered — a man who had somehow formed an erroneous idea of
> my possibilities. Catching sight of me, he asked sternly,
> 'What's that thing doing down there?'
> The master in charge could only reply that whether it was
> crass ignorance or invincible stupidity he wotted not, but there
> it was. The Headmaster merely remarked that if that thing —
> meaning me — was not up there or near it, pointing to the
> head of the form, before the close of work it was to be severely
> caned; and left the room.
> It is pleasant to record that the rest of the form achieved
> undreamed of heights of stupidity in order to avert the worst,
> but Kenneth, who was unused to being 'savaged by big, beefy,
> hefty, hairy men called masters' promptly burst into tears of
> horror and bewilderment.
> What maggot tickled the brain of the Headmaster on that
> occasion I never found out. Schoolmasters never explain, never
> retract, never apologise.

After this episode the headmaster was almost uniformly kind to Kenneth.

They could be brutes. That great sailor, Sir William Goodenough, encountered one at Temple Grove.

> The majestic figure of Mr Waterfield, the headmaster,
> pervaded all. The cane, or rather a very thick ruler that he used
> in place of it and with which he once broke a boy's finger, an
> act that caused that tremendous being to shed tears, and the
> birch — more familiarly known as the swish — came easily to
> his hand, and it was a real experience to see the manner in
> which with his left hand he drew the lapel of his frock coat
> across his breast and applied the weapon with a swing that would
> do credit to a plus-two golfer. I experienced it.

One of the worst brutes of the lot, a case study for a psychiatrist, was the Reverend R.S. Tabor, headmaster of Cheam School. Started in 1660, in the belfry of Cheam Church, it received a big uplift when there was an outrush of whole families from London fleeing the Great Plague. By 1863, when Sir Ian Hamilton went there, it was reputed to be the most famous preparatory school in England. 'Upon the portals of the school', says Sir Ian, 'are carved the letters R.S.T. When, on my visit to Cheam after the South African War my eyes lit upon that sign, my blood went cold'.

Soon after his first arrival, he was summoned to the headmaster's study.

Screwing up my courage I tapped at the door. Mr Tabor was seated at a big desk, facing the window, with his back to me. When I came in he got up and patted me on the head. So wide from the mark and so unexpected was this opening that it took me quite aback and almost broke me up. Had I begun to blubber I should have been as putty in his hands, but luckily he added, 'let us pray!' Now, though only a ten-year-old, I knew as much about prayers as many grown-ups; I had been prayed over and prayed over since my birth and to me prayers seemed very much just one of the ways ministers had of making boys do something they didn't want to do . . . I felt much better and as the prayer rumbled on we three, Mr Tabor, myself and the Almighty, seemed to be in entire agreement that it would be a good thing if I was good.

So soon as we had risen from our knees Mr Tabor said, 'Now, dear boy, I want you to help me work towards a better and purer Cheam. I know that some of the boys have been rough and unkind. Are they "good boys"?' 'Yes, sir, they are all very good boys'. 'Do you ever hear a bad word spoken? Be careful with your answer. I don't mean silly words like "By Jove", though they are certainly objectionable. I mean any blasphemous allusion to the Almighty. Have you ever heard that vile word "Damn"?'

Even as he spoke he seemed to be changing before my eyes. His face was losing its rounded form and becoming sharpened; his lips were becoming thin. He repeated, 'Be very careful what you say. Have you, or have you not, ever heard a boy say "Damn"?'

Now I had never said damn myself since I had used it over
the knot in the tail of my tie; but Horace Flower never
spoke to me without saying "damn" and I could have named
another dozen. So I tried to wriggle off by saying, 'I have never
said "damn", sir'.

'Answer me, and do not prevaricate' – and as he spoke his
face began to appear to me as that of a wolf. So I feel some pride
at being able to put it on paper that my nerve held and I gave
nobody away. What happened during the next five minutes still
makes me feel bad. All the more, then, do I regret that I
cannot say who, or what, inspired a little brat like myself
to stand firm against the chief terror of my life; the face of a
clergyman changing into that of a werewolf which, in one
second, could bury its fangs in the throat of a child.

The strength was not in myself; nor could mere fear of the
other boys have saved me. Perhaps it was just the wish of
every decent British boy – to play the game. So I said, looking
down on the floor to avoid his eyes, 'No, sir. I have never
heard a bad word at Cheam'.

In a moment Mr Tabor had seized me by the upper part of
my left arm, driving his nails into the fleshy part three or four
inches below the armpit. Having got a good grip he shook
me violently, backwards and forwards, completely skinning a
surface of several inches and making a raw, discoloured sore.
Next he dragged me up to the wall by the window; put me
with my face to it, made me stretch my arms to their fullest
extent, palms uppermost and said, 'Don't you dare move'.

So there I stood until, by degrees, my arms began to droop
at the elbows. I could hear the scratching of Mr Tabor's
quill. He must have forgotten all about me. My elbows
dropped a little more.

Of a sudden and without warning, a couple of paralysing
blows from clenched fists struck the funny bones of each elbow.
'You may go now', said Mr Tabor, opening the door (I could
not). 'Go up to your bedroom and stay there; you are excused
dinner. And don't forget it, you have made a bad start at
Cheam'.

So upstair I went in an agony of despair. As luck would
have it, on the first landing I met the matron, Mrs Scrivener,
who had pity, stroked my head and brought me a piece of

bread and butter at dinner time telling me not to give her away. However, after some seventy-six years I dare say she won't mind.

Sir Ian records how, on a subsequent occasion, he managed to station himself in front of a large picture hanging on the wall. This was a tip he had been given by other boys who had suffered in a similar way. By looking in the glass he was able to watch the stealthy approach of Mr Tabor, 'like a tiger stalking its prey', and by straightening his arms at the critical moment, to save his funny bones.

Lord Dunsany narrowly escaped the tiger. 'Fortunately for him', says his biographer Mark Amory, 'the Reverend R.S. Tabor had been succeeded by his much pleasanter son, Charles. He had a gift for imaginative abuse, once calling a boy "a confusticated piece of toasted cheese".'

It goes without saying that there were good headmasters as well; good teachers and good men.

The voice was important. H.W. Massingham, the great radical journalist, who went to Norwich Grammar School at the age of ten, remembers the headmaster, Augustus Jessop.

Of stature and mien to impress schoolboys as Arnold had impressed Rugby, and for beauty and sonority his voice equalled, I think, Gladstone's. I shall never forget his reading of the collect 'Lighten our Darkness', with which he used to close afternoon school, so that to an imaginative boy the growing gloom of the winter's day seemed to be shot with spiritual light.

It was not only how he said it. What he said was equally important. Of the Reverend E. St John Parry, headmaster of Stoke House at Seaford, Mark Tellar records:

He used a string of strange expletives to accompany each thump. 'You abomination of the gentiles'; 'The perversest of perverse sticks'; 'You lump of impermeable clay'. When he had exhausted his repertoire he would draw back from the victim and, gazing at him over his pince-nez which, in his agitation, had several times fallen from his nose, he would slowly utter a last ejaculation of despair, 'You horrible animalcule'.

The eyes were important, too. As General Sir Douglas Brownrigg remembers.

The Reverend the Marquis of Normanby, as Lord Mulgrave, had taken Holy Orders and had acted as tutor to various boys preparing for public school. When he succeeded his father it occurred to him that he could afford to live at home if he could augment his income by running a school. Thus it came about that his ancestral home became a private school.

It had eleven years of existence and gave Lord Normanby time to influence for good a great many young lives. On no one can his influence have been greater than on me, lacking as I did all the normal associations of home life. [His father, also a regular soldier, was serving abroad during most of Douglas's early life.]

At that time Lord Normanby had lightish brown hair brushed straight back over a rather narrow head, leaving bare a high forehead. Beneath this forehead was a straight, thin nose, a firm and rather stern mouth and a small, but very determined chin. But it was the eyes that mattered. Those eyes could search the heart of a small boy and compel the truth; they could look severe, but could never be unjust, and they could soften into depths of kindness as the stern mouth relaxed into a radiant smile. There has never been anyone quite like him.

At, or near, the top of any poll of great headmasters must stand Pat Knox-Shaw, who was head of St Peter's, Seaford, before, during and after the Second World War and Chairman of the IAPS. Many of the boys whom he taught have written of him with affection. The following is from Christopher Pirie-Gordon, of the Foreign Service.

Pat is, without question, the outstanding personality in the history of St Peter's. What was his secret? Why was he so liked and admired by the boys, their parents and, later, their sons, his staff, his fellow headmasters and, indeed, all who knew him? He was not particularly brilliant and I doubt if his busy life allowed him the time to be deeply read. But he seemed to know the answer to most questions that came his way and the confidence which he inspired was automatic and complete.

The answer may have been a total absence of self-importance and of even the most elementary guile or pretence. He treated everyone as equals, especially the boys (until they showed that they weren't when he could become bleak). He taught as though he was giving a briefing to brother officers for an incursion into strange territory where he had had the good fortune to have made a previous reconnaissance and was consequently able, through no special merit of his own, to give helpful hints. Above all he was amusing. His conversation at table was fun. It was not witty. Wit can be unkind and Pat was never that. Talking to him was soothing to the juvenile ego.

It is clear from the above extracts that the same man might be viewed very differently by his staff, by the boys, by their parents, or by an outside observer. In one case disparate opinions can be compared. *The Rise of the English Preparatory School* by Donald Leinster-Mackay the best and most fully documented study of these institutions. In it Mackay writes:

Pupils who, like Stephen Spender, claimed that they were unhappy at preparatory school because of the constant ragging and the penchant of the headmaster for using the cane were, as men of letters, prone to exaggeration. True the regime in many schools had to be a combination of kindness and rigour.

Just such a school was St Aubyns at Rottingdean where Mr Stanford, in the 1890s eschewed corporal punishment and administered his discipline through a good conduct marks system . . .

When he was succeeded by Mr R.C.V. Lang, who had been an assistant master under Mr Stanford, the tone of the school improved immeasurably, since Lang was better able to put into practice the theories of his predecessor.

Thus the independent observer. It happens to be possible, however, to see both Mr Stanford and Mr Lang from the viewpoint of a boy under them. The account of Mr Stanford comes from James Strachey Barnes, who was at St Aubyn's between 1898 and 1902. A second extract, under 'Discipline' from his book *Half a Life*, will make it clear that he was a boy of outstandingly independent mind.

Mr Stanford, the headmaster, was one of a few early pioneers who regarded the use of the birch as an outworn barbarism. He set himself to demonstrate the practicability of running a school and keeping his boys in order by a system of good conduct marks and appealing to their sense of corporate responsibility and honour.

Unfortunately, although he had many kind and generous qualities, and although he meant exceedingly well, he vitiated his good intentions by certain deplorable defects. He habitually indulged in unconcealed favouritism. He also broke the spirit of his own excellent theoretical precepts; for though he spared the rod, he made use of a far crueller weapon; mental terror, by means of an uncontrollable temper. Also he was a bad psychologist. He failed to understand any boy that was not cast in the mould of a modernised little Lord Fauntleroy. Hence it was largely due to him that, though I had every disposition to be happy (being exceptionally good at both work and games) I came to loathe my schooldays with a bitter resentment resulting, in that I was not an easy person to put under, in a violent spirit of rebellion.

For a boy's account of Mr Lang we have the recently published book *The Life of my Choice* by Wilfred Thesiger.

St Aubyn's had a good reputation when my father decided to send us there. Unfortunately just before we arrived, a new headmaster, R.C.V. Lang, took over. He was unmarried; his sister looked after him. He was a large, imposing man who had been a noted athlete and I am sure he created a favourable impression on my parents. In fact he was a sadist, and after my father's death both Brian and I were among his victims. The school motto was 'Quit you like men: be strong', an exhortation not without relevance to some of us boys. He beat me on a number of occasions, often for some trivial offence. I had to kneel naked by the side of my bed. I remember crying out the first time, 'It hurts' and Lang saying grimly, 'It's meant to'.

For two or three days after each beating I was called to his study so that he could see I was healing properly. Though I had never been hurt like this before, strangely enough I bore him no resentment for these beatings, accepting them as the penalty for what I had done. It never occurred to me how disproportionate was the punishment to the offence.

After we had been at school for about three years Arnold Hodson, who had been Consul in Southern Abyssinia, was staying with us at the beginning of the holidays. One evening he said, jokingly, 'I don't suppose you get beaten at school nowadays, not like we were in my time'. Neither Brian nor I had told our mother about these beatings, but now, incensed, I pulled down my shorts and showed him some half-healed scars. Years later I learnt that Hodson went down to Sussex and told the headmaster that if he beat either of us again he would have him taken to court.

# 13

# MASTERS

Hardly a book of reminiscences, when it reaches the prep school period, omits a description of the assistant masters. If the unworthy seem to predominate over the worthy and the conventional over the unconventional, this is only a reflection of the impression these often untrained men made on the boys entrusted to their care and instruction.

In the earliest examples, such as the first school attended by Tom Brown – said to be closely based on Twyford – they could be obnoxious, but were of less importance.

> The two ushers at Tom's first school were not gentlemen and were very poorly educated. They were only driving their poor trade of usher to get such living as they could out of it. They were not bad men, but had little heart for their work and, of course, were bent on making it as easy for themselves as possible. One of the methods by which they endeavoured to accomplish this was by encouraging tale-bearing, which had become a frightfully common vice in the school in consequence and sapped all the foundation of schoolboy morality.

From Sir Osbert Sitwell we have a famous blast against the whole tribe:

> How I loathed them, no doubt unjustly. I saw them . . . as so many uninterested and mentally lazy men, who tired themselves out with physical exercise to such a degree that they were fit for little else. They would return from the football field drenched and dripping with green sweat, panting and hollow-eyed and with an incipient death-rattle in their knotted throats. Naturally they were not inclined to exert themselves again until the following afternoon, when they would play once more; even their pipes, in the masters' room, could not bring them solace.

A few Latin tags, a knowledge of the more reputable parts
of the Bible, an aptitude for footer and cricket – and, of course,
fives; that, they knew, was what got most gentlemen
comfortably through life. But while, of course, they liked
every boy to be of the same mental height, with nothing odd,
or 'weird' as they would have said about him, yet they did not
actually *want* unusual boys to be beaten to death in the
dormitories, for that, too, would have been unconventional and
would interfere with the games; and so to a certain extent they
exercised a watchful attitude, at first sight apparently
kindly, but really very impersonal over their charges.

As teachers, then, you might judge them from what I say
to have been uninspired, but you would underrate them. They
may not have been on the grand scale, but they possessed
magic nevertheless; they could, with a few words, tear every
plume out of British history and render Latin, from being a
dead language, into one that plainly could never have lived.
Indeed, a few terms of their tuition exercised a great influence
upon at least one of their pupils. Learning ceased to interest
me. I became too miserable even to try to learn. Moreover my
state of wretchedness and the perpetual inquisition, 'Where were
you when the head beak sent for you?' and 'Why weren't you
kicking about on the football field?' obliged me to develop the
habit of lying and thereby forced my powers of invention.
Certainly it was those first months at my first school which
produced in me the elements of novelist and story-teller.

For a glance at the other side of the coin we have the views of the
golfer, Bernard Darwin.

When one grows a little older, at a public school, masters
take on a variety of aspects, some of them ridiculous. They
become the objects of mimicry for those possessing the
requisite talent. At a private school one may like some and
dislike others, but they have all a certain godlike quality.
Their learning is generally believed to be profound. Their clothes
are intensely interesting and I have the clearest recollection of
the shape of their collars. In one of the volumes of Sir Osbert
Sitwell's entrancing autobiography he seems to me
unreasonably hard on some of his private schoolmasters for

being blues or good at football. How different from me! I could have wished for far more blues; we had two and that was something. Mr Alington, who was the brother-in-law of Dr Williams the Headmaster, was a soccer blue and I believe myself to have seen him, arrayed in a dark blue and white shirt, in which he dribbled very slowly and gently through our serried ranks that hurled themselves against him in vain, like waves on a lighthouse.

As tolerant as Bernard Darwin, if less stilted, is M.M. Cahill, who was at Summer Fields from 1936 to 1940. He mentions a point which may have escaped other critics of the teaching staff:

It is, of course, well known that all prep-school masters are as old as God. They bumble around with one foot in the grave doing their best to implant seeds of knowledge in ground so stony that lesser mortals would think twice before even applying for planning permission. Some of them are plainly off their chump and mooch to and fro clutching pocket volumes of Shakespeare from which they are liable to declaim if you haven't the sense to keep your distance. But the horrifying thing is that these desiccated wrecks, good only for the garbage can, are really fresh-faced lads, bulging with blues and honours degrees, who are just beginning to climb the first rungs of their occupational ladder.

And, for a last general view, Nicholas Monsarrat:

Sitting above us all the time, like a thick layer of crust on an ill-mixed loaf, was the staff. We knew them all very well and yet we knew nothing about them; they were grown-ups – remote, possessed of the last word on everything, ten foot tall, incomprehensible. We knew nothing of their feelings, except their feelings towards us, which were likely to be severe. We could only go by rumours of past excesses (He once pulled someone's hair *right out*) and by the amount of noise they made when they were angry.

One cannot avoid a measure of sympathy. Not all boys were as difficult as Schopenhauer (who appears under 'Rebels'), but to find oneself faced, at the same time and place, by the young George Orwell, Cyril Connolly and Cecil Beaton and to have to deal with the acerbic character of the first, the analytical ability of the second and the dulcet charm of the third, must have called for a balance and a capacity not normally to be found in a young man. It has also to be remembered that the master in question was probably untrained. The headmaster might have academic qualifications and powers of control. An assistant, having neither, would have to rely on what Ben Travers calls 'the rule of fear'. If he were capable of inspiring neither fear nor respect, the boot would be on the other foot. Giles Romilly records:

> My last term was enlivened by an addition to the staff – a man called Handicap. The name itself would have been a pretty considerable disadvantage to any young master. Mr Handicap lacked the qualities which exact respect from boys; he was small and rabbity, with steel-rimmed spectacles and a weak voice. Almost from the first day he was ragged mercilessly. We had discovered, by some devilish sixth sense, that he would be easy game. And easy game he was. When he took us for walks on the Downs, we threw snowballs at him, pretending we had aimed them at someone else. 'I say, sir, have I hit you? Oh sir, I am sorry.' His impotent fury was a delight to watch. I wrote ribald verses about him, which were recited in chorus when he tried to give us physical training in the gym. He has since become the headmaster of his own school. I wonder how the boys behave there.

Midway between the timid Handicaps and the fearsome Croomes and Gullivers who are to be met shortly, there are always some members of the staff who are remembered with affection. Michael Powell says:

> Very little remains in my memory of the other masters except for Godfrey, the music master, a character as eccentric as any of the characters that appear and disappear in my films. He was either Scottish or Northern Irish and larger than life. I can see his great ill-shaven face, red and weather-beaten, with craggy eyebrows over blazing blue eyes. His hair was pepper and salt and cropped short. It seems to me that he always wore the same suit of clothes; a brown tweed knickerbocker suit, the jacket in the Norfolk style with a belt of the same material,

the breeks buckled below the knee. He loved to teach us to bawl out traditional songs, like Aiken Drum:

> 'And he rode upon a ladle, a ladle! a ladle!
> He rode upon a ladle and his name was Aiken Drum.'

This quaintly named hero also 'ate up all the bawbee baps'. It wasn't until I was in Scotland that I found out that a bawbee was a threepenny piece and a bap a sour-dough bun.

Godfrey loved ballads and would chant 'Phadraig Crohour' and 'Cockles and Mussels' with a passion that transformed him.

> 'Oh Phadraig Crohour was a broth of a boy
> And he stood six foot eight
> His arm was as round as another man's thigh
> 'Twas Phadraig Crohour was great.'

And I can still hear his musical, whisky-harsh baritone, half crooning, half whispering:

> 'For the green grass is growing
> O'er Phadraig Cro-hho-oo-oor.'

He was a figure of fun to most of the boys and we were inclined to bait him, rather as one baits a bull, half fearfully, because he would not hesitate to throw his song book at the head of an unruly or unmusical pupil. Also he was armed with his conductor's baton and would certainly use it to keep order. He never wore a mortar-board and gown like the other masters, so seemed closer to us; a big truculent bear of an old boy. It was my first experience of an artist.

Sir Rupert Hart-Davis was at school during the First World War.

The masters were all too old or too unfit for military service. We were taught copper-plate handwriting by a gentle, bearded old man called Mr Adamsez. We had to copy out these valuable couplets:

> 'Work hard, play hard.
> Xenophon was a Greek.
> Use your toothbrush daily.
> Hack no furniture.'

Says Lord Home:

The master to whom I, and countless others, were most indebted was a teacher of classics who, for some forgotten reason, we christened Bunko Brown. He was a rather forbidding figure, invariably dressed in a greenish-brown herring-bone tweed suit and a stick-up collar which, with a large drooping moustache and plastered-down hair, produced a portrait of unrelieved gloom. But as an interpreter of Virgil and Ovid he was a genius. He could even bring alive the interminable campaigns of Caesar.

And everyone remembered Allan Madden with pleasure; first, because of his wit and secondly because he truckled to no one, not even the headmaster.

Allan Madden, a classical scholar of Westminster and Christchurch, came to the Dragon School straight from University in 1927. He was a fellow of infinite jest whose many *bon mots* were still being quoted in the Common Room long after he had moved on to a Headmastership.

His quick wit could be disconcerting. At one staff meeting someone raised the question of boys who asked 'to be excused'. 'Any schoolmaster who knows his job,' said the headmaster, 'can tell whether such a request is genuine'.

'Well, headmaster,' said Allan, 'personally I was engaged here as a teacher, not a water-diviner'.

Bel Bailey, writing in *Prep School*, recalls one notable character:

Blair was generally well liked though he kept a large stick by his desk to use 'fairly often' as an old pupil later recalled. It was agreed that he was fair and had no obvious favourites – as important then as now. He had a knack of never being patronising and retained his characteristic detached amusement. He gave up his spare time freely to brighten their rather dull lives after school hours. He took them to search for Puss Moth caterpillars on the black poplars, or to collect marsh gas from a nearby stagnant pond. He would encourage their hobbies, even introduce them to oil painting and gliding – in fact share his own wide ranging interests with his pupils.

Blair's industry on the boys' behalf extended to writing
them a play to act at a local hall at the end of the school
year. This play was called *King Charles II* and revealed his
Cavalier bias. The boys revelled in the play and he made them
suits of armour, labouring over brown paper and glue each
evening.

But this typical schoolmaster's life, of taxing over-activity
followed by spells of despondency and boredom, was not the
whole of his life by any means. In Hayes, in that year of
1932, Eric Arthur Blair was slowly undergoing a total
transformation, like his favourite Puss Moth eggs.

He was becoming George Orwell.

And now for the monsters.

In his hilarious *tour de force, The Moon's a Balloon*, Niven describes
his experiences at a preparatory school (unnamed) near Worthing.

I had not been long at boarding school before I discovered
that life could be hell. There was a great deal of bullying
and for a six-year-old the spectacle of a gang of twelve-
year-olds bearing down on him cracking wet towels like
whips can be terrifying.

For the most part, the masters were even more frightening.
It would be charitable to think that they were shell-shocked
heroes returned from the hell of Mons and Vimy, but it seems
more probable that they were sadistic perverts who had been
dredged up from the bottom of the educational barrel at a
time of acute manpower shortage.

One, a Mr Croome, when he tired of pulling our ears half
way out of our heads (I still have one that sticks out almost
at right angles thanks to that son of a bitch) and delivering,
for the smallest mistake in declension, back-handed slaps that
knocked one off one's bench, delighted in saying, 'Show me
the hand that wrote this', and then bringing down the sharp
edge of a heavy ruler across the offending wrist.

He took the last class on Friday evening and I remember
praying every week that he would die before then so that I could
somehow reach the haven of Saturday and Sunday and the
comparative safety of the weekend.

I don't think I have ever been so frightened of a human

being in my life. Once he made me lean out of a fourth floor window – a stupefying height for a little boy – then he shut the window across the small of my back and laid into me mightily with a cane.

Ben Travers was the author of a series of farces which, flashed out by Tom Walls, Ralph Lynn and Robertson Hare, gave audiences at the Aldwych Theatre years of delight and which, revived today, show no evidence of senility. In his autobiography, *A-sitting on a Gate* he introduces another ogre.

'You'll finish on the gallers,' said Mr Gulliver.

He delivered his awful prophecy on my untidy blond head and I crept back to my humble place in the form, an insignificant, woefully grubby, Eton-collared creature, uncommonly little for the age of ten.

There was no uniformity of type among assistant prep-school masters in the 1890s. The Abbey School, Beckenham boasted several unique and formidable specimens on its staff, but Mr Gulliver towered above the lot. I wonder how old he really was at that time and how large. A red waistcoat spread at its base to embrace his notable paunch. He sported the popular feature of his time, the moustache luxuriant, and this he had a habit of twirling with both hands simultaneously, with the action of one swimming. His rapid, if slightly provincial, voice was thunderous. His breath would whistle through his great nostrils like a steam exhaust. His eyes were swords.

To me he quite genuinely filled the role of the earthly and visible representation of the God of Wrath. It was the rule of fear which in those days at school – and in many cases at home – formed the basis of a child's upbringing. It was fear and fear alone which brought me a beating on that occasion. For what had been my crime?

This – we did sums and, when we had done what always seemed a grievously large number of these sums, Mr Gulliver read out the answers and we had to put 'R' or 'W' against each sum. The results were not questioned; it was left to our honour to report whether we'd got the sum 'Right' or 'Wrong'. Mr Gulliver was wont to read out the answers too quickly for my convenience and that morning, getting behindhand and a little muddled in my 'R' and 'W' marking I had, quite inadvertently and in my eagerness to catch up, slipped in an 'R' where a 'W' should have been. Some devilish intuition prompted Mr Gulliver to forego his credulous custom and to inspect our books.

Now, sixty years later, I recall most vividly the agony of the moment when he discovered my fallacious 'R'. His face came slowly round into mine. His green eyes pierced me with accusation. The huge moustache bristled down upon me and the great hairy nostrils whistled condemnation. I tried to gibber some honest explanation, but the panic of the culprit unmasked must have been only too clear. I suppose I realised the utter hopelessness of trying to assert the truth and sticking to it. I sank back from that awful Kitchener moustache and my quivering lips found themselves somehow blurting out the pitiable false admission, 'Oh, s-s-sir, the temptation was too great.'

Such cowardly surrender to intimidation seems contemptible even in a frightened ten-year-old. But I have never really got much better in this respect. My reason for capitulating to Mr Gulliver was probably much the same reason as that which, throughout my professional career, has instructed my immediate acceptance of modification – and even downright rejection – of my work, with the implication that everyone knows better than I do. Indeed, my reason for writing of Mr Gulliver, his terrifying beating and even more terrifying forecast of my finish, is that the incident supplies a perfect example of that inability to assert myself which has been my most marked characteristic throughout the whole of my sensitive seventy years.


Ben Travers has told, against himself, the story of one of his earliest plays, which had been accepted, 'subject to a measure of editing', by a famous actor-manager. He watched him reading the script, his blue pencil descending remorselessly on line after line of the dialogue. Finally, seeing one of his favourite witticisms about to disappear, he ventured a protest.

'I thought,' he said, 'that that was rather a good joke.'

'It *is* a good joke,' said the great man. 'It's an excellent joke. Put it in your next play.'

Mr Gulliver had much to answer for.

And now for something completely different. Something that would have been inconceivable to boys of an earlier generation. The school is Heddon Court, Cockfosters. The master under discussion is the young John Betjeman.

The other staff were not just carping or being stuffy when they complained of John's subversive influence. He *was* subversive. Sir Jasper Hollom was struck by the way in which John provided diversions for himself on a dull Sunday afternoon 'when a lot of small boys had to be pushed out to take fresh air and exercise and all they could do was admire the dripping rhododendron bushes'. John's approach was different from any other master's. 'Anybody else would have started with some degree of order; he started with the idea of introducing some degree of disorder, in a way which caught the imagination of the young . . . There was a long frontage on the road past Heddon Court, along which a certain amount of traffic and a few buses went. One of his ideas to keep small boys reasonably occupied and yet amused on a Sunday afternoon was to go out, conceal a quantity of small boys in the bushes, fling himself down in an artistic heap on the road as one who had been run over, and wait till a bus came along, when everybody would climb out to rescue him. Whereupon he scampered away into the bushes and a lot of jeering boys appeared to the discomfort of the would-be Samaritans'.

The prank was also remembered by Robert Vernon Harcourt who told John, in a letter of 1959, 'The betting on the first car stopping or driving over you was about even and many grubby peppermint creams changed hands when the result was known'.

# 14

# MATRONS

Next in importance to the headmaster's wife, sometimes ranking even ahead of her, was the matron. She was closest to the boys and, inevitably, became a deputy mother. Being women first and matrons second they varied widely in character and the reaction to them of their young charges varied accordingly.

In some institutions their position was one of considerable dignity and power. Geoffrey Rawson remembers:

> We lived in wards, each presided over by a dame. In one sense, notwithstanding the eleemosynary nature of her employment our dame was *une grande dame*. She had her own apartment, her own maids and her dress was like that of the Queen. When she made her rounds of inspection, her entourage was an impressive one, including the head boy and the two ward maids with the porter bringing up the rear. Her forty subjects stood to attention at the foot of their beds. She was 'Ma'am' to us all. Her moral and disciplinary sway was complete and I now suspect that her seeming innocent eye saw more than we suspected. If it was a case of bowels or bad breath, or teeth, or a cough or a pallid languor, or other childish ailment, she was quick to interrogate us in her room. Then the appropriate bottle was taken down and the horrid draught administered, among which I recollect Parrishes Food, Syrup of Squills, Iron Tonic, Rhubarb Pills and red flannel pads for weak chests. Her accumulated wisdom and experience as wife and mother no doubt fitted her admirably to be Mother of Forty. Her success in her vocation was proved by the way we ran to her with our hopes and fears, our pleasures and pains, our ardours and disappointments.

Her influence might, with a certain type of boy, become more than merely impressive. In rare cases it could be inspirational; as it was with C. S. Lewis. On the collapse of 'Oldies', which sank, unlamented, in 1910 and following a brief stay at Campbell College, he went to a school which he calls 'Chartres'.

No school ever had a better Matron, more skilled and comforting to boys in sickness or more cheery and companionable to boys in health. She was one of the most selfless people I have ever known. We all loved her. I, the orphan, especially. Now it so happened that Miss 'C', who seemed so old to me, was still in her spiritual immaturity, still hunting, with the eagerness of a soul that had a touch of angelic quality in it, for a truth and a way of life. Guides were even rarer then than now. She was (as I should now put it) floundering in the mazes of Theosophy, Rosicrucianism, Spiritualism; the whole Anglo-American Occultist tradition. Nothing was further from her intention than to destroy my faith. She could not tell that the room into which she brought this candle was full of gunpowder. But the result of Miss C's conversation did not stop there. Little by little, unconsciously, unintentionally, she loosened the whole framework, blunted all the sharp edges, of my belief. The vagueness, the merely speculative character of all this Occultism began to spread – yes, and to spread deliciously – to the stern truths of the creed. The whole thing became a matter of speculation. I was soon altering 'I believe' to 'one does feel'. And oh, the relief of it. From the tyrannous noon of revelation I passed into the cool evening twilight of Higher Thought, where there was nothing to be obeyed, and nothing to be believed except what was either comforting or exciting. I do not mean that Miss C did this; better say that the Enemy did this to me, taking occasion from the things she innocently said.

The reaction of some boys might be more flippant. Captain T.G. Wells, when at Summer Fields, used to sing 'Nurse Hayes has no stays' and propagated the rumour that she had eloped with a man from London. He says: 'She looked after our health with care. She was pretty free with the slipper and with quinine as an instant cure for colds'. Or it might be amusement tinged with appreciation. Giles Romilly, who was critical of most of the staff, says:

I was rather fond of Matron. She was an immense woman.
Her face had a comical shapelessness and her figure was like a
sack in which everything had been shaken down to the bottom.
The school had no need of an early morning bell, because when
she moved the floorboards rang and her 'good morning' was a
thunder-clap that not even the heaviest sleeper could ignore.

Graham Greene, who found being at his father's school difficult in
so many ways, remembers an occasion when a kindly gesture by the
matron upset him.

The matron, Miss Wills, embarrassed me on my seventh
birthday by kissing me when I brought her a piece of my
birthday cake, so that I returned to the family circle angry
and shattered by the experience. My Aunt Nono wrote some
verses on the subject in the School House Gazette; 'Miss Wills
kissed me when we met. As I took my birthday cake in . . .'
and I had the uncomfortable sense that now the incident would
never be forgotten.
It had been immortalised by art.

A well-known character at Sherborne Prep School is recalled by
Oliver Holt in a privately printed memoir. She was known to all,
affectionately, as the Cat.

At bed time, when fatigue had forced Matron to replace the
nobbly black shoes she wore during the day with a pair of
carpet slippers, she would heave along the dormitory corridor
with a loud flip-flap which sent us scurrying into bed. She
would come, as Lady Macbeth did, bearing a taper. 'All well
'ere?' she would enquire, her hand at the switch of the
gas-flare on the wall bracket, the light shining on her
steel-rimmed spectacles, her high-coloured cheeks, her
white apron and long, stiff, cylindrical cuffs. Sometimes she
would catch the eye of a grinning boy and say, 'Goodnight,
Johnny 'Ess. Go to bye-byes', or point to another whose eyes
were half closed with sleepiness.
'There, there. Look at little Master Baker, now —

> Blinky Eye
> Pickled Pie
> Went to bed and told a lie.'

Out would go the light, and if in jocular mood she would recite the following exhortation –

> 'Pleasant Dreams
> Sweet Repose
> Don't lie on your chest or
> you'll 'urt your nose.'

But usually it was just 'Goodnight, All', and we could hear the Goodnight, Alls repeated with diminishing distinctness as she flapped further and further along the corridor.

A. C. Liddell, who was at Temple Grove as a boy, and subsequently himself became headmaster of a preparatory school, notes that with even the most formidable matrons strings might be pulled.

> Every night and morning we filed before the matron, a deep-bosomed old dame, who dealt out two or three ferocious strokes with a hair-brush onto our heads as we passed under her. Oddly enough the good lady had been a maid at my father's private school, so was kind to me in her way, tempering the blows of her hair-brush by saying that my forehead reminded her of my father's.

But one feels some doubt whether anything could have softened the heart of the ogress remembered with terror by Roald Dahl.

> There was a boy in our dormitory during my first term [at St Peter's, Weston-Super-Mare] called Tweedie who, one night, started snoring after he had gone to sleep.
> 'Who's that talking?' cried the Matron bursting in. I remember looking up at her from my pillow and seeing her there silhouetted against the light from the corridor and thinking how truly frightening she looked. I think it was her enormous bosom that scared me most of all. My eyes were riveted to it and to me it was like a battering ram, or the bows of an ice breaker, or maybe a couple of high-explosive bombs.
> 'Own up,' she cried. 'Who was talking?'

We lay there in silence. Then Tweedie, who was lying fast asleep on his back with his mouth open, gave another snore.

The Matron stared at Tweedie. 'Snoring is a disgusting habit,' she said. 'Only the lower classes do it. We shall have to teach him a lesson.'

She didn't switch on the light, but she advanced into the room and picked up a cake of soap from the nearest basin. The bare electric bulb in the corridor illuminated the whole dormitory in a pale creamy glow.

None of us dared to sit up in bed, but all eyes were on the Matron now, watching to see what she was going to do next. She always had a pair of scissors hanging by a white tape from her waist and with this she began shaving thin slivers of soap into the palm of her hand. Then she went over to where the wretched Tweedie lay and very carefully she dropped these little soap flakes into his open mouth. She had a whole handful of them and I thought she was never going to stop.

What on earth is going to happen? I wondered. Would Tweedie choke? Would he strangle? Might his throat get blocked up completely? Was she going to kill him?

The Matron stepped back a couple of paces and folded her arms across, or rather underneath, her massive chest.

Nothing happened. Tweedie kept right on snoring.

Then suddenly he began to gurgle and white bubbles appeared around his lips. The bubbles grew and grew until in the end his whole face seemed to be smothered in a bubbly foaming white soapy froth. It was a horrific sight. Then, all at once, Tweedie gave a great cough and a splutter and he sat up very fast and began clawing at his face with his hands. 'Oh,' he stuttered. 'Oh, oh, oh, oh no. Wh – wh – what's happening? Wh – wh – what's on my face? Somebody help me.'

The Matron threw him a face flannel and said, 'Wipe it off, Tweedie. And don't ever let me hear you snoring again. Hasn't anyone ever taught you not to sleep on your back?'

With that she marched out of the dormitory and slammed the door.

# 15

# READING

The reading of poetry is not often a voluntary occupation in preparatory schools. On Sundays, in earlier times, nothing but selected devotional works were permitted. H.A.L. Fisher, the great historian, writes in his *Unfinished Biography*:

> In compensation for this comprehensive abridgement of
> private reading on Sunday, the Headmaster gathered us together
> in class and took us through Keble's *Christian Year* at the rate
> of one poem per week. We were called upon to read these poems
> aloud and to explain them, verse by verse and line by line. I
> believe that good judges concede to Mr Keble not only a
> rare piety of soul, but also a vein of genuine poetry, but I am
> sure that he is not a poet to put before boys.

Cyril Connolly's headmaster established the Index with papal authority. There were acceptable poets – a list starting with Chaucer and ending with Henry Newbolt; and there were unacceptable ones – Donne, Dryden, Blake, Browning, Fitzgerald and, not surprisingly, Oscar Wilde. He enunciated a few general principles:

> A poem is good either because it is funny or because it makes
> you want to cry. Some funny poems make you want to cry; that
> is because you are not a healthy little boy. You need more
> Character. The best poems have the most beautiful lines in them;
> these lines can be detached. They are purple patches and are
> Useful in Examinations. *Greyselegy* is almost all purple patches
> . . . Nobody wrote so many purple passages as Tennyson and
> he had character too. (*Bury the Great Duke*; *Charge of the Light
> Brigade*; *The Revenge*). Kipling is the only great poet alive
> today. Poetry is romantic, purple, a help in time of trouble
> . . . It is also something to be ashamed of, like sex and (except
> with the Chaplain) religion.

In spite of this magisterial warning, a lot of earlier reading had been religious. Wilson Harris, journalist and editor of *The Spectator* for twenty-one years, remembers:

> The earliest literature to which I applied myself was a series of large, thin, distinctly improving publications, of which I can remember three in particular. 'A Peep Behind the Scenes', 'Christie's Old Organ' and 'Jessica's First Prayer'. Whether these entertaining and instructive romances are obtainable now I know not. It is well over fifty years since I set eyes on them.
>
> To these should be added 'Robinson Crusoe', 'The Swiss Family Robinson' and 'Black Beauty'. Also a poor imitation of that excellent work called 'Beautiful Joe', about a dog, instead of a horse; the Chronicles of the Schönberg-Cotta Family and Dean Farrer's absurd 'St Winifreds, or the World of School'. Who the Schönberg-Cotta Family was, and what was chronicled about it, I have forgotten completely, but it could be discovered as I have often seen copies of the book on second-hand book barrows.
>
> And then there was 'Gulliver's Travels'. There was a copy of that dangerous work in the house, but my mother had done her best to make it innocuous by the rather drastic method of cutting out, with a pair of scissors, whatever she deemed it desirable to cut out. This had the disadvantage, of course, of removing also whatever was on the other side of that particular page. But I got the hang of the thing pretty well, including what I was not meant to get the hang of.

Gordon Hake, doctor and poet, was at a school which he does not name, but describes as 'a monastic one which, three hundred years before, had been the house of mitred abbots'. Here an undiluted diet of religious works might have been intended. But a different type of book was apt to infiltrate.

> Many of the boys were great readers of forbidden stories and smuggled books into the school, the penalty for which, on being found out, was a flogging. The books in question were romances of enchanted castles; of beautiful young women, the prisoners of tyrants, of subterranean passages and solitary

cells. I would give much to possess a circulating library of
that day, such as the one I discovered at Seaford and devoured
whenever my holidays came round.

Sooner or later the boy found that he could read for himself easily
enough to enjoy whatever book happened to fall into his hands at that
magical moment. Says David Christie Murray, novelist, traveller and
*Times* special correspondent:

> I can recall quite easily the time when I could not read and
> the recollection of one superb moment is very often with
> me. That moment came with the reading of a story entitled,
> 'The Mandan's Revenge' or 'The Riccarree War Spear'. It came
> from the pen of Mr Percy B. St John and may still be found
> in some far away number of Chambers' Journal.
>
> I have never gone back to that story. I have never had the
> courage to go back. It would be something like a crime to
> dissipate the halo of romance and splendour which lived about
> it; as I know most certainly I should do if I read it over
> again.

As time went on a more modern sort of reading list appeared. For
instance, Robert Speaight says:

> I read – well, not anything I could get my hands on, for I
> was always choosy – but the usual things, Rider Haggard,
> Anthony Hope, the early Buchan and Conan Doyle. The
> modern adventure story had been ruined for me by sex,
> speed and violence.
>
> Sherlock Holmes I read now with the same pleasure I did
> then and I am constantly finding myself in good company.
> T.S. Eliot once told me that he thought 'The Speckled Band'
> one of the great short stories in the English language; and, when
> I recalled to him the classic opening chapters of 'The Hound
> of the Baskervilles', his slow, slightly sepulchral voice completed
> the quotation, 'Mr Holmes, they were the footprints of a
> gigantic hound'.
>
> Only a few years ago Armstrong Gibbs introduced me to
> Stevenson, but my passion was for Scott and I looked down my
> nose at the boys who were still satisfied with Henty. At home

I read Scott's novels in a cumbersome edition, two columns to a page, straining my eyes in the summer twilight. At The Wick Miss Tring used to lend me the fat closely printed volumes from her library, until, one day, I was laid low by a mysterious fever. The school doctor was a saturnine character called Utoff, with a stoop and curly grey hair whom I instantly cast for the role of Professor Moriarty. 'If the boy doesn't get better,' he said, 'I shall bring the leeches to him tomorrow'.

Not even the hint of medieval medicine either reduced my temperature or interrupted my reading of 'The Fair Maid of Perth'. The following day Dr Utoff made his desperate diagnosis.

'This boy's temperature,' he said, 'is due to excessive reading of the works of Sir Walter Scott. Put him onto Conan Doyle'.

This passion for Sherlock Holmes is echoed by the well-known theatrical producer Basil Dean. He was badly bitten.

Upon a memorable wet afternoon I encountered Mr Sherlock Holmes beneath the light blue covers of the *Strand Magazine* with its hansom cab bowling down Fleet Street and the shouting news boys holding up the contents sheet. The atmosphere of suspense created by that first story was so strong that I lay awake all night, shivering, in contemplation of the dangers lurking behind the wardrobe. When my mother found out about it, I was forbidden to read any more Sherlock Holmes, but this was too much. I retired to the most unlikely, and therefore safest, place. Seated on the throne I read the latest issue. Sometimes I was too frightened to come out afterwards, so that my mother thought that I had been taken ill 'in there'. Ultimately the ban was withdrawn, provided I learned my Sunday collect first.

The reading list was by no means static, as Adrian Alington, novelist as well as schoolmaster, mentions.

Literature had its phases and fashions. Gods were raised up and as inexplicably cast down. Henty was admired, was derided. Harrison Ainsworth and Stevenson were the men, or else it

was Rodney Stone and the Adventure of Charles Augustus
Milverton, or the Solitary Cyclist that held the field; only to
give way to Rider Haggard or a renascent Henty. 'The Hill' at
one time enjoyed a vogue, due to its being read aloud with
great emotion by Miss Billings on Sunday afternoons when it
was too wet for a walk.

The abominable Scaife, the admirable Caesar were loathed
and venerated.

And the changes might be caused, or accelerated, by extraneous
circumstances. The 1914–18 war damaged the reputation of many
generals. Paul Spillane, in his *History of St Andrew's*, shows that it had
an equally deleterious effect on the reputations of authors.

The reading habits of the boys were significantly changed by
the war. Westerman and Henty went out of fashion. Nobody
was interested in 'The Sea-Girt Fortress' or 'The Lion of St
Marks'; nobody wanted to go 'With Roberts to Kandahar' nor
yet 'With Kitchener to Khartoum'. A new breed of author
took over the market with such titles as 'The Secret Service
Submarine' and 'The Secret Service Airoplane' (contemporary
spelling). Commander Lawless R.N. and Buckle of
Submarine V2 fought gallantly for king and country. Heroes,
most of whom seemed to be named Frank, uttered such
deathless lines as, 'Come on you cowardly bunch of cads, one
British seaman is worth the whole blithering pack of you'. While
detective novels were banned, titles such as 'Count Dracula',
'Ultus, the Man from the Dead' and 'The Clutching Hand'
were approved dormitory reading. But the basic literary diet
consisted of the colossal annuals, 'Chums' and the 'Boys' Own
Paper'. Once in the school they became public property and
were avidly read by anyone who picked them up. The B.O.P.
was full of useful information, while 'Chums' largely contained
armchair soldiers' interpretation of events on the Western
Front. Anti-German schoolboy literature was a not unnatural
product of the First World War. It still flourishes.

Graham Greene found one compensation for attending a school of
which his father was the headmaster. The school library was open to

him in the holidays as well as in the term time. And the effects of
what he read were profound.

[When I had finished with nursery reading] I came on Henty.
I particularly liked the dull historical parts. 'The XIVth Hussars
proceeded in close order to the top of the ridge. On the right
flank were the Second Ghurkas –' Rider Haggard I discovered
after Henty. My favourite, of course, was *King Solomon's Mines*,
but the later adventures of Quartermain bored me . . . What a
happy chance it seemed in those days, to be the son of the
headmaster, for in the holidays all the shelves of the library were
open to me, with thousands of books only waiting to be
explored.

The influence of early books is profound. So much of the
future lies on the shelves; early reading has more influence
on conduct than any religious teaching. I feel certain that I
would not have made a false start, when I was twenty-one,
in the British American Tobacco Company, who had promised
me a post in China, if I had never read Captain Gilson's *Lost
Column*, and without a knowledge of Rider Haggard would I
have been drawn later to Liberia – which led to a wartime post
in Sierra Leone? And surely it must have been *Montezuma's
Daughter* and the story of the disastrous night of Cortez'
retreat which lured me, twenty years afterwards to Mexico.
*The Maneaters of Tsavo* on the other hand fixed in me a boring
image of East Africa which even Hemingway was powerless
to change.

Finally, Noël Coward, who demonstrates an affection for a type of
reading which appealed also to George Orwell.

About this time I took a fancy for the most tremendously
hearty schoolboy literature. I read avidly week by week
*Chums, The Boy's Own Paper, The Magnet* and *The Gem* and
loved particularly these last two. *The Gem* appeared on
Thursday or Friday and was devoted to the light-hearted
adventures of Tom Merry and Co. *The Magnet* came out on
Tuesdays and dealt with the very similar adventures of Harry
Wharton and Co. As far as I can remember the dialogue of the
two papers was almost identical, consisting largely of the

words 'Jape' and 'Wheeze' and, in moments of hilarity and pain respectively 'Ha Ha Ha' and 'Yow Yow Yow'. There was a fat boy in each. In *The Magnet* it was Billy Bunter, who in addition to being very greedy and providing great opportunities for jam-tart fun (Ha ha ha! – He he he! – Yow yow yow!) was a ventriloquist of extraordinary ability and could make sausages cry out when stabbed with a fork. They were awfully manly, decent fellows, Harry Wharton and Co, and no suggestion of sex, even in its lighter forms, ever sullied their conversation. Considering their ages, their healthy mindedness was almost frightening. I was delighted to find in a newspaper shop the other day that *The Magnet* was unchanged, excepting its cover which used to be bright orange and is now white. I read a little of it with tender emotion. There they all were, Harry Wharton, Frank Nugent and Billy Bunter, still 'Ha-ha-ha-ing' and 'He-he-he-ing' and still, after twenty-four years, hovering merrily on the verge of puberty.

# 16

# PETS AND CRAZES

The keeping of pets depended on the tolerance of the authorities – or, at least, in keeping those authorities in happy ignorance. Eden Phillpotts outlines the obstacles.

There were difficulties in the way of maintenance, though happily the desks were constructed for ventilation. Not that they were really made for ventilation, but the ink pots were let into holes at the top of each desk and through these holes, when the inkpots were removed, pure air descended to the fauna beneath and refreshed them, while the exhausted air also escaped in the same way. Thus the most understanding chaps always kept their inkpots out of these holes as much as possible, with good results for their specimens. But in the case of very large fauna, especially two young moles which I had managed to catch and kept in a box of earth renewed as often as possible, and also as in the case of Forrester Minor's specimen, a live and very young rabbit . . . the danger of ventilation was very great, because these fauna gave off a distinct scent, which might have ruined all if it had come to Mr Paget's nose – him being our form master.

In Maurice Baring's school, St George's, Ascot, there seems to have been a measure of tolerance. More so than when the young Winston Churchill was there.

During the summer the rage the boys had for keeping caterpillars in breeding cages, for collecting butterflies and keeping live stock was allowed full play. I myself invested in a green lizard which, although it had no tail, was otherwise satisfactory and ate, so a letter of mine of that date says, a lot of worms. I also had a large fat toad which was blind in one eye but, for a toad, affectionate. But the ideal of the boys was a natterjack toad – whatever that may be.

At the school known as 'Chaytors' similar enthusiasms were encouraged. Says Adrian Alington:

Most old Chaytorians would recall the bug-collecting craze, when the field would be dotted of a half holiday afternoon with ardent naturalists armed with little boxes. Great was the rivalry between collectors, while the craze endured, to secure the largest and most uncommon 'spec'; heated the arguments on the merits of this insect and that.

It must not be supposed, however, that all boys were captivated by these pursuits. As soon as they became a sort of substitute lesson a spirit of opposition surfaced.

The historian A.J.P. Taylor writes in *A Personal History*:

Nature study was my special bugbear. I tried one variety after another. I tried Aquarium. My tadpoles died. I could not catch newts. My tank smelled. I tried Astronomy and could never identify the stars. I even tried Lichen, the dreariest study known to man. Worst of all was the Flower List. This was a great printed sheet issued to each boy, with the names of some 200 flowers and space for even rarer ones. We had to collect these flowers on our Sunday walk and then name then to Mr Jones the next morning. Some boys scored well over a hundred in no time. I never got more than half a dozen. Daisy, dandelion, buttercup. Then what? My flowers had all withered by Monday and the water in my jam jar stank. The whole affair was a nightmare to me.

Unlike these staff-propagated activities, the 'craze', in its simplest form, was the property of its instigators. 'Some', says Anthony Cheetham, of Summer Fields, 'like conker fights in the autumn, are probably permanent fixtures. Others seem to make no sense at all. Perhaps they were just a working off of excess energy. But in their day *they were the sole form of activity separate from organisation or interference*'.

Nicholas Monsarrat, at The Leas, Hoylake, lists a few of them.

There were stilts and pogo-sticks and keeping ferrets – vile tempered, acrid smelling, horrible to rabbits and owners

alike. There was Couéism . . . There was photography:
beginners had Box Brownies, experts wielded VPKs (or Vest
Pocket Kodaks); we all did our own developing, 'fixing', and
printing in wooden frames, under sunlight.

There was roller-skating, and this again involved a sharp
social distinction; unless you had ball-bearing skates you were
pretty well a social out-cast. There was conkers – demolishing
each other's chestnuts. (Unscrupulous players boiled their
chestnuts for extra hardness and then denied it.) There was a
brief craze, limited to one boy, which made us all passionate
with envy.

This child of good fortune, this lucky swine called
Blackburn, had a father recently returned from America; and
the father had brought his son back something so modern, so
dazzling, so unbelievably scientific and ripping, that no one
else could top it.

It was a wireless set, *inside a match box*.

Though no one dared to say so, there was not very much
to it; a 'cat's whisker', a piece of quartz and two plugs for
outside wiring. Nor was there anything for us to listen to.
Broadcasting, though apparently all the rage in America,
was not to reach England for more than a year. Yet there it
was, in all its mysterious glory; an actual wireless set in a
match box.

We sat round it, shushing each other vehemently, while
Blackburn fiddled with the cat's whisker and produced small
scratching noises. 'If there was a programme, you could hear
music', he said importantly. 'My pater heard Paul Whiteman'.
We were enthralled, deeply envious and disconsolate.
Blackburn had achieved an enormous edge on everybody.

Monsarrat's list is far from exhaustive. As Graham Greene remembers there were war games.

When I was a bit older (about twelve) I would play with
Hugh, who was six, an elaborate war game, based on H.G.
Wells's book *Little Wars*. In the holidays we were able to use
the big tables in the School House dining-hall. We would push
two tables together and lay out a whole countryside. There
were roads marked in chalk and cottages and forests of twigs

and a river which had to be crossed. One game might last a week, with perhaps two hundred men on either side, quick raids by cavalry and slow advances by infantry, measured on lengths of string, mêlées which led to the capture of prisoners and bombardments with the two 4.2 naval guns. It was 1916, but war was still glamorous to a child.

There were tops. Richard Meinertzhagen, who appears under 'Fighting', notes in one of his quieter moments:

> When I was at Fonthill there was a delightful fashion-craze in
> the school. Most boys, including me, had masses of tiny
> wooden tops, beautifully fashioned from strange woods. They
> were but half to three quarters of an inch in diameter. Our
> ambition was to have as many as possible spinning at the same
> time and of as many different sorts of wood. They were spun
> by hand. It taught me my woods – rose, elm, oak, eye-maple,
> ebony, satin, holly, yew and the rest. At one time I was
> supreme, with twenty different sorts of woods.

The more intelligent the boy, the more abstruse were his pursuits likely to be. Alan Turing, the outstanding mathematician, father of the modern computer and presiding genius at the code-breaking establishment at Bletchley, was at Hazelhurst Preparatory School under a Mr Darlington. His biographer writes:

> Maps were an old interest; family trees he also liked and the
> particularly awkward Turing genealogy, with its leaps of the
> barometer from bough to bough and its enormous Victorian
> families, exercised his ingenuity. Chess was the most social of
> his activities ('There was not going to be any Chess
> Tournament because Mr Darlington had not seen many people
> playing, but he said, if I asked everyone who could play and
> made a list of everyone who had played this term, we would
> have it. I managed to get enough people so we are having it').

Kenneth Tynan, the well-known critic, writer, producer and literary adviser to the National Theatre was in the junior section of King Edward's School, Birmingham. He was eleven years old when he began his lifelong hobby, the cultivation of famous men and women. His biographer, his widow Kathleen Tynan, writes:

Between 1938 and 1941 he indiscriminately hounded the
famous to secure their signatures. Here was the beginning of a
lifelong passion for stars. As a correspondent he was both
persistent and impressive. The comedian, Tommy Handley,
thanked Ken for his charming letter which he read out to the
cast of his radio programme, *Itma*. 'You haven't missed a single
point in the whole show'.

The political world had its pen poised for Master Tynan.
Winston Churchill's private secretary sent Churchill's
autograph in May 1939. The Prime Minister, Neville
Chamberlain, and his wife signed in the same month. The
following year the War Cabinet was bagged. Lord
Beaverbrook, at the Ministry of Aircraft Production,
thanked Ken for his £1 contribution to a Spitfire and added,
'I am most grateful to you for helping us in this way to drive
the Nazis from our skies –'

Joseph Kennedy, the United States Ambassador to Great
Britain, wrote, in April 1940, that 'it is heartening to know that
one's sincere efforts in difficult times are not misunderstood.
May I add that if you write such a graceful letter when you are
twelve, you should be of diplomatic calibre when you reach
man's estate.'

Of all crazes, possibly the most curious and unlikely is the one
recorded by Anthony Cheetham. He explains how it arose. It seems
to be broadly descriptive of all of them.

First, an original idea, then slavish imitation. A boy arrived
back at the beginning of term with two knitting needles and a
ball of wool. In no time this unmasculine innovation had
aroused intense enthusiasm. Parents were bombarded with
requests for knitting equipment and soon the school resounded
to the clack of knitting needles. Jagged multicoloured
scarves besprinkled with dropped stitches began to make their
appearance. Those who could not knit were regarded with
disdain, whilst the boy who had mastered both plain and purl
was admired by all. Then suddenly enthusiasm waned.

It seems unlikely that knitting will have much attraction for the
boys of this technological age. Adrian Ward-Jackson, writing in 1964,

says, 'Boys treasure change. First typewriters, then wireless, gramophones, intercoms and tape recorders. Has anyone got a portable TV yet?' Nearly thirty years later the answer is 'Certainly. Rather old fashioned, though.'

# LANGUAGE

Like all close communities, preparatory schools develop their own language. This is not the complete and somewhat affected vocabulary by which some of the older public schools demonstrate their antiquity. It is rather the allotting of names to certain objects and persons, and, on the negative side, the imposing of taboos.

Says Compton Mackenzie:

> Prep schools used to be the preserve of much lore and language. At Colet Court, for instance, we used the good old English word 'lam' and always threatened a 'lamming' instead of a 'licking'. Yet nobody across the road at St Paul's ever used the word 'lam'. We called money 'chink' at Colet Court; at St Paul's it was 'tin'. Then there was a way to be rid of an obligation by being the first to call 'Fain I'; which we may feel Shakespeare once shouted in his Stratford schooldays.

Nicholas Aldridge, in *Time to Spare*, says:

> Schoolboy language proper is hard to keep track of. We have 'gut' for 'tuck', which a later generation called 'guzz'. As to the food provided by the school itself, a rich and varied menu of names, usually uncomplimentary and sometimes positively nauseous, exists in most such institutions, ranging from the starkly descriptive 'stodge' to more imaginative flights of fancy such as 'matron's leg'. These tended to be universal terms for food which probably differed little from school to school; sago looked like frogspawn wherever you were eating it.
>
> The Molesworth books of Ronald Searle and Geoffrey Williams contain a number of terms that have been used at Summer Fields. 'Chiz' and all its variants may possibly derive from '(hard) cheese' i.e. bad luck; its parallel 'swiz' incorporating elements of 'swindle'. One might also say 'swizzle' and 'swee' suggesting a French pronunciation of the root form. 'I claim big

swee' or 'I claim chiz' were common cries at the injustice of fate. 'Bish' is a relatively common prep school word for a mistake, but how many other schools used 'skiv' to denote not the domestic staff, but a boy who became (theoretically) subservient to another for payment?

'Be my skiv for half a sweet ration a week?'

Skivs and slaves, who were unpaid, but bound by loyalty, blackmail or fear, were expected to do the bidding of their masters and this was one of the ways in which gangs were formed. But such arrangements were often of short duration. Feeling secure in his freedom the liberated one might turn and 'cock a snook' at his erstwhile lord, a gesture performed by thumbing the nose and twiddling the fingers – admirably expressive and often accompanied by some such derisive chant as, 'So derdle erdle er to you'.

Masters were referred to by traditional names. 'All German masters,' says Lord Dunsany, 'were called "Fink" and all French masters "Bun", whilst the butler was "Jumbo".' The prohibitions were rigid. Nicholas Monsarrat encountered them at the first of the two schools he attended, St Christopher's.

The word 'brother' was, for some reason, taboo. One spoke of 'my major' or 'my minor' . . . Spurned even more scornfully were the tender terms 'mother' and 'father'. These had now become 'mater' and 'pater' – or, collectively, 'my people'. Sisters were never mentioned. I lived in constant terror that someone would find out what my sister was called. Nicholas itself was bad enough, and never, never, *never* to be written on envelopes. But Felicity! . . .

Even a more sophisticated boy like Maurice Baring fell foul of this prohibition.

One day my sister, Susan, unwittingly caused me annoyance by writing to me and sealing the letter with her name, Susan. The boys saw the seal and called out, 'He's got a sister called Susan; he's got a sister called Susan'. Sisters should be warned never to let their Christian names come to the knowledge of their brothers' school fellows. This kind of thing is typical of private school life.

Gilbert Murray, distinguished writer and scholar, who became both Professor of Greek at Oxford and Professor of English at Harvard, went to Southeys School, where he faced one of the problems of language at a very early age. He cannot have been much more than ten at the time.

The bad language was a very great shock to me when I first came away from home. It seemed to me so much more wicked than anything I had imagined before. It was the badge of the manly, vicious way of looking at the world which was the ideal of life to many. I was once or twice criticised for not swearing and felt myself something of an outcast in consequence.

Pretty soon I made a bargain with the powers above. I had a strong objection to obscene language, but I thought I must satisfy popular feeling by swearing. I did it in a manner of calculation. I got little or no pleasure, but in order to be less unpopular I deliberately swore at every second sentence. A few weeks later my friend Willie Watt and I were crossing a paddock and I advised him that he should take the road 'because the damned grass was so blasted wet'. Watt was older than I. He must have been about thirteen. He said he didn't see the good of swearing when you weren't angry. I was so delighted to hear my own sentiments from another that I agreed with him warmly; at which he seemed much surprised and asked why, then, I swore so much. It had never occurred to me before, that when I was swearing to please people, anyone would actually be displeased with me for that very reason.

It is, of course, true that obscene words could be used in total innocence. Francis Brett Young, novelist and poet, was at a school called Iona at Sutton Coldfield. Says his widow, Jessica:

Francis had just discovered the poems of William Shenstone and at a tea party, one Sunday, the Rector teased him about this and asked him if he could remember anything Shenstone had written.

He thereupon recited, with great confidence, a passage of turgid blank verse from Shenstone's 'Lines on a Distant Prospect of Halesby Abbey'.

144

> . . . the luxurious priest
> Crawled from his bedded strumpet
> muttering low
> An ineffectual curse.

When the visitors had gone his mother asked him if he had any idea what a bedded strumpet was. He said, 'No. But I thought they were lovely sounding words'.

Rarely, but only very rarely, a boy could rise superior to all fashion and tradition. Such a one was Micky Wall, John Osborne's friend.

Micky Wall's technique of containing adults was the pre-emptive strike. Even when he gave voice to what seemed to me the unsayable, his gravity ensured that his reward was no more than a half-hearted cuff. It is hard to convey the impact of those sallies, which certainly did not rely on wit, but on transported cheekiness. Rude, naughty, or invented words exploded with inevitable shock. Propriety and dignity had a whiff of shot, as if innocence, in the form of Micky, was keeping them on their toes.

For example, he was ever ready to coin a meaningless phrase or invent a word. During a long fiery afternoon in Mr Jones' pit of Scripture and whacking, he was challenged about the contents of a toffee tin under his desk. 'What is that you're playing with, Wall?' 'It's my gzoo.' 'What's in that tin?' 'My gzoo, sir.' 'And what's that?'

Looking eagerly helpful Micky held up the tin and took out various toy animals, elephants, giraffes, lions, antelopes. 'These, sir. This is my gzoo.'

Mr Jones looked upon Micky's ark as if it were the ark of the covenant rather than of Noah. The creatures of the pit waited for Welsh flame to strike and consume the blasphemer. Mr Jones stared; nostrils flared for the whiff of evil. Instead of dragging Micky to damnation by the ear, he flung down his palsied cane and mumbled, 'Well, put it away. We don't want to see it.'

Elijah's chariot had lost a spoke.

# 18

# MYTHS

Preparatory schools, like other primitive communities, are a fruitful field for myths. Lord Berners, the composer, aesthete and eccentric who installed a harpsichord in his car and adorned his dogs with diamond necklaces, recalled his days at Elmley in *First Childhood*. He writes: 'This kind of emotional masochism has existed through the ages and is not confined to the very young. If a student of folklore was able to live for some months in a preparatory school disguised as a small boy, he might be enabled to make some illuminating discoveries as to the origin of primitive myths and the growth of primitive religions'.

The myths might be autogenous, generated by an over-imaginative boy. Edward Frederic Benson, third son of that Edward Benson who became Archbishop of Canterbury, was a prolific writer credited with ninety-three books of fiction, biography and drama. He is generally considered, now, to have been too prolific for his own good, a judgement curiously foreshadowed when he was at Temple Grove.

The minds of children, as they grow, have those diseases which are incident to childhood much as their bodies have. I had my measles of sentimentality and having got over that I developed a kind of whooping-cough of lying. I used to invent and repeat extraordinary experiences which had their root in fact but were embellished by my imagination to scenes of unparalleled magnificence. For instance, coming back from summer holidays at Le Havre the crossing was an extremely rough one. All night the waters broke over the decks, heavy and solid and certainly an unfortunate traveller came into our cabin drenched through. All next day, as I travelled to Temple Grove, my imagination worked on these promising materials and I told my admiring school fellows that we had barely escaped shipwreck. The waves, which certainly did deluge the decks, I represented as having poured in torrents down the funnels extinguishing the furnaces so that we had to stop until the fires were relit. Out of the passenger who had come into our cabin I constructed a Frenchman, who was supposed to have said, in broken English, 'Ze water is not coming over in bucketfuls, it is coming over in shipfuls'.

So vividly did I imagine this that before long I really half believed it. Again, the next winter holidays were marked by a heavy snowfall . . . and I seized hungrily on the incident. On returning to school I added further embellishments; that I personally drove the horses which brought my father's carriage home along the steeply glazed roads.

There were more of these fictions, which I cannot remember now, all of which had some exiguous foundation of fact and great was my horror when an implacable enemy handed me, one morning, a scrap of paper in the manner of an ultimatum headed BENSON'S LIES. And there below, neatly summarised, were all the stories which I thought had been listened to with such respectful envy.

The enemy added darkly that 'they' (whoever 'they' might be) were considering what they were going to do about it. I suppose that consternation was graven on me, for he stonily added, 'Yes. You may well turn pale', and I pictured this damning text being handed to the headmaster, who would send it to my father.

What the public upshot was I cannot remember, but by the aid of this terrifying medicine I made a marvellously brisk recovery from that particular disease of boyhood.

The myth might be believed by its originator, or possibly only half believed. Roald Dahl went to two preparatory schools; at seven to Llandaff Cathedral School and at nine to St Peter's, Weston-Super-Mare. *Boy*, the book in which he wrote about them, is unquestionably a classic.

One of the other boys at Llandaff, whose name was Thwaites, told me I should never eat Liquorice Bootlaces. Thwaites's father, who was a doctor, had said that they were made from rats' blood. The father had given his young son a lecture about Liquorice Bootlaces when he caught him eating one in bed. 'Every rat-catcher in the country' the father had said, 'takes his rats to the Liquorice Bootlace Factory and the manager pays twopence for each rat. Many a rat-catcher has become a millionaire by selling his dead rats to the factory'. 'But how do they turn the rats into liquorice?' the young Thwaites had asked his father.

'They wait until they've got ten thousand rats,' the father had answered, 'then they dump them all into a huge shiny steel cauldron and boil them up for several hours. Two men stir the bubbling cauldron with long poles and in the end they have a thick, steaming rat-stew. After that a cruncher is lowered into the cauldron to crunch the bones and what's left is a pulpy substance called rat-mash'.

'Yes, but how do they turn that into Liquorice Bootlaces, daddy?' young Thwaites had asked and this question, according to Thwaites, had caused his father to pause and think for a few minutes before he answered it. At last he had said, 'The two men who were doing the stirring with long poles now put on their wellington boots and climb into the cauldron and shovel the hot rat-mash out onto a concrete floor. They run a steamroller over it several times to flatten it out. What is left looks rather like a gigantic black pancake, and all they have to do after that is to wait for it to cool and to harden so they can cut it up into strips to make the bootlaces. Don't ever eat them', the father had said. 'If you do, you'll get ratitis'.

'What is ratitis, daddy?' young Thwaites had asked.

'All the rats that the rat-catchers catch are poisoned with rat poison', the father had said. 'It's the rat poison that gives you ratitis'.

'Yes, but what happens to you when you catch it?' young Thwaites had asked.

'Your teeth become very sharp and pointed', the father had answered. 'And a short stumpy tail grows out of your back just above your bottom. There is no cure for ratitis. I ought to know, I am a doctor'.

We all enjoyed Thwaites's story and we made him tell it to us many times on our walks to and from school. But it did not stop any of us, except Thwaites, from buying Liquorice Bootlaces.

There might be myths about the staff. Humphrey Lyttelton records:

> Of course we had legends, which were quickly passed home through the medium of the Sunday letter. One of the masters used to allow himself the mild luxury of a glass of stout every day at lunch in the communal dining room. He was labelled 'The master who was drunk in class'. Then there was 'The oldest master in England', 'The best Latin master in Europe' and, best of all, 'The tallest master in the World'. We also clung to the romantic belief that the head gardener, whose name was Smith, was the same Smith who had been our headmaster's predecessor and we wove elaborate stories about 'The headmaster who became a head gardener'.

On myths about other boys, Alfred Percival Graves writes in his autobiography:

> We noticed that one of the boys, called Ward, a pale wistful faced little fellow, did not prepare his lessons regularly overnight, but was always ready with them in the morning. This struck us as strange and we decided to watch him. Potter and another boy were detailed for the task. They reported next morning that Ward had got up quite quietly in the middle of the night, dressed, lit a candle, gone downstairs to his locker in the school-room below, unlocked it, taken out his book and sat down by the table. There he worked at and finished his sums and prepared his Latin grammar with great rapidity. He then put his books carefully back and returned to our bedroom, where he undressed, put out his candle and went back to bed.
>
> During the whole of this performance, the two witnesses declared, Ward's eyes were staring strangely, he breathed as if in sleep and his movements were unnaturally noiseless. Convinced that this was a case of somnambulism, we reported it to the authorities who put Ward into the doctor's hands. He was never known to sleep walk again and was, therefore, compelled to prepare his lessons in the normal way. Had Potter and the other boy romanced about Ward? I wonder.

Or about other schools. Arthur Marshall says that for some reason the boys at Stowe were considered artistic and unrobust. There was a story current that when Oundle played them at rugger a shrill sound had been heard from the bottom of a loose scrum. It was a scream of agony and a voice was heard to shriek, 'Humphrey, for pity's sake. You're standing on my hair'.

Or they might be about ghosts. Says Lord Berners:

The covered gymnasium adjoining the swimming bath was supposed to be haunted by a whining banshee. One evening Arthur and I plucked up sufficient courage to do a little psychic research. The great empty court looked ghostly enough in the grey twilight and as we stood there, quivering with fear and excitement, we distinctly heard a faint but unmistakable sound of whining. If it had occurred to either of us that the uncanny sounds emanated from a dog kept by one of the assistant masters in an outhouse at the further end of the gymnasium we would have deliberately set aside so obvious an explanation. Having obtained the thrill we were seeking, we were determined to enjoy it whole-heartedly.

But the most prolific source of legends between the two World Wars was, unquestionably, the intriguing possibility of German spies.

Sometimes it was simply a question of a name. Robert Graves mentions the trouble he ran into at all stages in his school career from his unfortunate middle name, von Ranke, and we are told that the boys of St Andrew's, Eastbourne, were convinced that one of the mistresses, who had the unfortunate name of Muller, must be a German spy. Sometimes the evidence was there, though not firm enough, one would have thought, to convince a boy like Denys Buckley who was to attain such a degree of eminence in the law:

One day I and two or three others were hanging over the gate leading to the farm. A monoplane came flying low over the farm buildings. As it did so the farmer came out of the doorway and raised his hands to his eyes as he stood looking up at the plane. We were convinced that we saw him remove a mask from his face so that he could be recognised by a fellow spy in the plane, to whom he was signalling. With patriotic fervour we immediately reported the event to the headmaster. There was no sequel.

Sometimes there really was cause for alarm. H.E. Davis, a boy at Summer Fields, in his contribution to Richard Usborne's anthology on that school, writes:

During World War I we were heavily infected by spy fever. We were always on the lookout for suspicious characters and there was a small coterie of anti-espionage enthusiasts with whom I became associated.

Alongside the railings that separated the playing fields from the farm there used to be a public path. The spy-hunters had noticed that an elderly gentleman with pince-nez glasses took a stroll most afternoons along this path. He would often pause to watch the cricket. The spy-hunters decided that this old man might well have sinister intentions. After all, Port Meadow, with its crazy box-kite aeroplanes, was not far off and a Zeppelin had been reported over Oxford one night. There were rumours that flashed signals had been exchanged from ground to air.

A conference was called and a plan was laid with concealed positions for all participants. At a given signal they would surround the old man and conduct him to Doctor for interrogation. Doctor had not been informed of the plans.

At his accustomed hour the old man approached, peering short-sightedly through his pince-nez. (Who but a German would wear such glasses?) He paused and the boys were on him. His loose raincoat provided a useful hold.

'What's all this?' the victim demanded angrily. It was a shock to his captors to find that he did not have a guttural accent or say 'Donner Wetter!' They told him that he must come and see Doctor. They shouted to the cricketers that they'd caught a spy and the cricketers came to help. A procession formed up, the spy closely guarded by his captors, the cricketers following.

Doctor . . . came briskly out onto the lawn, megaphone in hand. In his clear and precise voice he demanded an explanation. Like a Greek chorus the procession answered, 'Please, sir, we've got a German spy'. They came to the sunken fence. Doctor was there to meet them, a dangerous glint in his eye. Some of the cricketers decided to sneak back to their game.

Doctor was wise in the foolishness of small boys. He handled the affair with tact and firmness. An apology was made to the old man and 'we're very sorry, sir' followed him as he departed, now in good humour. But the spy-hunters were ordered to the study and they waited with apprehensive glances at the corner where the cane was kept. Doctor said it was unpardonable to be rude to a stranger and there was no excuse at all for being rough with an old man. The tension eased. Finally Doctor said he believed the boys had acted with the best of patriotic motives and that their conduct would be overlooked. The case was dismissed, to the disappointment of other boys waiting within earshot of the green baize door, hoping to hear the familiar swish-bang of the cane.

Sometimes the boys were not content simply to report their suspicions to the headmaster. More enterprising, they determined on personal action. Christopher Pirie-Gordon, later to lead an adventurous life in Palestine during the Mandate and to end up as Consul General in Florence, describes such an occasion.

The first, or master spy, was the mathematics master. When one came to think of it, he was an obvious choice. He had smooth black shiny hair, drove a powerful car (it made so much noise that it must have been powerful) and he was an expert in photography; all attributes of the professional spy. He first gave himself away by taking a pair of binoculars on a walk and studying, through them, one of the deserted sentry huts on the cliff top. Clearly an assignation was being arranged at the hut – a natural meeting place for spies, being conspicuous and difficult to get at. But an assignation meant a fellow spy. Vigilance should enable us to discover his identity.

It was my friend Derek who accomplished this. By close observation he had discovered that the assistant matron was really a man. And if a man, clearly a German.

He had actually penetrated to the assistant matron's bedroom and there had found, insolently displayed on the top of a chest of drawers, a pair of dark glasses and a bottle of hair dye. Nor was this all. Confident that he was on the right track, and that the police, if not the school authorities, would back him up, he had opened one of the drawers. And there the full truth had been revealed, for, nestling among the garments of an apparently female nature, was a safety razor.

'And when you look close,' said Christopher, 'you can see that she – he, I mean – wears a wig'.

At bed time that evening we both looked closely. There was no doubt about it. The assistant matron looked closely at us in return and remarked that we looked pale. Was there anything wrong with us?

There seemed to be a sinister undertone to her question, and when she insisted on us having a spoonful of Parrishes Food we managed, by distracting her attention, to tip it into a flower vase. She wasn't going to silence us that easily.

What are today's myths? In thirty or forty years' time we shall find out. Extra-sensory perception? Automation? Character transposition?

# 19

# FIGHTING

The climactic, no punches-barred, schoolboy fight seems to have been the province of the novelist rather than the biographer, and was, in any event, more likely to occur in the public than in the preparatory school. Memorable combats splatter with youthful blood the pages of *Lorna Doone* and *Tom Brown's Schooldays*. Hugh Walpole in *Jeremy at Crale* and P.G. Wodehouse in his early school stories, carried the tradition into this century. But if such serious organized fights do occur in the modern preparatory school, the principals seem reluctant to discuss them.

Possibly they are ashamed of such outdated, ritual blood-letting. Richard Usborne, essayist, editor of *A Century of Summer Fields*, and expert on all matters connected with P.G. Wodehouse, looked back upon this matter with ambivalent feelings.

> 'Tom Brown's Schooldays', read too early, left a nasty and
> unacknowledged residue. It made us think that if we came
> to the end of our prep school years without taking part in a
> fist fight, hitting in the face, we had not proved ourselves men.
> I am thankful to say that I came through a decade of boarding
> schools without being forced to fight anybody. But in my
> last years at prep school I twice picked hit-in-the-face affrays
> with smaller boys (naturally) for no reason that I can
> retrospectively claim other than that *I had to have a fight*. Sorry,
> Stubbs. Sorry, Scott-Ellis. That's all it was and I'm still ashamed
> of myself and still a great hater of 'Tom Brown's Schooldays'.

Some fights were less serious than others. In this one we meet the remarkable Powys boys. Littleton Powys was the second of the eleven children of the Reverend Charles Powys. Three of his brothers, John, Llewellyn and Theodore, became writers and Littleton was a noted athlete. All four went to Sherborne Preparatory School, of which Littleton subsequently became headmaster. He records:

The two bigger boys who shared our dormitory found pleasure
in making the two little Powys boys, John and myself, fight.
They must have known something of the boxing ring and
staged the fight accordingly. At each end of the dormitory
a chair was placed on which we had to sit when the round was
over and by each chair stood one of these boys with sponge and
towel in hand. I remember writing to my mother; 'Johnny
and I had a fight last night. He licked me. I hope I shall
lick him tomorrow'. Imagine what a wound that must have
dealt to her loving heart.

Another fight, involving the Terriss brothers, was, as their biographer Arthur Smythe says, 'quite a family affair'.

From Littlehampton William Terriss [actor and dramatist]
went to Windermere College. His brother, known to his
friends as Bob, and two cousins were among his school fellows
and here it was he engaged in his first regular fight which
might be described as quite a family affair, since the
antagonists were William and one cousin and his brother and
the other cousin were seconds. The scene of the encounter was
a space behind some bushes at the far end of the playground
and the fight was carried out with due formalities. Round
after round was contested and it was only when it became
apparent that neither would gain any material advantage that
the seconds brought the contest to a close; and, as is usually the
case in school fights, the contestants were the best of friends
afterwards.

A boy to whom fighting seemed to be a form of ritual as much part
of the programme as lessons and games, was Frank Benson, knighted
as an actor-manager and founder of the company that bore his name.
He records:

From church, it seemed but a step to the pugilistic encounters
which took place as a sort of introduction to morning
prayers. The formula of the challenge was, 'Will you meet me
before prayers in order that I may punch your head?' I admit
that at that time I saw no incongruity in the arrangement. I
confess that I had a mania for fighting boys bigger than myself

and a cowardly abhorrence of getting licked by a boy of my
own size and weight. The point is stressed because it bears out
my bias in matters theatrical. It was a cause of much trouble
in after years and it was at a somewhat advanced stage in
my manhood that this cowardly characteristic was overcome
and disappeared. I did not much mind hard knocks and
defeat at the hands of those I was not expected to conquer; I
did mind them and shunned getting them from those I
might be expected to excel. I was sufficiently honest with
myself to realise that this was no noble championship of the
weak against the strong, but the vanity of a strong dislike of
being overcome by the weak.

Some fights were more serious. Here is Richard Meinertzhagen, born
in 1878, traveller, soldier, General Allenby's Intelligence Officer, orni-
thologist and writer. His first school, to which he went accompanied by
his brother, Dan, was at Aysgarth, in Wensleydale. The life was spartan,
but he enjoyed it and protested vehemently when he was taken away
and sent to Fonthill, which was supposed, by his parents, to be a more
fashionable establishment. Meanwhile:

I had my first fight at Aysgarth in June 1886. J was nine years
old. There was a boy in the school called Brown. He was
known as 'the cannibal' and would boast that he loved eating
little boys and that he did, in fact, do so at home, a story which
we, of course, believed. He had a nasty habit of biting us in
the leg and one day he bit Dan. I flew at him and a fight
then ensued, but the sergeant separated us before much
damage was done. I had a tooth knocked out and a rib bruised
and Brown was bleeding like a pig from some hits in the face.
I wrote to my mother:
'Brown the cannibal broke one of my teeth and hurt my side.
Sergeant told me to go to Mrs Humphreys [the matron] and I
did and she said I must report the cannibal to Mr Hales which
I did and he sent for Brown and his face was all bleeding
where I hit him. We are both swollen much today. But Brown
is worst.

Giles and Esmond Romilly, the sons of Nellie Hozier (Winston
Churchill's sister-in-law) and Colonel Bertram Romilly, are a prime

source of information about all aspects of preparatory school life in the 1920s. Esmond, the younger of the two, was a left-wing rebel who started his conflict with the right at an early age. By the time he was sixteen he had helped to found an anti-public school magazine entitled *Out of Bounds* and had attracted the further attention of the press by running away from Wellington.

In other places in this book Giles and Esmond Romilly discourse on masters, matrons, dancing and discipline. The current extract is more serious stuff. It is Esmond who is speaking.

I had an open feud with Hoskins which culminated in a bare-fist fight. If I forget everything else about Seacliffe, I am sure I shall remember that fight.

One afternoon, when we were out for one of our many walks over the Downs, Hoskins and I lagged behind the rest of the school until we were alone. Then we took off our coats and began to hit each other hard in the face. It was an extremely painful affair and has made me dislike boxing ever since. Suddenly, after a good many blows had been exchanged, my opponent collapsed on the ground, lay there groaning for a few seconds, then relapsed into complete silence. I was absolutely terrified. In vain I shook him. It was a genuine knockout, but I was by no means proud of my handiwork only terrified of the consequences.

[Hoskins was restored, with the help of the master taking the walk and they returned to school.]

I expected the heaviest punishment. I had provoked the quarrel and Hoskins was still dazed. But I had just been ill with some sort of rash and Mr Lancaster [the headmaster] told me that, to his sorrow, he would be unable to administer corporal punishment for this reason. 'Romilly, you will go up to your room and stay in bed. Your books will be taken away'. Personally I had never felt more in need of a good rest.

My adversary was not so lucky.

'Hoskins, you will go up to my room and wait for me there'.

Mr Lancaster's room was at the bottom of my dormitory. From my bed I could hear poor Hoskins' squeals of pain and, for once, my conscience was troubled.

A fight could, on rare occasions, be a formal and communal affair. Sir George Newnes, who created (*inter alia*) *The Strand Magazine, The Westminster Gazette* and *Titbits*, recalls such an occasion. He was at Silcoates Hall, in Halifax. When the boys marched, in crocodile, to chapel, they were jeered and jostled by the town boys.

After a time these insults became more than Ted, George's older brother, could bear and as he and his schoolmates were going home one Sunday he found an opportunity to enquire of one of the tormentors, 'Will six of you fellows fight six of ours?' The challenge was accepted and there and then it was arranged that six chosen warriors from Silcoates should meet six from Halifax at eleven o'clock next night.

The excitement in the dormitories may be imagined when our six 'men' were selected; and after that tremendous question was settled, ways and means had to be found of getting the army out of the school-house when the great moment came. Ted Newnes was, of course, the leader of the six, but his excitement was as nothing compared to the wild excitement of George, the 'baby' of the school, who promptly invented all manner of means of despatching the warriors to the battlefield down in the town. He, and others of the younger boys, promised to procure ropes and let them down from the upper windows and haul them up again when they came home triumphant.

To the intense annoyance of the conspirators, the moon shone brightly upon Silcoates as the hour for the departure of their army arrived, but ropes supplied by a gardener who had been caught up in the general enthusiasm were ready and ten lads were lowered into the garden, six to fight and four to see fair play. They stole, unseen and unheard, to the appointed place chosen as far away from the beat of the police as possible. The Halifax lads fought pluckily, but those from Silcoates fought better and remained victors. 'You know what we have been fighting for?' said Ted Newnes, as he shook hands with the conquered. 'In future you will have to leave us alone'. And from that day forth no procession of Silcoates boys was molested in the streets of Halifax.

The last word on this matter is from G.K. Chesterton. His opponent in the fight which he describes was Edmund Clerihew Bentley, originator of the verse form which bears his middle name and author of the classic detective story, *Trent's Last Case*.

Boyhood is a most complex and incomprehensible thing. Even
when one has been through it, one does not understand
what it was. When I first met my best friend I fought with
him wildly for three quarters of an hour; not scientifically and
certainly not vindictively. (I had never seen him before and I
have been very fond of him ever since.) But by a sort of
inexhaustible and insatiable impulse, rushing hither and
thither about the field and rolling over and over in the mud.

I believe our minds were entirely mild and reasonable and
when we desisted from sheer exhaustion and he happened to
quote Dickens or 'The Bab Ballads' or something I had read
we plunged into a friendly discussion on literature, which has
gone on intermittently from that day to this.

There is no explaining these things.

# 20

# POLITICS

It would be surprising if political questions greatly exercised the minds of schoolboys; minds crammed to overflowing with more important topics: food, games, lessons and the moods of their headmaster. However, they may be affected by what is going on in the outside world, if it jeopardizes their popularity.

'When I admitted that I was a South African,' says Nicholas Ward-Jackson, who was at Summer Fields between 1953 and 1957, 'they immediately dubbed me "Mau Mau", and called me by that name for years – sublimely unconscious that South Africa is several thousand miles away from Kenya'.

Oliver Messel was even more unfortunate. In his case it was his name.

> To make things even more tense for the fledgling pushed out of the home nest, it was war time [Messel went to school in 1913]. Dachshunds were put down and faithful old German governesses stoned and interned. Plates and other German products were smashed in the hysteria. My name, of course, was German. Fiendish little schoolboys quickly caught on to that and their taunts and torments knew no bounds.

Jack Seeley, Lord Mottistone, was the son of a noted radical and attracted immediate ill treatment, and the name 'Spawn of Satan', by announcing his attachment to the Liberal Party as soon as he arrived at his ultra-conservative school.

It was, however, exceptional for children to arrive with their beliefs established. One of these was Naomi Mitchison who, although only six years old, had perceived that political attachment was a matter of status.

> There would be political pamphlets which I could put into envelopes or deliver to the neighbours. I remember collecting for some earthquake fund – in the West Indies perhaps? – and

saying, 'They are people like us'. That is to say, 'Not mere
natives'. However, this was not entirely a matter of colour.
When the Russo-Japanese War got into the British press, several
of the boys at the Dragon School, including my brother,
drafted a letter to show their sympathy with the brave little
Japs. No doubt this was a matter of unsympathy with our
rivals, or enemies, the Russians, whom we thought of as
bear-like and constantly throwing babies out of sledges to feed
the ravening wolves of the boundless steppes. Now I wanted
to sign the letter too; I must have been six and it was really
a matter of status. So they all questioned me on what I knew
about the war. I had heard so much that my answers were
thought adequate and I was allowed to sign. In due course
a letter came back, I suppose from the Japanese Embassy, and
was taken in triumph to school to be handed round and admired.

It is less clear how Rupert Brooke had attained such fixed feelings,
but he had certainly done so.

There was bloodshed in the Transvaal and a pro-Boer faction
held a public meeting in Rugby. Mrs Brooke, always interested
in what was going on, thought she would look in. Having sat
down, she couldn't believe her eyes. Rupert was sitting aloft
with the platform party. He had followed the same impulse
as his mother and, being conspicuous as the youngest present
by many years, had been called up by the Chairman to
demonstrate to the world that even small children were being
moved to protest against the country's injustice to the Boers.

In politics, as in every other aspect of school life, an important
factor was the opinion of the headmaster. The three boys who follow
all became men of mark and were none of them likely to accept
tamely the view of authority. Sir Patrick Hastings QC, later to become
Attorney General in the Labour Government of 1924, early declared
his adherence to the left.

I was held up to public ridicule by the headmaster before the
whole school for announcing that I was a Liberal. The chief
ground for complaint was that Liberals were people who
wanted to burn down churches. I was quite unable to refute this

somewhat remarkable statement, which I can only attribute
to being in some way associated with the disestablishment
of the Welsh Church, but I continued to adhere to my previous
announcement amidst universal disapproval.

Leonard Woolf, later husband of Virginia, author and founder of
the Hogarth Press, was overwhelmed by the sight of Mr Gladstone
driving along the front at Brighton.

There was not a corner or crevice of the headmaster's mind
that was not obstinately conservative. The only comment
that I remember him to have made on public events was
continual abuse of Mr Gladstone, whom he regarded as the
author of all evil. One day, when the school was walking back
from Brill's Baths along the front, Mr and Mrs Gladstone
drove by in an open victoria. All the way people recognised
him and waved, or took their hats off to them. He did not
look at all the kind of criminal anarchist and traitor whose
portrait Mr Burman had drawn for us.

My instinct has been, from a very early age, to disbelieve
anything I was told 'on authority'. At the age of thirteen I
think I had already seen far enough through him to accept
anything he said, (except about Latin verbs) with some
reserve, and the sight of Mr Gladstone's eagle-like eminence
sunning itself in the victoria confirmed my silent determination.
If Mr Burman was a Conservative, I would be a Liberal.

And finally Maurice Baring, though unfairly treated, keeps his cool.

The headmaster was a virulent politician and a fanatical Tory.
On the 5th November an effigy of Mr Gladstone used to be
burnt in the grounds, and there was a little note in the School
Gazette to say that there were only seven Liberals in the
school, the least of whom was myself. The Gazette went on
to add that 'needless to say, the school were supporters of
the Church and the State'.

One day someone rashly sent the Head a Liberal circular.
He sent it back, weighed down with some coppers inside,
so that the recipient would have to pay 18 pence on receipt
of it.

One day there was a by-election going on hard by. All the school were taken, with blue ribbons in their jackets, except the seven Liberals who were told to stay at school and work. One of the renegades was Basil Blackwood. He took the matter very calmly and drew offensive caricatures of the Conservative politicians.

# 21

# DISCIPLINE

Until quite recently, in most preparatory schools a serious breach of the rules was punished by a beating from the headmaster. In bad schools beatings were frequent; in good schools they were rare. That being so, it might be questioned why the few schools that had abandoned corporal punishment altogether did not advertise the fact and gain an influx of pupils. There is no certainty, however, that this course would have been effective.

Contemporary feeling on this topic can be judged from a notice in the agony column of *The Times* of 3 February 1911 which said:

> 'Uncle, afflicted with sole guardianship of healthy nephew
> aged twelve, would be glad to receive information of a school
> conducted on good old-fashioned lines, free from all maudlin
> modern ideas, where the sound rule, 'Spare the rod and spoil
> the child' is strictly observed.'

And on 6 February 1911:

> 'Uncle presents his compliments and thanks to correspondents
> for their assistance to him in his search for a boys' school of
> the sound old type. To the senders of many pamphlets dealing
> with the alleged evils of physical punishment for the young he
> can only say that these pamphlets form the strongest possible
> argument for regret that their writers were not thrashed
> daily in their youth.

In his autobiography, *The Early Years*, Alec Waugh says that prep school boys, being at their age more turned on by sadism than by sex (and unaware of any connection between the two) found detailed accounts of beatings gripping, while public school boys were uninterested in them. There is a reasoned judgement on this subject in the *Life of George Orwell* by Christopher Hollis.

There was a trait in Orwell's character which drove him on to accept unpleasant experiences in order to prove to himself that 'he could take it'. He did not deny that corporal punishment was, within its limits, effective for its purpose – that his work improved after a beating. He objected to corporal punishment because it was, he said, 'obscene'. Like Macaulay's Puritan with bear-baiting, he objected to it not because it gave pain to the boy, but because it gave pleasure to the master – a very reasonable objection, but not at all the point that troubled Cyril Connolly's more fragile bottom.

Before he went to The Old Ride, at Branksome near Bournemouth, Francis Chichester, yachtsman and aviator extraordinary, had been to a school, which he does not name, at Ellerslie, about seven miles from Barnstaple.

My first term I was up for a beating seven times. The headmaster, who was a big, powerful man, sent one up to one's dormitory at a fixed time. Here one waited beside one's bed. Being kept waiting was the worst part and I couldn't stop myself from trembling. He made us strip off our trousers and beat us on the bare bottom. But not always. Sometimes he made us strip off and bend over and then didn't beat us. Outside the windows of that dormitory there were creeping plants like Cape gooseberries with bobble-shaped fruit dangling in the wind. Waiting there I used to see the sparrows flitting among this creeper and this stayed in my memory as a picture of misery. After a year or so my parents took me away from this school; but not because of the tough conditions, only because I was always ill there, which was a nuisance.

There were alternatives, none of them noticeably more pleasant. Lord Berners remembers Elmley.

Mr Gambril [the headmaster] had a stock of tortures. He would pull one up by the hair near one's ears. He would hit boys on the shins with a cricket stump. He had a way of pinching his victims that was positively excruciating. Whenever I tried to do the same thing to a boy smaller than myself it never seemed to be quite so effective.

He excelled also in the administration of mental tortures. The mark books were always examined at meal-times. He would examine them in a leisurely way and call up any boys who had been given bad marks. It would be difficult to describe adequately all the horror and agony that being 'called up' entailed. It nearly always involved the pinching and hair pulling, but more often than not you were sent back to your place with instructions to come to the Headmaster's study as soon as the meal was over. This meant further tortures, culminating in a caning. The actual punishment, however, was less agonising than the suspense of waiting to be called. If one received a bad mark during the morning, the luncheon hour would be spent in an agony of fear. Mr Gambril looked through the books at random, so that it was a matter of chance whether one would be called up at luncheon or supper.

I can still remember that terrible, devastating panic that seemed to paralyse the digestive organs and deprive one of appetite and if, as often happened, the fatal summons was delayed till supper-time, it was impossible to eat anything during either meal. I find it hard to believe that this particular form of terrorisation can really have been good for growing boys.

Mr Gambril occasionally gave vent to a sort of grim humour and invented punishments that were highly capricious and fanciful. I remember once, in a blithe gather-ye-microbes-while-ye-may spirit he made one of his victims go down on his hands and knees and lick a straight line on the floor in front of the assembled school.

When the punishment did not fall on the author himself he was able to take a more dispassionate view of it. Major-General Sir Archibald Anson was at Temple Grove School, East Sheen, at that time the great preparatory school for Eton. Dr Pinckney was the headmaster.

Dr Pinckney was a very skilful administrator of the cane and birch. From the 'little school' we used to be sent down to his table, where he held his class in the middle window of the 'big school' to hold out a hand which received one or more cuts with the cane. One punishment for a greater offence was named a 'tight breech'; to administer this, the culprit was laid in a position bending over the Doctor's leg, while he pulled his trousers tight with one hand and applied the cane with the other. For a still greater offence the boy was laid face downwards across the Doctor's table, when two of the class held each a leg and two others held each an arm and the head boy of the class placed a Latin Grammar in his mouth to bite to relieve his feelings during the operations. On more than one occasion I assisted at this function. It was no easy matter to hold on to the arm or leg of a wriggling boy undergoing this description of torture.

Not all headmasters were sadists. And occasionally ill-health saved the boy from punishment. It will be remembered that Esmond Romilly had a bit of luck here, as also did Guy Boas, as he recounts in his book *A Teacher's Story*.

Discipline [at the St Leonard's branch of Summer Fields] was certainly milder than under Dr Williams. I only once remember getting into serious trouble, which was for organising the tossing of a fellow pupil – now a distinguished publisher – on a blanket in the dormitory because he refused to sing 'Onward, Christian Soldiers' before going to sleep. When the penalty, and the future publisher, were at their height Mr Compton made a sudden and massive appearance and I was led off for retribution.

Remembering that I had been confided to him on account of a breakdown in health, instead of leading me, clad only in pyjamas, to his study for the cane, Mr Compton considerately chose his dressing-room, where he administered four resounding strokes with his razor-strop, which sounded like pistol shots to my friends who were listening awe-struck at the door. The strokes, in fact, caused me no sensation whatever. When, accordingly, I emerged from the ordeal smiling I was regarded by my companions, including the publisher-to-be, with no little respect and admiration.

Most schools used some form of good mark–bad mark system. If backed up by more stringent sanctions it could work well enough, as Christopher Pirie-Gordon wrote in his privately printed memoir of St Peter's, Seaford:

The school was divided into three sets, Reds, Whites and Blues, symbolised by the three shell cases and the three little wooden men on their ladder. 'Blacks' and 'golds' were the currency in which the little men dealt.

Two blacks could be cancelled out by one gold. After lunch each day the Captain of the School, standing on the Headmaster's left, would record the day's bag. Four blacks in one week, if unredeemed by a gold, could result in painful consequences. A double-black, almost always fatal, would be awarded for some grave crime such as 'Impertinence' or 'Cheating'. Its announcement would be followed by the Headmaster's prominent blue eyes assuming a fish-like expression and the dread words, 'Come and Explain'. I heard of, but never met, a double gold. At the end of the week the score would be added up and the little men moved up, or down, the ladder accordingly.

As Esmond Romilly points out, the system could degenerate into farce.

The 'Plus' and 'Minus' system was about the stupidest that could ever have been evolved. Each boy was given each week a small green card, like a golf-scorer, on one side of which he marked plusses and on the other side minuses. The minuses were given for misbehaviour of any kind, from spilling a glass of water to walking about naked in the passages. A plus was awarded for a variety of actions from reading a 'good' book to opening a door for a master. At one time the situation became perfectly ludicrous, for wherever a master went, he would be followed by a swarm of boys all intent on opening some door for him. If a boy made a sufficient nuisance of himself, the master would award him a plus to get rid of him. If he continued to make a nuisance of himself, then the probability was that he would be given a minus for performing the same action.

There were headmasters with original ideas. Peter Howard was the author of a number of books and plays, also an accomplished athlete, an international rugby football player and a member of the bobsleigh team that broke the world record at Cortina D'Ampozzo. He was at

Crescent House Preparatory School. His biographer, Anne Wolrige-
Gordon writes:

> Among Peter's enjoyments at Crescent House was collecting
> birds' eggs. Many of the boys did this and one of them possessed
> a small egg with spots on it which Peter much coveted. He
> stole it and put it in his desk.
>
> The owner reported the loss to the headmaster who ordered
> that all desks be searched. The egg was found in Peter's desk.
> He was ordered to return the egg in front of the class. But
> that was not all.
>
> Peter owned a pen-knife. It was his most treasured
> possession. It had a thing for taking out corks, a thing for
> taking stones out of horses' hooves and three different blades
> for cutting. 'You stole that egg,' said the headmaster. 'You give
> him that knife.'
>
> 'To give the boy my knife,' said Peter, 'it was as if
> something had been ripped out of my guts.' But he handed it
> over.
>
> He had learned the penalty of theft.

Other headmasters had even more original ideas. Sir Cedric Hardwicke, the famous actor, was sent, in 1903, at the age of ten, to a
day preparatory school at Stourbridge.

> Mr Rupert Deakin, the Headmaster, was a tyrant, but an
> extraordinary one. He had a flaming red beard and a voice
> like a bull. One of his self-imposed penances was to conduct
> our weekly singing lessons. I recall this pillar of a man, with
> head flung back and mouth gaping in a circle of red whiskers,
> roaring out the incongruously gentle ditty; 'Run, little rivulet,
> run. Run in the beams of the sun.'
>
> One of his fancies was inventing original punishments for
> familiar schoolboy crimes. He favoured an old-fashioned caning
> for major offences, but for minor ones he sentenced the boy
> to eat dog biscuits at tea-time, in place of the customary
> bread and jam.
>
> I was served more than my share of Spratt's Ovals, allegedly
> the delight of every dog, to the indignation of my mother,
> who attributed every illness I had to this enforced champing

of inhuman fare. Each time I reported that I had been given another serving she sped off to school to have it out with Mr Deakin.

I enjoyed having a champion and started telling her about punishments I had not actually suffered, simply to get her to hurry to school and tell them off. Needless to say these imaginary woes were followed by real ones as soon as Mr Deakin caught me out in my lies.

But pride of place must go to Thomas Pellatt, head of Durnford House, Langton Matravers ('T.P.' to boys and masters alike). It was he who first kindled Laurence Irving's interest in matters theatrical, with a performance of *The Babes in the Wood*. Laurence was one babe, T.P.'s daughter, Hester, was the other, while the moon was an acetylene bicycle lamp manipulated by the science master. It was in connection with this performance that the incident now related occurred.

For T.P. the play was the thing, and nerves or no nerves, with the performance only a fortnight hence I should have to be rushed. And, after a particularly halting rehearsal, rushed I was, up to the empty sickroom, and told not to come down until I had learned my part. I tried to concentrate, but my attention wandered to sheets of foolscap strewn upon the table – T.P. working on another play I supposed. These were a welcome distraction, but on closer inspection the sheets appeared to be covered with verses written in a boyish hand. The first I read began; 'I love to see Minnie make water . . .' With growing alarm I discovered that sheet after sheet was covered with rhymes, puerile but uniformly prurient; the shock of reading them all the more startling, because, unlikely though it sounds, smutty anecdotes and conjectures on the mysteries of sex were ignored by the boys of my time (with this evident exception) as subjects of conversation.

I scented a trap. For some reason or other this ignoble exercise was to be planted on me. In a few minutes I was word perfect in my part and fled the room to report this to T.P. I waited anxiously for the row I thought those damning sheets must presage. No mention of them was made and the identity of the poetaster was never disclosed.

Years afterwards I told T.P. of the incident and asked if he remembered why he had shut me up with such incriminating evidence. He chuckled; yes, of course he remembered it, but had forgotten that I had been a party to it. Having heard a boy reciting to a friend a piece from his repertoire he rushed him, as he had rushed me, up to the sickroom and told him to write out all the dirty poems he knew. Typically T.P. had devised the perfect punishment for the offence. By the time the wretched and ashamed boy had finished his anthology I imagine that he and the man he became, was forever sickened of such stuff.

# 22

# REBELS AND NON-CONFORMERS

There were boys who refused to conform to the system and held out against it; some passively, by their attitude and comments, others actively.

A very early example was Arthur Schopenhauer, who was born in Danzig in 1788. His father was fanatically Anglophile and determined that Arthur should receive the benefits of an English education. He therefore packed him off to a school at Wimbledon, kept by a Mr Lancaster ('a man much esteemed by others and by himself').

Patrick Bridgewater, in his recent study of Schopenhauer's early years, writes:

> That Arthur Schopenhauer reacted strongly against English bigotry and the type of education of which this is the product, is hardly surprising. These are matters which call for discussion, but first we need to consider the personal antipathy between Arthur and his English headmaster, for young Schopenhauer was, of course, the sort of pupil that headmasters have nightmares about. He not only walked with a slouch, was untidy and given to fighting, but he was sarcastic and outspoken to the point of being loud-mouthed. To make matters worse, he was highly intelligent and highly articulate. He was not only the proverbial 'little horror', but was more intelligent, better educated and more sophisticated than his English headmaster.

James Strachey Barnes also proved a difficult pupil. He was at St Aubyn's, Rottingdean, between 1898 and 1902 and his opinion of the headmaster, Mr Stanford, has already been recorded. It will be remembered that in that passage he says, 'I was not an easy person to put under', a point borne out by this extract from his autobiography, *Half a Life*.

First there was the Boer War; and a wave of astonishing flag-waving, patriotic jingoism came with it, like a mad hurricane, to sweep the country. Schoolboys were second to none in catching the infection. So here was a grand opportunity for me as a professed atheist.

'Suppose you had to choose between your country and your God. Which would you choose?'

This was the cunningly contrived dilemma wherewith I impaled the consciences of my poor little comrades, their cheeks aglow with patriotic fervour on the day Mafeking was relieved. How could they answer anything but 'My country'.

'In that case,' I said, with ruthless logic, 'your country *is* your God. Why haven't you the courage to confess your true faith and declare yourself an atheist as I do?'

One little boy, not knowing what to do, confided his difficulties to the headmaster, Mr Stanford.

[This earned Barnes a *mauvais quart d'heure*, but he was not deterred from his self-imposed duty to upset his school fellows.]

About a year later I approached an older boy with a new dilemma. 'Do you believe in ghosts?' I knew he did not and he duly confirmed my assumption.

'Then what about this blooming Holy Ghost you profess to believe in every Sunday? Sucks!' I had him there; and he saw the fun of it. He thought it awfully good. He began trying it on others. Very soon it was running round the whole school. Then it came to the ears of Mr Stanford. 'Who had started this horrible blasphemy? The culprit must come forward and confess.'

Nobody did, but he knew full well it was I.

Sir Mortimer Wheeler was a remarkably gifted man. Archaeologist, writer and artist, he was president, member, or corresponding member of nearly every archaeological society of importance in the world. He saw very active service in both World Wars, winning an MC in France in the First and raising and commanding an artillery regiment which took part in the Battle of El Alamein in the Second. His trouble at school was simple. He disliked organized games.

173

By and large my school was of no great moment to me save that it confirmed in me certain prejudices which I had developed in contact with my father. The prejudice he had most in mind was against organised ball games of every kind for which he maintained 'a deep-seated and barely tolerant contempt'.

However, says his biographer, Jacquetta Hawkes, this total avoidance of the playing fields was achieved without any loss of standing among the other boys. Indeed, when he was thirteen and in the classical fifth, one of the football teams made him an honorary member, appointing him to draw their posters and programmes for them and nominating him as 'their R.A.'

This assignment he may be said to have combined with his classical studies, for the first poster he devised for them showed 'a full Bacchus trying to kick a goal'.

George Gordon Coulton, historian, fellow of St John's College, Cambridge, was the author of the magisterial four-volume *Life in the Middle Ages*. He started his education at Thursby School, Lynn, in which, he warns us, 'there was little discipline'.

Alan Hardwick, one of the oldest boarders, was a favourite of Mrs White [wife of the headmaster, the Reverend Thomas White] and was in many ways privileged. He was good looking, high spirited and as mischievous as a monkey. Alan, as we all knew, had sworn by the nine Gods that he would never take the cane. But at last there came some obviously 'canable' transaction and we were all agog to see what would happen after prayers next morning. He appeared with a heavily bandaged hand; he had cut it that morning, he said, in breaking an indispensable bedroom utensil. White would take no such excuse. Hardwick must hold out his left hand. He held it out for a moment; then started aside, like an unbroken colt and ran out of the schoolroom. In the face of a threat of expulsion he at length submitted and accepted a few formal cuts.

Another time, however, it was the culprit who won.

Charlie was the youngest child of a worthy citizen of conspicuous musical talents, whose yard lay back to back with our playground. Charlie was a pampered little urchin, dressed with artistic taste and my only surviving memory shows him in the middle of the schoolroom, whimpering, while the headmaster bent over him, cane in hand.

'What are you saying?' thundered White. 'What? If I cane you your father will take you away from the school. We shall see, we shall see.'

But, in fact, Charlie was sent back to his place and there was much envious murmuring among us who knew that our homes would be only too ready to endorse the sentence of the headmaster.

David Garnett, the novelist, who made his name with his novel *Lady into Fox*, went first as a day boy, later as a boarder, to a school which he describes, in his autobiography *The Golden Echo*, as being five miles from Cearne on Westerham Hill.

One morning, after prayers, the headmaster told us that his son (aged twelve) had been discovered committing the most filthy and unmentionable wickedness by getting into another boy's bed. There followed a public thrashing in which two canes were broken and the boy bit his father in the leg. I had not the remotest idea what it was all about, but this scene made me decide that I would kill any master who beat me.

It was not long before I had an opportunity to test my determination.

In the absence of the headmaster in London his partner, Mr H, lost his temper with me during a lesson and told me to see him after school. I went to his room and, to my surprise, he made me bend over and caned me. It did not hurt much, but I was furious at what I felt was an outrage and an insult.

As I was leaving the school buildings I noticed a crow sitting on a fence about a hundred yards away. Mr H had a .22 rifle and was in the habit of shooting at crows. I went back to his study, much to his surprise and told him about the crow. He came out with his little rifle and looked, but said the crow was too far off.

He often let favoured boys carry his rifle and sometimes allowed them to have a shot. If I could have got the rifle into my hands I would have shot him. Disappointed at not being able to commit a murder to vindicate my honour, I got onto my bicycle and rode home. Was I abnormal, or was there something wrong with my bringing up?

Richard Meinertzhagen, whose first fight, at Aysgarth, has been described, moved, unwillingly, to more fashionable Fonthill. This was presided over by Walter and Ashton Radcliffe, both over-indulgent in the use of the cane. Meinertzhagen recalls that he returned home after the first term 'my back and legs wealed with green and purple stripes'. However, it was not to be a one-sided encounter.

When I returned to Fonthill in September 1889, my moral temperature had sunk to zero. I had murder in my heart and was determined to fight my own battles in my own way and with the best weapons I could muster . . . For the first week or so I was left in peace, but I knew it could not last. On October 10th the usual technique was followed in the classroom; an impossible question asked, no effort made to reply and then the stick was sent for. A boy called Fraser was the one always sent to fetch it and the beatings invariably took place in front of the whole class.

I was beyond myself with passion and recognised murder in my heart. I wanted to kill. I seized the stick before anyone could stop me and struck Walter [the joint headmaster] on the head as hard as I could; he put up his hand to ward off the stroke, but it was too late. I saw the gash and the blood beginning to spurt from the wound on his forehead; then I upset his high desk, throwing his inks and papers all over the room and hurled the stick, a heavy holly one, through the large plate glass window with a crash. Everyone in the room was completely taken by surprise and I fled up to my bedroom, terrified and half mad and at once gave way to tears and prayer. Walter soon followed, but left the room without saying a word. I knew I had won, but expected instant expulsion.

Sir Edward Blount, of Imberborne Manor, quite close to Fonthill, was a business friend of my father and had asked me to his house several times during my first term − in fact I had permission to go to his house whenever I wished. He was a dear, kind old gentleman and gave me much wise advice.

That evening I broke out of my room and ran to Imberborne. I was in the depth of despair, bruised and

bleeding from a beating Walter had given me just before
going to bed for losing my temper. I arrived breathless and
in tears. I told him I had run away from school because I had
been beaten and would be expelled for striking Walter. He
made me show him my back, which was green and blue with
bruises and some nasty weals down my legs. My vest was
discoloured with blood and sticking to me. I shall never forget
his 'Good God Almighty, this is most shocking. Now, you
stay here till I return.' He gave me a bedroom and I went to
bed feeling safe at last.

What happened I never knew, but after breakfast the
following morning Blount walked me back to school and I went
in as though nothing had happened. Neither Walter nor
Ashton ever referred to my absence and I begged old Blount
not to tell my parents. All I know is that there was no more
systematic beating or cruelty.

# 23

# Running Away

The ultimate gesture of the oppressed or the non-conformist was to remove himself; usually making for home or for friends in the neighbourhood, but sometimes simply running.

It was an action not universally approved even by the other boys. Walter Farquhar Hook is writing from his preparatory school at Tiverton.

> My dear Mama,
>     You will, with me, pity that wicked boy Henry George Salter, who is now publicly expelled from this school; and his master, Mr Richards, blotted his name from the register, Oct. 30 1811 that it may be handed down to generations.'

There follows an account of how this 'wicked boy' enticed another to run away with him, having borrowed a watch, which he afterwards sold, saying they would go to London, where he would persuade his grandmother to leave him her immense fortune, which he would divide with his companion.

The runaways were captured and Salter wrote a contrite letter, upon which young Walter observes, 'Well, so far one would think him to be Salter the penitent, but I say Salter the hypocrite;' and he goes on to relate how this naughty boy repeated his escapade, borrowing and selling another watch; after which he was expelled in the awful manner described at the beginning of the letter.

The volume of Hook's *Life and Letters* contains, unfortunately, no further reference to Salter. A boy of such ingenuity and persistence must have gone far. Further than Thackeray.

> On one occasion [records his biographer Gordon Ray], Thackeray was driven to run away. He was still small for his age and the older boys made a pet of him and encouraged him to develop his budding powers of caricature. An unflattering sketch that he had made of an usher was discovered

by Dr Turner and to escape punishment he took to his heels. But coming to the end of the lane that led to the school he 'was so frightened by the sight of Hammersmith High Road that he ran back again, and no one was wiser'.

Alfred Gatty and his small friend did at least reach London, although it seems they were bundled back to school as soon as they got there. Gatty subsequently became a distinguished clergyman (there is a hint of this in the choice of provisions he took with him); and wrote a number of books, including *A History of Sundials*.

Alfred Gatty who, at the age of seven, was taken in a post-chaise to Temple Grove, a distinguished school, 'numbering among its pupils sons of the nobility and rich parents', hated it so much that he and a friend saved some crusts of bread from breakfast and with these packed in a small box, together with a prayer book, ran through the private grounds and, dropping from a wall six feet high into the road, set forth for London, a distance of eight miles. The old wooden toll bridge at Putney was their first obstacle; so Alfred offered to pawn his small black silk handkerchief; which offer the good natured man allowed without security.

Unquestionably the most resolute runner-away was Lionel Dunsterville, who was the original 'Stalky' of *Stalky & Co*. He gives a number of reasons for taking this step. Judging from Kipling's account of the school in his autobiography, the third reason ('the tyranny of masters and boys') may have been the compelling one.

About my second or third year at school I ran away to sea, during the summer term. In taking this action I was impelled by many considerations. I had a great love for the sea which has never left me. I wanted freedom and adventure – something on the lines of being wrecked on a desert island where one found, conveniently to hand, all the things one needed, not forgetting a parrot and a Man Friday.

I wanted to get away from the tyranny of masters and boys, to get out into the wide world, to make my own way in life, to find a gold mine and return in a few years and say, Ha ha!

My effort ended in complete failure. I sought employment
with the small coasting brigs and schooners, but they
laughed at me and told me to go back to school. It worried
me that they should spot so easily that I was a schoolboy when
I had taken, as I thought, great pains to disguise myself.

I must have been away about three days and two nights,
getting a crust of bread here and there at farms, a turnip or
two from the fields and sleeping in the thick Devon hedges at
night. At last hunger compelled me to surrender and I made
my way back to the school to give myself up. As I crossed the
football field I was spotted by various people who 'captured'
me and rather boasted of their capture. This annoyed me more
than anything. To be regarded as a 'capture' when one was really
a 'surrender'. Quite a different thing.

I was taken before the Head, who showed considerable tact
in his treatment of me.

Although I had failed to get to sea, I had had an interesting
time and the excitement caused by my recapture helped me to
feel somewhat of a hero. The fact that I should have to undergo
a severe licking and perhaps be expelled, did not worry me
in the least. I was very, very hungry. And the thought
uppermost in my mind was that they would have to give me
some food.

So I was full of assurance as I was marched by the Sergeant
into the awful presence of the Head. I expected him to leap from
his desk and do or say something dramatic, but to my pained
surprise he continued writing and seemed barely aware of
my presence. The silence was unnerving. Nothing beyond the
sound of my own breathing and the ticking of the clock.

At last the Sergeant ventured to attract attention by clearing
his throat, on which the Head asked him what he wanted,
without even turning round.

My assurance was trickling out of me fast. It trickled to the
last drop when I heard the Head say, 'Dunsterville? Dunsterville?
Oh yes, now I remember. The boy who ran away.' Then,
turning on me he asked, 'And what do you want?'

What did I want? This was quite a new proposition. I had
thought it was they who wanted me, but the Head assured
me that that was not so at all. Having run away my name had

been erased from the rolls and that settled it. I no longer
belonged to the college, and so, 'What did I want?'

Visions of cups of hot tea and plates of nice meat and bread
faded from my mind and I burst into tears. No amount of
beating or reproaches could have made me weep like that, or
feel such a worm.

To cut a long story short, the Head saw that, like a
condemned criminal, I was given plenty of good things to
eat. Then there was a public licking before the whole school
in solemn assembly, which somewhat restored my assurance.
And there the matter ended.

Coming to more modern times there is one curious example from
Summer Fields – curious in that Philip Slessor, who was there just
after the First World War, gives no reason for his action. 'Bear' is the
formidable headmaster. Miss Peirce (who really did spell her name
that way) was the matron.

Early in my first summer term the shocked whisper ran from
the Vinery to Chapel. 'Slessor's done a bunk.' Bunk, indeed,
I did, trotting wretchedly down the Banbury Road into
Oxford on a sticky hot day. I must have made a woefully
appealing picture, for a tender-hearted girl in the post office
– blessings on her growing grandchildren – actually bought back
from me a 3/6d book of stamps, my entire capital and not
officially negotiable at that.

I set up temporary headquarters in a sleazy baker's-shop cafe
near the station, where, again, the appearance of a dusty,
lachrymose little boy must have touched some female heart,
for they let me telephone an aunt in London. Some hours later
my distracted and travel-stained mother collected me from the
kindly custody of the Oxford police – tocsins having been
sounded – and we were driven back to Summer Fields, in the
small beetle-shaped 'baby car' of the period, by a gentle
tow-headed young master called Barber. Miss Peirce must
have taken over guard from there; meanwhile my poor parent
was eventually convinced that the condign punishment, which
I must inevitably receive next morning for the trouble I had
caused, would not be administered with the knout or the cat.
Indeed, though the 'Bear' dealt with me faithfully, the

punishment made its impression more by precept than by pain.

One boy, by rare determination, achieved all his objectives. Sir Peregrine Worsthorne attended two preparatory schools. The first, for a few terms only, was Ladycross, at Seaford. The second was Abinger Hill.

There was an eccentric at Abinger Hill. He was extremely precocious sexually and took an excessive liking to me. But the liking took the form of threatening to strangle me.

To begin with I was rather fascinated. He was older and bigger than me and full of worldly knowledge. Detachable shirt collars were his hobby and he collected them as other boys collected butterflies or stamps. His favourite was an outsize Van Heusen white evening collar and it was with this, he confided, that I was to be privileged to have my neck wrung. I was terrified. But I had been sworn to secrecy. The torment went on for quite some weeks, until one day the date was fixed. I was to meet him in the woods at such and such a time.

It never occurred to me to go to the headmaster. The idea of seeking protection seemed out of the question. I was entirely under the boy's spell. So far as the school went, he was, in my mind, the dominant force from which there was no conceivable escape. So there was only one thing to do; run away. Nobody who has not been at boarding school can have much idea how radical such a solution would appear to a nine-year-old boy. My decision to run away was certainly the most courageous I have ever taken in my life. At my time of life, I had never been on a train unaccompanied; had no idea, in any case, of how to get to the railway station some fifteen miles away. To this day I have no recollection of how I did overcome the difficulties. I must have walked to the station and borrowed money there for a ticket to Waterloo. I do remember, very clearly, arriving at Waterloo, because at that point I made a decision which was later to cause me trouble. I went to the cinema there which used, in those days, to show continuous newsreels, not because I wanted to, but because

I dreaded going home. How could I possibly explain to my parents why I had 'run away'? Anything to put off that fateful confrontation.

Eventually, of course, I could delay no longer. To my infinite relief my parents were out to dinner and the servants put me to bed. My mother, however, was summoned home soon enough and through floods of hysterical tears I told my story. The relief of getting it off my chest was indescribable. I was told not to worry, to have a good night's rest and she would see what was to be done in the morning.

Unbeknown to me she then telephoned the headmaster.
*My mother*: Sorry to be ringing you in the middle of the night, Mr So and So, but I am very worried about Peregrine.
*Headmaster*: Worried about Peregrine? Why on earth? The dear boy is doing very well. Of course, he's fast asleep in the dormitory by now. It's long after the boys' bedtime, you know.
*My mother*: Fast asleep he may be, but he's not in the dormitory, headmaster, he's right here at home and I suggest you get up to London right away and explain what's been going on.

This the headmaster did, without a moment's delay and I was woken in the small hours to repeat my story to him. He tried to bluff a bit. Hadn't I been imagining things? In any case, when had I left the school? How had I got to the station? He wanted to know the full details. So I told him. Not forgetting to mention the newsreel film part. That gave him the opportunity. He turned to my mother with a smile. 'I think, Mrs Worsthorne,' he said triumphantly, 'Peregrine may have been feeling in need of a little holiday, weren't you, dear boy?'

That damned newsreel. I could see that even mother felt that it was rather a frivolous thing to do in the circumstances, casting doubts on the genuineness of my tribulations. How little grown-ups understand, I thought, not for the first time or the last.

But I refused to go back to school while X, my kinky admirer, remained. A few days later, I was told by my mother that she had heard from the headmaster, who had checked up on X. He *had* been expelled, from several other schools, for strange offences. My fears, in short, had not been made up or exaggerated. So X was duly removed and I was able to return to school.

# 24

# GREAT MEN IN SHORT TROUSERS

Many notable men have appeared in other chapters. Lord Home and Lord Dunsany, the imperturbable Edward Boyle and the unhappy Oliver Messel; Graham Greene, C. Day Lewis and George Orwell, 'Tall, pale with flaccid cheeks. Large spatulate fingers and supercilious voice,' says Cyril Connolly. 'He seems to have been born old. "You know, Connolly," he once said to me, "There's only one remedy for all diseases." I felt the usual guilty tremor when sex was mentioned, and hazarded, "You mean, going to the lavatory?" "No, I mean death," Orwell said.'

Here are half a dozen others from different walks of life. First, a further description of one of the remarkable Powys boys, from Malcolm Elwin's *Life of Llewelyn Powys*.

Llewelyn, as his letters show, was an exceptionally backward boy. At eleven he wrote and spelt like a child fresh from the nursery; even at nineteen the future master of prose wrote 'recieved' and 'innocense' and missed an 'm' from 'com(m)union'. He drew better than he wrote; the sketches monopolising most of the space in letters to his mother suggested a natural talent for drawing. Many of his boyish letters had a telegraphic terseness, like one in the autumn of 1896.

Dear Mother, Highest I have ever been was third last week. Can't write long. Went along the river with another boy. Boy fell in. Sketch.

Louis MacNeice, the poet, was sent at ten, to Sherborne Preparatory School, 'at that time a happy place' says the *Dictionary of National Biography* under its headmaster, Littleton Powys — an expression which suggests that it was less happy later. Louis was a boy who suffered from 'a poignant sense of the impermanence of things'. Here he shows another side to his character.

Once we had a fancy dress dance and while most of us got ourselves up in conventional guises, such as clowns or pierrots or Red Indians, one odd and original boy naturally thought of something odd and original to go as; An Ancient Briton. For this he made himself a loin cloth of a piece of old sacking and a necklace, coronet and bracelets of fossils shells and pieces of wood. Shortly before the dance was due to begin he ran out into the yard and rolled in the mud − to add, as he put it, verisimilitude to his get-up; and throughout the dance, in which he steadfastly refused to take any part, he sat glowering in a corner and growled when approached. The boy afterwards gained well deserved fame as the poet Louis MacNeice.

There are two accounts of Alfred Harmsworth. From H.G. Wells:

Alfred Harmsworth was born in 1865, a little more than a year before me and he seems to have entered Henley House School when he was nine or ten years old. He made a very poor impression on his teachers and became one of those unsatisfactory, rather heavy, good-tempered boys who in the usual course of things drift ineffectively through school to some second rate employment. It was J.V. Milne's ability that saved him from that. Somewhere about the age of twelve master Harmsworth became possessed of a Jelly-graph for the reproduction of MS in violet ink and with this he set himself to produce a mock newspaper. J.V., with the soundest pedagogic instinct, seized upon the educational possibilities of this display of interest and encouraged young Harmsworth, violet with copying ink and not quite sure whether he had done well or ill, to persist with the *Henley House Magazine* even at the cost of his school work. The first number appeared in 1878; the first printed number in 1881 'edited by Alfred C. Harmsworth' and I possess all the subsequent issues up to the end of 1893 when Milne transferred his school to Streete Court. During my stay at Henley House I contributed largely and amongst others who had a hand in the magazine was A.J. Montefiore, who was later to edit *The Educational Review* and A.A. Milne (aged six, at his first appearance in print) the novelist, essayist and playwright.

And at a somewhat later date from A.A. Milne himself:

At Penshurst Place we had arranged to meet an Old Henley
House Boy called Alfred Harmsworth. It was he who had started
the Henley House School Magazine in 1881 and he was now
starting 'Answers' . . . My one vivid memory of him on this
occasion was, naturally, concerned with food. We had been over
Penshurst Place, we had lunched and, for whatever reason, the
grown-ups wanted to be rid of the children. So we were sent into
the village to buy ourselves sweets. And Harmsworth pulled out
a great handful of pennies, just as if he had been selling
'Answers' personally round the corner, and poured them into our
pockets with an ease of manner which convinced us that he was
already the millionaire which he was afterwards to become.
'Isn't he rich?' we said to each other. 'I *say*'.

Here are two boys, destined to become heads of the armed services;
one in the First World War, the other in the Second.

Lord Trenchard, Father of the Royal Air Force and Godfather, in
the opinion of many, of the modern Metropolitan Police Force, was
at Allen's Preparatory School at Botley. He early displayed mental
independence.

The boy's dislike of being forcibly fed with useless knowledge
betrayed itself. Though mathematics presented few
difficulties, he had no ear for words and his writing was
atrocious. The illogicalities of English spelling endlessly
baffled him. When the correct letter arrangement was set
beside his own he would ask himself with brooding belligerence,
'Why?' Perhaps as an assertion of disbelief he went on spelling
this word 'Yi' for many years.

Admiral of the Fleet Lord Cunningham (A.B.C. to the Navy) was,
with Alanbrooke and Portal, in the small committee which, under
Churchill – and sometimes in spite of him – directed our efforts in
the 1939–45 war. His father was Professor D. J. Cunningham. Before
he joined HMS *Britannia* at fourteen, Andrew was at Stubbington
House School, Fareham.

One supposes that the teaching was really cramming. We were

required to perform prodigious feats of memory, such as
memorising the dates of all important events from the landing
of Julius Caesar to the accession of James I. I can still
remember much of what I learnt there and the older masters
were wizards at driving knowledge into the heads of the
unintelligent. On one occasion the history master 'Vip' Isaacs
– 'Vip', I may add, being short for Viper – said to me in
withering tones, 'What an extraordinary thing that so clever
a father should have such an idiot for a son!'

Occasionally it was the boys who made predictions about them-
selves. In two cases they proved remarkably accurate.
Lord Curzon was at a school called Wixenford, in Hampshire. Says
Lady Carmichael:

Many of the boys who were at Wixenford afterwards entered
politics. One of these was George Curzon, who was there with
his two brothers; and began there a friendship which was kept
up to the end.
    He was a very studious little boy and said to Tom
Carmichael in those early days, 'Tom, we shall be at the head
of this school before long.' And they were. Even in those early
days George Curzon kept a commonplace book and used to speak
of some day being Viceroy of India.

And Oscar Wilde:

Oscar, at eleven, became a boarder at Portora Royal Junior
School, Lough Erne. While his elder brother, Willie,
studied the prescribed text books and excelled at both work
and games, Oscar read what pleased him. Nor did he care
for either cricket or football. 'I never liked to kick or be
kicked.' But he was certainly no milksop, in spite of the fact
that he wore his hair quite long, like a girl's. 'Nearly everyone
went in for athletics – running and jumping and so forth.'
He added, 'No one appeared to care for sex. We were healthy
young barbarians, that was all.'
    A schoolboy contemporary who remembered Oscar at
Portora has recorded that he was an excellent talker, his
descriptive powers being far above the average. A favourite

place for the boys to sit and gossip in the late afternoons in wintertime was a stove which stood in the Stone Hall. Here Oscar was at his best. His friend, Edward Sullivan, who was a son of the Lord Chancellor of Ireland has recalled that at one of these gatherings a discussion took place about an ecclesiastical prosecution which was making a considerable stir at the time. Oscar seemed to know all about it. Indeed, he made a remark of curious prophetic insight. He told us there was nothing he would like better in after life than to be the hero of a *cause célèbre*.

# 25

# THE DARK GODS

In this chapter it is important to look at dates. Many of the contributors to this collection were born around the turn of the century. Philip Slessor was at his preparatory school just after the First World War. And George Melly, the only one who can rank in any way as a 'modern', was at his during the 1930s. Most of the others are Victorians; an era of such smothering respectability that piano legs were draped in bloomers and a reference by young Chuzzlewit to having seen something 'with the naked eye' was held to be the height of impropriety. Naturally this carried over into the schools, and headmasters who felt it their duty to enlighten their boys about conception wrapped up their meaning as discreetly as the piano legs.

This produced results which were sometimes ludicrous and often amusing, but which, as Harold Anson points out, could also be dangerous. Nowadays, although the topic itself is just as important, it has, mercifully, been stripped of its mystery. Under the cold and unexciting heading of 'Biology' the reproductive function is explained to children at an early age. The only question is whether, perhaps, it is taught too early. Total innocence can be oddly attractive.

The actor Emlyn Williams records:

'Tyd yma' hissed an older boy. Nine he must have been. 'Sit here.' I was an obedient child and it was arithmetic. I settled next to him at the back. Beside him sat two round-faced, fringed, knickerbockered nobodies, but there was adventure in the air. I waited for sweets to be passed. Nothing. They were all looking guilelessly at the teacher. I was puzzling what they – when I saw, with the candid eye of childhood, that behind the long desk they had undone their buttons and were sitting on nonchalant hands with three pink shells impudently on display. A display only to the chill morning air, for nobody could see it but me. Feeling daring I followed suit, sat on my hands, and turned the same look of blank

innocence on to Miss Dawson. The lesson ended and with it
the cherubim show. I never saw it repeated and never heard
it referred to.

It was not always by official explanation that hints of the truth
about their exciting bodies reached boys. Occasionally it was by accident. Ernest Raymond remembers:

One day I was climbing the rope in my school's empty
gymnasium. It was because of my desire to be as muscular
as Percy Wilkinson, whom I then hero-worshipped, that I
would go so often into the gymnasium and exercise alone
on the horizontal bar, parallel bars, bridge ladder and rope.
By now I had developed good arm muscles and sometimes
I would ascend the rope to the very ceiling, using arms alone,
my legs properly extended below, toes together and pointing to
the floor. But more often I raced as quickly as I could up the
long rope with my legs doing their full share around it.
And on this day I was more than half-way up when I halted
and hung there because of an unexpected pleasure between
my loins that stirred breathless delight in throat and heart. I
hung there to let it endure, and it endured . . .
   There was no emission at this age of twelve, only delight.
   Why did I tell no one of this unforeseen experience? What
reason was there for something like shame? Did this reasonless
doubt and shame come from out the long tribal past behind
my birth?
   After this I would sometimes go back to the empty
gymnasium in the hope of knowing again this curious, gasping
ecstasy that was the gift of the rope. More often than not I
failed to find it, but there were times when I succeeded and then
I would hang there for quite a time in the empty gym while
it played its exquisite game upon me.
   Thus did the dark gods within me speak to my innocence.

The actor Roland Culver, who had the same experience, recalls it
more sardonically and concludes:

No doubt this sexual experience when rope climbing might
lead psychiatrists to suppose that it created in me a lifelong

passion for ropes. But it is not so. Through my teens and early manhood I never gaped goggle-eyed at a rope with any unnatural longing. Ropes, after my prep school days, were things to heave on, to trim a sail on or chuck over an anchor.

Alec Waugh was five years older than his more famous brother, Evelyn. Like Ernest Raymond he achieved fame with his first book, *The Loom of Youth*, but never really reached that high pinnacle of popularity again. He summarizes the matter when he says: 'We were not only incurious, but did not know that there was a secret involved'.

One of the features of Fernden in my time, possibly in consequence of our being a small school, with ourselves the first generation of senior boys, was a complete sexual innocence. N.G.B. [the headmaster, Mr Norman Brownrigg] lectured us on the functions of our bodies, but no reference was made to sex. When Mrs Brownrigg, at the end of my second year, had her second baby, we learnt something of the facts of maternity, but nothing about paternity. We were not only incurious, but did not know that there was a secret involved. When N.G.B. shortly before I left gave me a talk about the dangers that awaited me at a public school – 'How can you ask some pure woman to be your wife if you have been a filthy little beast at school?' – I had no idea what he was talking about.

One curious aspect of sexual development did, however, manifest itself, though we did not recognise it as such – how could we, since we did not know that such a thing existed? During my last year we indulged in a form of flagellation, belabouring our bared posteriors on bath nights with knotted bootlaces and hair brushes. This was partly due to a pleasure in inflicting pain, partly due to a desire to show courage under pain – and as such it showed a kinship with the initiation ceremonies of the Red Indian braves – but it had a very definite sexual basis. Once when we were discussing our experiences in the changing room a boy, pointing to a rampant display of masculinity, remarked that it was funny he 'always got like that' when we discussed beatings.

Boys could sometimes be brought face to face with the sordid side of sex. If they were as tough and independent minded as Randolph Churchill it may have surprised them, but done them no great harm. It seems to have upset his father more than it did him.

I suffered one disagreeable experience at Sandroyd when I was about ten years old. There was a young assistant master who made some pretext for me to go and see him in his room. When I got there he made me sit down beside him on the bed. He undid his trousers and caused me to manipulate his organ. I was much surprised, but stood in awe of him and cannot pretend that I found it particularly disgusting, or even that I had any sense of guilt until the housemaid came in without knocking to deliver his laundry. He went scarlet in the face and re-arranged his dress as quickly as he could.

I steered very clear of that young master after this and though the episode had not really left any deep scar on my mind, I was puzzled and worried about it. One day I told my sister, Diana, about this strange experience. The nanny overheard this and reported the matter to my mother, who told my father.

I remember very well how my father sent for me one morning when he was still lying in bed and having his breakfast and asked me about the truth of the matter. I told him the truth as I have always done. I don't think I have ever seen him so angry before or since. He leapt out of bed, ordered his car and drove across country – the round trip must have been well over two hundred miles. He returned late that night. He had seen the headmaster who told him that the young assistant master had already been dismissed on other grounds.

My father said, 'Never let anyone do that to you again'. This was the only homosexual experience I ever had.

It was not only boys. Girls, kept in equal ignorance, sometimes ran across inexplicable parts of the mystery. Dora, Countess Russell, was the second wife of Bertrand Russell, the philosopher, and collaborated with him both in his books and in the formation and running of a 'progressive' school at Beacon Hill.

I was told nothing whatever about sex, not even where babies came from. The books on anatomy and physics which did exist in the school library had certain dangerous pages stuck fast together. I really did not know the full facts about sex and reproduction until I was in my twenties. Four letter words I learnt much later. My cousin Dolly and I did speculate a bit. Once she told me that 'there was something that men had to get rid of from time to time and they gave this to women in Piccadilly'. Needless to say, the image that I formed of this transaction bore no resemblance to the reality.

The notion that children who are told nothing find out about these mysteries from other boys and girls was totally false in my case. For instance, I enjoyed the company of boys and was hardly ever without such companions and even admirers. We flirted, kissed shyly at party games, but we neither explored nor knew about sex.

Once only the physical reality intruded. I was crossing the school playground, deserted in the lunch hour, when a man attracted my attention over the side fence, exposing himself. I was alarmed, because I thought he had some horrible disease. But I decided not to show fear by running away. The incident left no emotional disturbance.

One of the unfortunate results of this reticence was that boys were often accused of crimes which only the blinkered minds of schoolmasters imputed to them. Sir Francis Chichester, speaking of his second school, The Old Ride, Branksome, says:

The headmaster, A.S. Philips, with his stubby round figure, walrus moustache (off which he would suck drops of soup) and big round spectacles which he pushed up his forehead, made his mistakes – but who doesn't? Perhaps one of the worst that I got involved in was when I was caught after Lights Out with everybody visiting some other boy in his bed. There was a most frightful hullabaloo about this and we were brought up for questioning, one at a time, for week after week and finally all flogged. We were told we were very lucky not to get the sack and I believe if we had not all been involved we would have. No one mentioned the word homosexuality and I would not have known what it meant if it had been mentioned. As we used to visit every other bed in turn I am quite sure that I must have known if any of the boys were interested in this vice. I don't think any of them knew anything about it, and that we merely used to go and swop yarns. The whole spice of the matter was that it was forbidden to talk after Lights Out.

Equally unfortunate in this respect was Cyril Connolly.

We took to visiting in our cubicles at night. One evening, after Lights Out, Ned Northcote and Frankie Wright were talking in mine when we heard Maud (the Matron) pass along.
    She went into Northcote's cubicle. No sign of him. She called out in a terrible voice, 'Where's Northcote?' I answered from my cubicle, 'I think he went to the lavatory'. We heard her go along to open the door and lost our heads, like rabbits chased by a ferret.
    Ned bolted the latch of my cubicle with a toothbrush and started to climb over the partition into his own. But Maud came and rattled it. 'Why is this door locked? Open it this instant'. I was afraid to. At last, with white face, Frankie opened it and she burst in. There was an eternity of waiting while our crime was reported and then the three of us were taken down and caned in our pyjamas. The locked door was evidence which our being a trio instead of the usual compromised pair could not palliate. It was Oscar Wilde over again.

This is where dates become important. Chichester and Connolly were at their schools in the first decade of the century and it is easier to believe in their innocence than it is to sympathise with the prurience of their headmasters. George Melly was born in 1926 and was still at his preparatory school when the Second World War broke out.
He is quite frank about the state of *his* knowledge.

My mother preferred, in general, the company of homosexuals, and from my earliest youth I had learned to equate wit and creativity with homosexuality. My loathed prep school master, already responsible for my left-wing bias, confirmed me in my admiration for effeminacy through his hysterical, and possibly ambivalent, hatred of it.

195

I was, on one occasion, slippered in front of the whole
school for insisting, despite warnings, that I would rather
go to the ballet than watch a game of rugger. In the face of
such a brute I felt impelled – as far as a twelve year old boy
could – to defend all these beautifully-dressed, graceful, funny
friends of my mother.

At the same time that very prep school, particularly after
its evacuation to Shropshire at the beginning of the Second
World War, was athrob with sexual experimentation of all
kinds. By the time I went to Stowe at the age of fourteen, I was
aware of, (if, in some cases uninitiated in) every variation of
homosexual love-making.

There were two ways in which the boys might find out, or try to find
out the truth. It could be by open discussion. Sir Compton Mackenzie's
autobiography runs to ten volumes. Here, from Volume One:

It was in the Summer term of 1893 that some of us ten year olds
got down seriously to solving the problem of how we had arrived
in this world. These discussions always took place by the outdoor
gymnasium in the north west corner of the playing fields.
Important clues, unearthed by close study of the Old
Testament, were argued over and we were all agreed how lucky it
was that we were able to read the Bible without being told 'that
it was not the sort of book young people should read'.

One thing we were nearly all agreed about. The baby must
come out of the mother's navel. What other possible reason
could there be for the belly-button? When a sceptic pointed
out that men had belly-buttons as well as women, we in
turn pointed out that men had breasts as well as women, but
that did not mean that they could be used for feeding babies.
No, no, no. We were not prepared to accept any other possible
exit for the infant. What we did want to know was what
happened before the infant was born; and we scanned our Old
Testament more carefully than ever.

And then, one day, a boy arrived with the facts. He had
discovered them in a book, hidden away at the back of his
father's study.

'With pictures, too,' he said and described to us those
pictures.

The shock of the information was so severe that, sitting as I was at the time of receiving it on the parallel bars, I lost my balance and fell off.

Or it might be by private information from some better-informed boy. Leonard Woolf was at Arlington House Preparatory School before going on to St Paul's. In the first volume of his autobiography (*Sowing*) published, like Ernest Raymond's, when he was eighty, he writes:

The only thing I learned thoroughly at Arlington House, other than cricket, was the nature and problems of sex. They were explained to me, luridly and in minute detail, almost at once, by a small boy who had probably the dirtiest mind in an extraordinarily dirty-minded school. I was at the time completely innocent and I had considerable difficulty in concealing from him the fact that it was only with the most heroic efforts that I was preventing myself from being sick.

However, I soon recovered; one had, indeed, to develop a strong stomach in matters sexual to stand up against the atmosphere of the school when I first went there. These facts are worth recording because they showed me, for the first time, at a very early age, the enormous influence a few boys at the top of a school exercise upon the minds and behaviour of the masses below them.

At the age of twelve I was not prudish. And I do not think I have ever been prudish after the nasty little X removed my innocence. But I have never known anything like the nastiness – corruption is hardly too strong a word – of the minds and even to some extent the bodies of the little boys at Arlington House when I went there.

However, by the time I left for St Paul's, in 1894, the atmosphere had changed from that of a sordid brothel to something more appropriate to fifty fairly happy small boys under the age of fourteen.

Information from official sources could be less disturbing, if more ambiguous. Philip Slessor, who was at Summer Fields between 1919 and 1923, writes, in his contribution to Richard Usborne's anthology:

Nowadays the newspapers are strident with controversy concerning sex education in schools, just as if it were something new. Forty years ago we, at Summer Fields, had the grave gathering known as 'Borva Class' at which boys leaving to go to public schools were assembled and Mr Alington started the proceedings with prayer. We were then – how well in my sere and sinful middle-age I remember it – given the authentic birds-and-bees story, with much talk, about it and about, all veiled in allegory. There was a dread note of forsakement by God if we did certain things (unspecified) and warnings of Torquemada agonies if we fell into various (unspecified) temptations. No diagrams, no iso-type sheets were shown; no biological or physiological terms were used. After further prayer we were cast into the outer darkness of our pubescent doubts and stood about on the gravel, gazing upon each other with a wild surmise. That was *all*?

Cyril Connolly found the information less ambiguous, but just as disturbing.

I was still ignorant of anything which I had not read in a book and just before I went to Eton a concerted attack was made on my modesty. My father struggled to explain the facts of life and the chaplain at St Wulfric's gave the boys who were leaving a seedy exhortation. The headmaster was more explicit. We were going into a world full of temptations, especially the Etonians; we must report any boy at once who tried to get into our bed, never go for a walk with a boy from another house, never make friends with anyone more than a year and a half older (eventually it would be younger) and, above all, not 'play with ourselves'. There was an old boy from St Wulfric's who became so self-intoxicated that when he got to Oxford he had put, in a fit of remorse, his head under a train. That miserable youth, I afterwards learnt, had attended all the private schools in England.

The topic could even be treated agreeably. Eric Maschwitz, television producer, administrator and author, attended Arden House Preparatory School before the First World War. It was owned by the brothers Ernest and Oswald Nelson. He says:

If sex reared its pretty head at Arden House it was usually most pleasant and normal. I myself received a hearty thrashing from Oswald Nelson for having written (at the dissolute age of eleven) a passionate love letter to Miss Elsie Craven, a young female person whom I admired in the London production of *Where the Rainbow Ends* (or was it in *Pinkie and the Fairies* – I forget). Her mother had returned it to the headmaster with an indignant note. We received no instruction in that side of life and left the school with the most confused idea as to how babies were born and what it was about little girls that made them so oddly exciting to dance with. My cousin, Philip Jordan, who was at another Midland school, maintains that on his last evening he was left by himself in the headmaster's study to read a booklet on sex written by a clergyman. He claims that the first chapter began with the words: 'If you have looked at your body when having a bath you may have noticed, about half way down, something that resembles a little bag, or purse –'

James Lees-Milne suffered from the eccentricities of his mother. Whilst introduction to the mysteries of sex was traditionally left to the last day at prep school, characteristically his mother considered it appropriate to open this, and other topics, with her eight-year-old son in the cab on the way to his first term.

She told me that the happiest time of my life was now dawning. The term always went by in a flash. I would soon be making the friends of a lifetime. 'Which reminds me,' she added, in rather portentous and uncharacteristic tone, 'your father would wish me to give you a little, just a little, piece of advice. About life generally'. She paused and then suddenly corrected herself, 'On the whole, it might be better if you asked the headmaster to explain all about the disgusting side of it'. And then, half to herself and half aloud, she added, 'Not that I myself have ever found it *exactly* that'.

Finally, we note that not everyone found this topic, even in retrospect, amusing. Harold Anson, who was the son of a country parson, sympathetically if narrowly brought up, went, in the 1870s, to a preparatory school called Ascham House at Bournemouth. Later he took orders and rose to be Master of the Temple. He sounds a warning:

I should grant now that I had been starved on the animal side.
The rather innocent Rabelaisianism of the small boy with
his healthy appetite for all that pertains to the growing puppy,
'Going up and down and round about the City' — all this seems
very wicked, and so I had been taught. I now see that much
of this outlook of the healthy sensual animal is not otherwise
than natural and good. Its suppression, or, in fact, the total
ignorance of there being anything to suppress, was what was
unfair and unnatural.

These nice little animals among whom I was suddenly
plunged, hardly any of them with much wrong about them,
were a terrible difficulty to the over-stimulated little boy that
I was, the companion of elderly parents and grown-ups and
unmarried sisters, with a natural taste for climbing up too
quickly to celestial abodes. To be recalled to the animal I
was, I now think, was necessary and essential; but to have to
encounter sexual animality as, first, a horrifying turning
away from God and all that a good home meant, and
afterwards as an attractive but shameful secret, was
altogether wrong, and it is hard to forgive the system which
inflicts so great an injury on a boy.

# 26

# BLUB SUNDAY

And so the last day of the four or five years' mixture of pleasure and pain arrived, and the boys marched out of the shelter of preparatory school and into a wider world. Cyril Connolly watched them go.

> Muscle bound with character the alumni of St Wulfric's would pass on to the best public schools, cleaning up all houses with a doubtful tone, reporting their best friends for homosexuality and seeing them expelled, winning athletic distinctions, for the house rather than for themselves, for the school rather than for the house, and prizes and scholarships and shooting competitions as well, and then finding their vocation in India, Burma, Nigeria and the Sudan, administering with Roman justice those natives for whom the final profligate overflow of Wulfrician character was, all the time, predestined.

Not all boys demonstrated this fine manly spirit. Sir Charles Oman, looking forward, wondered just what the preparatory school *had* prepared him for. Others looked back with simple nostalgia.

George Lyttelton's son Humphrey sobbed frantically through tea with the headmaster on his first day but soon recovered: 'There were no more tears – until the day he left'. Dunsany, too, cried when he went ('which was natural'); but also when he left. Alexander Florescu, son of the Romanian Ambassador, who was at Summer Fields through the Second World War, says that his saddest moment was on the day he left. Raymond Somerville records unashamedly, 'At the end of my last term I hid myself for a bit in the cloakroom and among all the coats had a private cry.'

Gerald Bullard, who left Summer Fields in 1929, says, 'I remember failing my Common Entrance first time for Eton. I believe it was because I spelt Eton "Eaton" and Thames "Tems". And the day I left the tears streamed down my face. I had a ghastly feeling of complete loneliness during my first two weeks at Eton.'

There was one function which the headmaster traditionally reserved for the last day. It was a formal farewell to the boys who were leaving, often accompanied by the gift of a suitable book and, as often, with an exhortation.

They were growing up; and they were going into a world of grown-up boys. On the assumption – more valid in earlier times than in this – that they knew nothing about sex, it was necessary that they should be both instructed and warned. For public schools, if not hotbeds of vice, had in them paths which led downwards.

Fifty years later, in verses understandably not included in the centenary anthology of Summer Fields which he edited, Richard Usborne wrote a resumé of what seemed to be the advice being dispensed to the dazed leaving boy in 1924 by the then headmaster, the Reverend E.H. Alington:

> Sex is not a subject set
> in the Scholarships . . . not yet.
> I must try to tell you now
> things about your bodies: how
> boys and girls are different:
> what God in His goodness meant
> when He gave us tools whereby
> we could love and multiply.
>
> Common are to either sex
> legs and arms and heads and necks:
> but in parts we seldom name
> boys and girls are not the same,
> Medical research has shown
> that, from thigh to collarbone,
> girls are thick where boys are thin,
> boys go out where girls go in.
> Boys have muscles on their chests:
> girls have two soft things called breasts
> (Coarse swine call these extra bits
> ugly names like bubs and tits):
> girls just have them there to carry
> milk for babies when they marry.
> Boys have penises, girls none:
> girls sit down for Number One.

You'll have pubic hair one day:
women have it the same way.

At your public school perhaps
you will find that bigger chaps,
roughly or by stratagem,
get you into bed with them.
Do not stop to reason why . . .
hit the buggers in the eye.
If somebody plays that game,
hit him first: then take his name:
then report him to his Dame.
She'll prescribe cold baths and rugger
regularly for the bugger.
Buggery is very bad.
Masturbation sends you mad.
You must all resist temptation:
God will punish masturbation.
Keep your trouser pockets sewn up
till you're well and truly grown up.
If you feel a warmth and stirring
in your private parts occurring,
thunder 'Satan, get thee hence!'
obdurate in innocence.

And a good deal more, in wilder and even more uninhibited terms.

# 27

# ADHERENCE OF REPUTATIONS

The publisher of this book recalled the fate of a boy at his preparatory school. It seems that the boy's mother had come down to attend some function. Clearly she was a lady of importance since she was seated on the platform. From this position of eminence it became clear that, owing to some failure in the arrangements that supported them, her stockings were coming down. From that point onwards in his life, even when they had forgotten his name, his fellows would refer to him as 'the boy whose mother's stockings were coming down'. The publisher, a man of impeccable veracity, alleges that he spotted the victim some forty years later approaching down Bond Street. The victim spotted him, too; and, at imminent risk to life and limb, hurried across onto the other pavement.

Nicholas Monsarrat suffered misery for three days because he didn't know how to ask the way to the lavatory. His nickname at school was 'the squit' – though more, he insists, on account of his size than of the inevitable outcome of such ignorance. Nor was he the only boy in the school with a derogatory nickname.

> A boy who had the misfortune to be sent to school on his first
> day wearing long black stockings, instead of the normal
> short grey ones, never lost the nickname 'girlie' which
> followed him like a curse. Serve him right, we thought. His
> people should have known better. They were a very common
> family.

Llewelyn Powys was called Lulu, which he can hardly have enjoyed, but the nickname could be unobjectionable. That notable sailor, Sir William Goodenough, writes:

> Did I have a fight or two? I daresay, but from what I remember
> I was a tame little fellow. The cynic says that the shortest
> thing on earth is human memory, but the following, I think,
> is remarkable. About forty years after I had left Temple

Grove, walking down St James's Street, I met a man who said to me, 'Temple Grove?'

    'Yes,' I said. 'I was there.'

    'Tadpole?'

    'Yes, that's me.'

The reputation could be undeserved. Stratton-Ferrier, hero of the famous Summer Fields–Horris Hill football match, recalls:

> Gerald Seager had one of his very rare off-days and he missed a couple of sitters. The headmaster swore he'd never seen anything like it since the famous day when David James skied the ball over the cross-bar from five yards in front of an open goal. The evil that boys did lived after them. Poor David James, immortalised for generations by this single, oft-told incident. Eternal infamy in this brief moment of zealous excess.

The reputation of masters could live on, too. The ineffective ones like Mr Handicap, and the terrifying ones like the Reverend E.H. Alington, known to the boys of Summer Fields as 'Bear'.

Says Stephen Pasmore:

> The fear of being wrong engendered in me by Bear lingers on. I recently parked my car on the edge of a common and was sitting in the car talking to my wife when I saw an elderly man coming towards us. I immediately felt guilty and thought he was going to reprimand me for trespassing. He passed by without taking any notice. It was only afterwards that I realised that the man's red face and flowing white hair had reminded me of Bear.

There were occasions, too, when the use of old and well-remembered nicknames raised no smiles. In his autobiographical poem, *Summoned by Bells*, John Betjeman writes:

> Before the hymn the Skipper would announce
> The latest, names of those who lost their lives
> For King and Country and the Dragon School.
> Sometimes his gruff old voice was full of tears
> When a particular favourite had been killed.

Then we would hear the nickname of the boy,
'Pongo' or 'Podge', and how he'd played 3Q
For Oxford and, if only he had lived,
He might have played for England – which he did,
But in a grimmer game, against the Hun.
And then we'd all look solemn, knowing well
There'd be no extra holiday today.

# GOING BACK

Apart from formal reunions there might be a number of reasons which induced Old Boys to return to the scenes of their youth. It might be to take part in a cricket week, or some other out-of-term function, or it might be to prospect for a job to fill in the years between leaving public school and more serious work. But mostly it was curiosity.

Herman Merivale, barrister, actor and author, had been to a school in the 1850s which he christened 'Little Dotheboys', kept by a Mr Wanks ('a gentle, handsome and generally ignorant clergyman'), also by his wife ('coarse, strong, loud and usually drunk') and four daughters. He had some miserable years there before going on to Harrow, where he was a little happier, but not much. It can only have been curiosity that took him back.

Many years afterwards, as an old pupil, I visited Little Dotheboys once more. It was a desert. Pupils there were few, if any. The school had gone to well deserved grief. The grounds and parsonage looked small and mean and miserable and deserted. I wondered from the heart of me how I could have thought the place so large. Mr and Mrs Wanks were still there, but quite ineffably run to seed and looking quarrelsome. For Nemesis had overtaken them. They both made much of me as I had then something of a name, but I do not believe that either of them remembered me in the very least. Apparently there were no hapless ushers left to keep up the tradition of some learning. Whether the four young ladies had departed I knew not; to happiness, I hope. Two of them were not unkindly girls. Mr and Mrs Wanks both pleaded hard with me not to forget them and to recommend the school, remembering what it had made of me; and rather sore of heart I went away and from that hour have heard of them no more.

The motive might be a desire for revenge. David Niven had not forgotten his treatment by Mr Croome.

> Years later, when I was at Sandhurst and playing in the rugby football fifteen, big enough and ugly enough to take care of myself, I had an over-powering urge to see that bastard Mr Croome again.
>
> I went down to the school, filled with vindictiveness. I don't know what I intended to do really, but when I got there I found the school deserted; its prison-like exercise yard full of rubbish and old newspapers. The fourth floor window, out of which I had dangled, was broken and open to the rain. It didn't even look very high.

Another man who had forgiven and forgotten nothing was Richard Meinertzhagen, a natural rebel. In his case the visit took place so long after his schooldays that there can have been no question of rediscovering the tyrants themselves. In retrospect, he wishes he had never made the visit.

> I returned to Fonthill in August 1962. The effect was disastrous. There was the old schoolroom, just as it had been, seventy-four years ago, with the headmaster's desk in the corner and, as I viewed the portraits of Walter and Ashton Radcliffe (joint headmasters in my time) my brain and body were flooded with hatred and horror such as I had not experienced for over seventy years, all increased by my mother's apparent indifference to the suffering of one of her children. My whole being went back seventy-four years to the time when I struck Walter Radcliffe and fled the school [see under 'Rebels and Non-conformers']. I was completely upset by my visit. It brought to the surface everything beastly in me and I did not recover until I returned to my hotel. It took nearly a whole bottle of Harvey's Bristol Cream to restore me to normal.

A number of schools which had previously been disagreeable places had later changed – usually on a change of headmaster – into something quite different. When Wilfred Thesiger went back to St Aubyn's he found the school the same, in a physical sense, but morally transformed.

Recently I went back to St Aubyn's to give a lecture and I
spent the night there. Time seemed to have stood still. The
boys wore the same grey shorts and jerseys; the band was
practising, marching and counter-marching on the playing field.
I attended morning chapel and neither the seating nor the
service had altered. In the dormitories I identified the beds
in which I had slept, with the same trays beneath them for
dirty clothes and the same chairs beside them. In the
dining-room, team photographs were ranged along the wall.
I recognised my brother in one of them; I myself had never
made the grade. In sixty years the school had hardly changed
in outward appearance. What was profoundly different was the
relationship of headmaster and boys. Between them I sensed
affection, confidence and trust. I had heard that St Aubyn's was
now one of the best preparatory schools in the country, with
a distinguished academic record. Having stayed with the
headmaster and talked to the boys I know this to be true.

Lord Berners also discovered a happier place:

The school chosen for me was Elmley. My father and uncles
had been there and it was considered to be one of the best
preparatory schools of the day. After the death of the
headmaster, Mr Gambril, it began to go downhill and now it
has ceased to exist as a school. When I went to visit the place
some years ago, with a view to refreshing ancient memories,
I noticed a definite alteration in the atmosphere; there was a
feeling of gaiety, of irresponsibility in the air that had been
absent in the old days. It had been converted into a lunatic
asylum.

From 1914 until its closure a few years ago, St Peter's, Seaford, was
fortunate enough to have, in succession, three headmasters all capable
of running a happy school. E.G. Turner, who is quoted in the
Introduction, furnishes the tail piece.

It was an evening in August, 1942. I was stationed near
Seaford and found time to visit the School. I wasn't quite sure
what to expect, but I soon found out. I stood for a moment
at the gate and gazed at the long grass on the playing fields, the

soldier's shirt hanging from the double cubicle window and the coal dump behind the site of the junior nets. I walked up the drive and was confronted by a mystified sergeant of a regiment which had come many hundreds of miles to take up a station, once occupied by the boys of St Peter's. Having satisfied himself as to who I was and why I was there, he persuaded me to sign the Unit visitors' book, which he found in the Orderly Room, better known as 'Clive'. I then wandered round the School. The dining hall still had two panels left, safe and intact, one recording the name of the boy who got 16 blacks and yet won the Set honours. The fives courts, piled high with wire and camouflage netting, reminded me of a happy afternoon.

In the hut I found the famous 'Dairy Farming in New Zealand' poster, now surrounded by modern pamphlets on careless talk and Savings Groups. I thought back and remembered the queue for eight goodies; the boxing, the wrestling, the skating, the cinema shows, the evening service and the deafening roars of the end of term cheering. I thought of Pollock as 'Shylock', of the beautiful girl that David Crerar made and of Toby Tankard as the hind legs of 'Dapple'. The tune of 'One Fish Ball' seemed still to ring round the walls, where parents sat and watched the concerts, breathless as little Willie spoke his much practised lines.

And then the Chapel. I had not seen it before and I was much impressed by its beauty and simplicity. Small, neat, compact, the little rows of pews were vacant, waiting. On the altar I found a Roll of Service – a simple list of humble service – of young fellows who have gone forth to do their duty. Some on that list have achieved fame; others have made the supreme sacrifice. But behind it all, I could not but feel that this was the fruit of seed sown in good ground and that, in the fatal hour, this fruit was good.

Around the School again, I found soldiers working and resting. They seemed interested to know what used to happen where they now toiled and slept. There seemed to be an uncanny sensation in telling a soldier where one spent one's schooldays. The guard mounting outside the eighth form window and a Bren gun carrier drawing up to the front door were strange scenes in familiar surroundings. The clock, they told me, would not work. I could not help feeling that it was waiting for the School's return.

And so in a few minutes memories of bygone days came back. The dip, the rush for prayers in the morning, first break, quiet time, double golds, B and J, soup after prep, the bathing buses and label days were all things that I had almost forgotten; but they all came back.

When I left St Peter's in 1936, I think I had a few tears in my eyes. Now I know why.

# Sources and
# Acknowledgements

All books were published in London unless otherwise specified.

I. ARRIVAL
Peter Green, *Kenneth Grahame*, 1959, reprinted by permission of John Murray (Publishers) Ltd; David Cecil, *Max*, Constable, 1964; *A Century of Summer Fields*, ed. Richard Usborne, 1964, reprinted by permission of Summer Fields School Trust Ltd and Richard Usborne; Maurice Baring, *The Puppet Show of Memory*, 1922, reprinted by permission of A.P. Watt Ltd on behalf of the trustees of the Maurice Baring Will Trust; Christopher Robin Milne, *The Enchanted Places*, 1974, reprinted by permission of Methuen London Ltd; *The Lyttelton Hart-Davis Letters*, Vol. 1, ed. Rupert Hart-Davis, 1978, reprinted by permission of John Murray (Publishers) Ltd; John Connell, *Wavell*, 1964, reprinted by permission of HarperCollins Ltd; *World of the Public School*, ed. McDonald Fraser, 1977, reprinted by permission of Weidenfeld & Nicolson Ltd; Ian Dall, *Sun Before Seven*, 1936; Thomas Hughes, *Tom Brown's Schooldays*, 1857; Nicholas Monsarrat, *Life is a Four Letter Word*, 1966, © The Estate of Nicholas Monsarrat, reprinted by permission of Mrs Ann Monsarrat; Hubert van Zeller, *One Foot in the Grave*, 1965, reprinted by permission of John Murray (Publishers) Ltd; Sue Arnold, *Boarding School Blues*, 1988, © The Observer.

2. FOOD
Nicholas Monsarrat, *Life is a Four Letter Word*, 1966, see above; F. Anstey, *A Long Retrospect*, 1936; Sir William Goodenough, *A Rough Record*, 1943; Major-General Sir A.E. Anson, *About Others and Myself*, 1920; Lord Edward Fitzmaurice, *George Leveson-Gower*, 1905; Nicholas Monsarrat, *Life is a Four Letter Word*, 1966, see above; Rupert Hart-Davis, *The Arms of Time*, 1979, reprinted by permission of the author;

Philip Masters, *Preparatory Schools Today*, A&C Black Ltd, 1966; Paul Spillane, *St Andrew's School*, privately printed, 1977, reprinted by permission of the author; Claude Blagden, *Well Remembered*, 1953; Philip Masters, *Preparatory Schools Today*, 1966, see above; Laurence Irving, *The Precarious Crust*, Chatto & Windus, 1971; Claude Blagden, *Well Remembered*, see above; A.A. Milne, *It's Too Late Now*, 1939, reproduced by permission of Curtis Brown Ltd.


3. FRIENDS
Maurice Bowra, *Memories*, 1966, reprinted by permission of Weidenfeld & Nicolson Ltd; John Connell, *Wavell*, see above; C. Day Lewis, *The Buried Day*, 1960, reprinted by permission of the Executors of the Estate of C. Day Lewis and The Hogarth Press; Bernard Darwin, *The World That Fred Made*, 1955, reprinted by permission of A.P. Watt Ltd on behalf of Lady Darwin, Ursula Mommens and Dr Paul Ashton; R.C. Robertson-Glasgow, *Forty-six Not Out*, 1948; L.A.G. Strong, *Green Memory*, 1961, reprinted by permission of the Peters, Fraser & Dunlop Group Ltd; Laurence Hanson, *Boy and Man*, 1952; Osbert Sitwell, *The Scarlet Tree*, Macmillan, 1950, reprinted by permission of David Higham Associates.


4. BULLYING AND COUNTER-BULLYING
Sir Hugh Walpole, *The Crystal Box*, privately printed, 1924; Sir Rupert Hart-Davis, *Hugh Walpole*, Macmillan, 1952; Hon. Henry Coke, *Tracks of a Rolling Stone*, 1905; General Ian Hamilton, *When I was a Boy*, 1936, reprinted by permission of Faber & Faber Ltd; Patrick Campbell, *My Life and Times*, 1967; Sir Francis Chichester, *The Lonely Sea and the Sky*, 1964, © Francis Chichester, reprinted by permission of Curtis Brown Ltd; Guy Kendall, *A Headmaster Remembers*, Gollancz, 1933; W.H. Dunn, *James Anthony Froude*, Oxford University Press, 1961; George Millar, *The Road to Resistance*, The Bodley Head, 1979; Maurice Collis, *Journey Outward*, 1942, reprinted by permission of Louise Collis; Randolph Churchill, *Twenty-One Years*, 1965, reprinted by permission of Curtis Brown Ltd on behalf of the Estate of Randolph S. Churchill © 1965; J.B. Seely, *Fear and Be Slain*, 1931, reprinted by permission of A.P. Watt Ltd; Compton Mackenzie, *My Life and Times*, 1963, reprinted by permission of The Society of Authors as the literary representative of the Estate of Compton Mackenzie.

## 5. A LITTLE LEARNING

Leo Tolstoy, *Boyhood*, 1854; Evelyn Waugh, *A Little Learning*, 1964, reprinted by permission of the Peters, Fraser & Dunlop Group Ltd; H.G. Wells, *Experiment in Autobiography*, 1934, reprinted by permission of A.P. Watt Ltd on behalf of the Literary Executors of the Estate of H.G. Wells; Giles and Esmond Romilly, *Out of Bounds*, 1935; Winston S. Churchill, *My Early Life*, 1930; Emlyn Williams, *George*, 1961, reprinted by permission of the Executors of the Estate of the late Emlyn Williams; *A Century of Summer Fields*, see above; Arthur Marshall, *Life's Rich Pageant*, Hamish Hamilton, 1984; Evelyn Waugh, *A Little Learning*, see above; L.A.G. Strong, *Green Memory*, see above; A.P. Graves, *No Return to All That*, 1930; A.A. Milne, *It's Too Late Now*, see above; Rev. Hiley, *Memories of Half a Century*, 1899; *A Century of Summer Fields*, see above; Rupert Hart-Davis, *The Arms of Time*, see above; Naomi Mitchison, *Small Talk*, The Bodley Head, 1973; Mark Amory, *Lord Dunsany*, Collins, 1972, reprinted by permission of Curtis Brown & John Farquharson Ltd; Bevis Hillier, *Young Betjeman*, 1988, reprinted by permission of John Murray (Publishers) Ltd; Roger Llombreaud, *Arthur Symons*, 1963, reprinted by permission of Unwin Hyman, a division of HarperCollins Publishers Ltd.

## 6. GAMES

F. Anstey, *A Long Retrospect*, see above; Ernest Raymond, *The Story of My Days*, 1968, reprinted by permission of A.P. Watt Ltd on behalf of Diana Raymond; *A Century of Summer Fields*, see above; Sir Alan Herbert, *His Life and Times*, 1970, reprinted by permission of A.P. Watt Ltd on behalf of Crystal Hale and Jocelyn Herbert; Bernard Newman, *Speaking from Memory*, Hutchinson, 1960; Paul Brickhill, *Reach for the Sky*, 1954, reprinted by permission of HarperCollins Ltd; Graham Greene, *A Sort of Life*, The Bodley Head, 1971, reprinted by permission of the Estate of Graham Greene; Paul Spillane, *St Andrew's School*, see above; Christopher Pirie-Gordon, *St Peter's: The Early Years*, privately printed, 1980; *A Century of Summer Fields*, see above; Lord Home, *The Way the Wind Blows*, 1976, reprinted by permission of HarperCollins Ltd; Christopher Pirie-Gordon, *St Peter's: The Early Years*, see above; George Melly, *Owning Up*, 1967, reprinted by permission of Weidenfeld & Nicolson Ltd; Maurice Baring, *The Puppet Show of Memory*, see above.

### 7. STEPS TO THE STAGE

Laurence Olivier, *Confessions of an Actor*, 1982, reprinted by permission of Weidenfeld & Nicolson Ltd; Roland Culver, *Not Quite a Gentleman*, 1979, reprinted by permission of HarperCollins Ltd; John Gielgud, *Early Stages*, 1939; Rex Harrison, *Rex*, Macmillan, 1974; Sir Frank Benson, *My Memoirs*, 1930; James Mason, *Before I Forget*, Hamish Hamilton, 1981; H. Montgomery Hyde, *Oscar Wilde*, 1976, reprinted by permission of Methuen London; John Russell Taylor, *Alec Guinness*, 1984, reprinted by permission of Pavilion Books; Elaine Dundy, *Finch, Bloody Finch*, 1980; Geoffrey Mansell, *Haunted Idol*, 1984; *A Century of Summer Fields*, see above.

### 8. MUSIC

Geoffrey Bush, *Left, Right and Centre*, 1983, reprinted by permission of the author; Laurence Olivier, *Confessions of an Actor*, see above; Charles Reid, *Malcolm Sargent*, Hamish Hamilton, 1968; Arthur Lawrence, *Sir Arthur Sullivan*, 1899; Humphrey Lyttelton, *I Play as I Please*, HarperCollins Publishers, 1954.

### 9. ENTERTAINMENTS

Giles and Esmond Romilly, *Out of Bounds*, 1935; Daphne du Maurier, *Gerald*, 1934; Ian Carmichael, *Will the Real Ian Carmichael*, 1979; Eden Phillpotts, *The Complete Human Boy*, 1930; Paul Spillane, *St Andrew's School*, see above; Cyril Connolly, *Enemies of Promise*, Routledge & Kegan Paul, 1938, reprinted by permission of Rogers Coleridge and White Ltd; Michael Powell, *A Life in the Movies*, 1986, reprinted by permission of William Heinemann Ltd.

### 10. LIFE

J.C. Masterman, *On the Chariot Wheel*, Oxford, 1975, copyright © J.C. Masterman 1975, reprinted by permission of Curtis Brown Ltd; Major-General Sir A.E. Anson, *About Others and Myself*, see above; *Charles Kingsley: Life and Letters*, 1877; Peter Green, *Kenneth Grahame*, 1959, reprinted by permission of John Murray (Publishers) Ltd; Christopher Robin Milne, *The Enchanted Places*, see above; Wilfred Thesiger, *The Life of My Choice*, 1987, reprinted by permission of HarperCollins Ltd; Cyril Connolly, *Enemies of Promise*, see above; Maurice Baring, *The Puppet Show of Memory*, see above; Nicholas Aldridge, *Time To Spare*, 1989, reprinted by permission of the author; Christopher Hollis, *The Seven Ages*, 1974, reprinted by permission of William

Heinemann Ltd; Robert Speaight, *The Property Basket*, 1970, reprinted by permission of David Higham Associates; David Niven, *The Moon's a Balloon*, 1961, reprinted by permission of Hamish Hamilton Ltd; Robert Graves, *Goodbye to all that*, 1929, reprinted by permission of A.P. Watt Ltd on behalf of The Trustees of the Robert Graves Copyright Trust; Norman Sherry, *Life of Graham Greene*, Vol. 1, 1989, reprinted by permission of Jonathan Cape Ltd; Charles Castle, *Oliver Messel*, 1986, reprinted by permission of Thames & Hudson International Ltd; Geoffrey Rawson, *Sea Prelude*, 1958; Bernard Darwin, *The World That Fred Made*, see above; Sir Charles Oman, *Memories of Victorian Oxford*, 1942.

11. CLOTHES

Siegfried Sassoon, *The Old Century*, 1938; Shelley Rohde, *A Private View of L.S. Lowry 1887–1976*, 1979, reprinted by permission of the author; Sir William Goodenough, *A Rough Record*, see above; James Lees-Milne, *Another Self*, Faber & Faber, 1970; Wilfred Blunt, *John Christie of Glyndebourne*, 1968; John Sherwood, *No Golden Journey*, 1973, reprinted by permission of William Heinemann Ltd; Douglas Ainslie, *Adventures Social and Literary*, 1922.

12. HEADMASTERS

C.H. Jaques, *A Dragon Century*, privately printed, 1977, reprinted by permission of the Dragon School; Colonel Sir Mike Ansell, *Soldier On*, 1973; C.S. Lewis, *Surprised by Joy*, 1955, reprinted by permission of HarperCollins Ltd; Lady Wester-Wemyss, *The Life of Rosslyn Wester-Wemyss*, 1935; Paul Spillane, *St Andrew's School*, see above; A.J.P. Taylor, *A Personal History*, 1983, reprinted by permission of David Higham Associates Ltd; *A Century of Summer Fields*, see above; Evelyn Waugh, *Ronald Knox*, 1959, reprinted by permission of the Peters Fraser & Dunlop Group Ltd; Peter Green, *Kenneth Grahame*, see above; Sir William Goodenough, *A Rough Record*, see above; General Hamilton, *When I Was a Boy*, 1936, reprinted by permission of Faber & Faber Ltd; Alfred Havighurst, *H.W. Massingham*, Cambridge, 1979, reprinted by permission of Cambridge University Press; Mark Tellar, *A Young Man's Passage*, 1952; Lieutenant-General Sir Douglas Brownrigg, *Unexpected*, 1942; Christopher Pirie-Gordon, *St Peter's: The Early Years*, see above; D.L. Mackay, *The Rise of the English Prep School*, Falmer Press, 1984; James Strachey Barnes, *Half a Life*, 1933; Wilfred Thesiger, *The Life of My Choice*, see above.

### 13. MASTERS

Thomas Hughes, *Tom Brown's Schooldays*, see above; Osbert Sitwell, *The Scarlet Tree*, 1950, reprinted by permission of David Higham Associates Ltd; Bernard Darwin, *The World that Fred Made*, see above; *A Century of Summer Fields*, see above; Nicholas Monsarrat, *Life is a Four Letter Word*, see above; Giles and Esmond Romilly, *Out of Bounds*, see above; Michael Powell, *A Life in the Movies*, see above; Rupert Hart-Davis, *The Arms of Time*, see above; Lord Home, *The Way the Wind Blows*, see above; C.H. Jaques, *A Dragon Century*, see above; *Prep School*, 1988; David Niven, *The Moon's a Balloon*, see above; Ben Travers, *A-Sitting on a Gate*, 1978; Bevis Hillier, *Young Betjeman*, see above.

### 14. MATRONS

Geoffrey Rawson, *Sea Prelude*, see above; C.S. Lewis, *Surprised by Joy*, see above; Giles and Esmond Romilly, *Out of Bounds*, see above; Graham Greene, *A Sort of Life*, see above; Oliver Holt, *Three Sherborne Memoirs*, privately printed, 1983, reprinted by permission of the author; A.G.C. Liddell, *An Ordinary Mortal*, 1911; Roald Dahl, *Boy*, 1984, reprinted by permission of Jonathan Cape and Penguin Books Ltd.

### 15. READING

H.A.L. Fisher, *An Unfinished Biography*, Oxford, 1940; Bernard Darwin, *The World that Fred Made*, see above; William Harris, *Life So Far*, 1954, reprinted by permission of Jonathan Cape Ltd; Dr Gordon Hake, *Memories of Eighty Years*, 1892; D.C. Murray, *Recollections*, 1908; Robert Speaight, *The Property Basket*, see above; Basil Dean, *Seven Ages*, Hutchinson, 1970, reprinted by permission of Martin Dean; Adrian Alington, *Chaytors*, 1933; Paul Spillane, *St Andrew's School*, see above; Graham Greene, *A Sort of Life*, see above; Noël Coward, *Present Indicative*, William Heinemann, 1937.

### 16. PETS AND CRAZES

Eden Phillpotts, *The Complete Human Boy*, 1930; Maurice Baring, *The Puppet Show of Memory*, see above; Adrian Alington, *Chaytors*, see above; A.J.P. Taylor, *A Personal History*, see above; Nicholas Monsarrat, *Life is a Four Letter Word*, see above; Graham Greene, *A Sort of Life*, see above; Richard Meinertzhagen, *Diary of a Black Sheep*, 1964, reprinted by permission of Messrs. Fisher, Dowson & Wasbrough; Andrew

Hodges, *The Enigma of Intelligence*, 1983, © Andrew Hodges 1983, reprinted by permission of the author; Kathleen Tynan, *Kenneth Tynan*, 1987, reprinted by permission of Weidenfeld & Nicolson Ltd; *A Century of Summer Fields*, see above.

17. LANGUAGE
Compton Mackenzie, *My Life and Times*, 1963, see above; Nicholas Aldridge, *Time to Spare*, see above; Nicholas Monsarrat, *Life is a Four Letter Word*, see above; Maurice Baring, *The Puppet Show of Memory*, see above; Gilbert Murray, *Autobiographical Fragment*, 1960; Jessica Brett Young, *Francis Brett Young*, 1962, reprinted by permission of David Higham Associates Ltd; John Osborne, *A Better Class of Person*, 1981, reprinted by permission of David Higham Associates Ltd.

18. MYTHS
E.F. Benson, *Our Family Affairs*, 1920; Roald Dahl, *Boy*, see above; Humphrey Lyttelton, *I Play as I Please*, see above; A.P. Graves, *No Return to All That*, 1930; Lord Berners, *First Childhood*, 1934; *A Century of Summer Fields*, see above; Michael Gilbert, 'School Days' from *Lilliput*.

19. FIGHTING
*World of the Public School*, ed. McDonald Fraser, see above; Littleton Powys, *The Joy of It*, 1937; Arthur J. Smythe, *William Terriss*, 1898; Sir Frank Benson, *My Memoirs*, Ernest Benn, 1930; Richard Meinertzhagen, *Diary of a Black Sheep*, see above; Giles and Esmond Romilly, *Out of Bounds*, see above; Hulda Freidrichs, *Sir George Newnes*, 1911; G.K. Chesterton, *Autobiography*, 1936.

20. POLITICS
Charles Castle, *Oliver Messel*, see above; Naomi Mitchison, *Small Talk*, see above; Christopher Hassall, *Rupert Brooke*, 1964, reprinted by permission of Faber & Faber Ltd; Sir Patrick Hastings, *Autobiography*, 1948, reprinted by permission of William Heinemann Ltd; Leonard Woolf, *Autobiography*, Vol. 1, 1960, reprinted by permission of the Executors of the Estate of Leonard Woolf and The Hogarth Press; Maurice Baring, *The Puppet Show of Memory*, see above.

21. DISCIPLINE

Arthur Harrison, *How Was that Sir?*, 1975, reprinted by permission of the Incorporated Association of Preparatory Schools; *ibid.*; Christopher Hollis, *George Orwell*, The Bodley Head, 1956; Sir Francis Chichester, *The Lonely Sea and the Sky*, see above; Lord Berners, *First Childhood*, see above; Major-General Sir A.E. Anson, *About Others and Myself*, 1920, see above; Guy Boas, *A Teacher's Story*, 1963; Christopher Pirie-Gordon, *St Peter's: The Early Years*, see above; Giles and Esmond Romilly, *Out of Bounds*, see above; Anne Wolrige-Gordon, *Peter Howard: Life and Letters*, 1969, reprinted by permission of Hodder & Stoughton Ltd; Sir Cedric Hardwicke, *A Victorian in Orbit*, 1961, reprinted by permission of Methuen & Co; Laurence Irving, *The Precarious Crust*, see above.


22. REBELS AND NON-CONFORMERS

Patrick Bridgewater, *Arthur Schopenhauer's English Schooling*, 1988, reprinted by permission of Routledge Ltd; James Strachey Barnes, *Half a Life*, see above; Jacquetta Hawkes, *Mortimer Wheeler*, 1982; G.G. Coulton, *Fourscore Years*, Cambridge, 1943, reprinted by permission of Cambridge University Press; David Garnett, *The Golden Echo*, 1954, reprinted by permission of A.P. Watt Ltd on behalf of the Executors of the Estate of David Garnett; Richard Meinertzhagen, *Diary of a Black Sheep*, see above.


23. RUNNING AWAY

W.R. Stephens, *Life & Letters of Walter Farquhar Hook*, 1879; Gordon N. Ray, *The Uses of Adversity*, Oxford, 1955, reprinted by permission of Oxford University Press; Arthur Harrison, *How Was that Sir?*, see above; L.C. Dunstervill, *Stalky's Reminiscences*, 1928; *A Century of Summer Fields*, see above; *World of the Public School*, see above.


24. GREAT MEN IN SHORT TROUSERS

Malcolm Elwin, *The Life of Llewellyn Powys*, 1949; Oliver Holt, *Three Sherborne Memoirs*, see above; H.G. Wells, *Experiment in Autobiography*, see above; A.A. Milne, *It's Too Late Now*, see above; Andrew Boyle, *Trenchard*, 1962, reprinted by permission of the author; Admiral Cunningham, *A Sailor's Odyssey*, 1951; Lady Carmichael, *Lord Carmichael of Stirling*, 1929; H. Montgomery Hyde, *Oscar Wilde*, see above.

25. THE DARK GODS
Emlyn Williams, *George*, see above; Ernest Raymond, *The Story of My Days*, 1986, reprinted by permission of A.P. Watt Ltd on behalf of Diana Raymond; Roland Culver, *Not Quite a Gentleman*, see above; Alec Waugh, *The Early Years*, 1962, reprinted by permission of the Peters Fraser & Dunlop Group Ltd; Randolph Churchill, *Twenty-one Years*, see above; Dora Russell, *The Tamarisk Tree*, 1975; Sir Francis Chichester, *The Lonely Sea and the Sky*, 1964, see above; Cyril Connolly, *Enemies of Promise*, see above; George Melly, *Rum, Bum and Concertina*, Weidenfeld & Nicolson, 1977; Compton Mackenzie, *My Life and Times*, see above; Leonard Woolf, *Autobiography*, see above; *A Century of Summer Fields*, see above; Cyril Connolly, *Enemies of Promise*, see above; Eric Maschwitz, *No Chip on My Shoulder*, Hutchinson, 1975; James Lees-Milne, *Another Self*, see above; Harold Anson, *Looking Forward*, Heinemann, 1938.

26. BLUB SUNDAY
Cyril Connolly, *Enemies of Promise*, see above; *A Century of Summer Fields*, see above.

27. ADHERENCE OF REPUTATIONS
Nicholas Monsarrat, *Life is a Four Letter Word*, see above; Sir William Goodenough, *A Rough Record*, see above; *A Century of Summer Fields*, see above; *ibid.*; John Betjeman, *Summoned by Bells*, 1960, reprinted by permission of John Murray (Publishers) Ltd.

28. GOING BACK
Herman Merival, *Bar, Stage & Platform*, 1902; David Niven, *The Moon's a Balloon*, see above; Richard Meinertzhagen, *Diary of a Black Sheep*, see above; Wilfred Thesiger, *The Life of My Choice*, see above; Lord Berners, *First Childhood*, see above; Christopher Pirie-Gordon, *St Peter's: The Early Years*, see above.

Every effort has been made to trace copyright holders. In some cases this has proved impossible. The author and publishers of this book would be pleased to hear from any copyright holders not acknowledged.

# INDEX